BRUCE JOHNSON

THE INAUDIBLE MUSIC

JAZZ, GENDER AND AUSTRALIAN MODERNITY

*un*tapped

ABOUT *UNTAPPED*

Most Australian books ever written have fallen out of print and become unavailable for purchase or loan from libraries. This includes important local and national histories, biographies and memoirs, beloved children's titles, and even winners of glittering literary prizes such as the Miles Franklin Literary Award.

Supported by funding from state and territory libraries, philanthropists and the Australian Research Council, *Untapped* is identifying Australia's culturally important lost books, digitising them, and promoting them to new generations of readers. As well as providing access to lost books and a new source of revenue for their writers, the *Untapped* collaboration is supporting new research into the economic value of authors' reversion rights and book promotion by libraries, and the relationship between library lending and digital book sales. The results will feed into public policy discussions about how we can better support Australian authors, readers and culture.

See untapped.org.au for more information, including a full list of project partners and rediscovered books.

Readers are reminded that these books are products of their time. Some may contain language or reflect views that might now be found offensive or inappropriate.

FOREWORD

Some years ago I organised a meeting of the UK branch of IASPM (the International Association for the Study of Popular Music) at Keele University. I can't remember now if we had a theme, but I did invite the late Jim Godbolt to be the plenary speaker. Godbolt had been involved with Mick Mulligan's jazz band in the 1950s. He was the author of his own sardonic memoirs of life as a jazz manager and agent and a well-respected historian of British jazz. He appears in this book, remembering the Graeme Bell Band's remarkable impact on the London jazz scene. A distinguished cove, then, if with a reputation for prickly eccentricity.

Keele is a campus university in the middle of England. Godbolt arrived from London late on the opening evening. This was the vacation. There was no one to meet him; the cafeteria was closed; the nearest drink was in the village pub, a mile or so away. He eventually tracked me down in the middle of the first IASPM session, a performance-with-lecture by avant-garde rock musicians which I wasn't about to leave. Godbolt was distinctly disgruntled.

The next morning, as I was walking from my cramped student room to breakfast, Godbolt leapt out at me from behind a bush. He was carrying his overnight case and a raincoat. He told me he was going straight back to London. Keele was a dreadful place and he had been treated dreadfully. When he got home he immediately wrote letters to my own university boss, to the vice-chancellor of Keele, to the editor of the paper for which I was then rock critic, to the mutual friend who had originally been our go-between. In each letter he described my rudeness and incompetence and asked that I be sacked. I wasn't but I did have some awkward telephone calls. People who knew Godbolt were unsympathetic: we warned you!

This is the sort of embarrassing memory I usually expunge—or embellish. Bruce Johnsons The Inaudible Music brought it flooding back. Not because Bruce isn't the very model of an enthusiastic colleague at IASPM meetings, but because his book shows so clearly the casual insensitivity with which popular music scholars (mostly formed by rock) have treated jazz which, as Johnson argues, has, in fact, a good claim to be the most important popular music of the twentieth century.

In Britain the world of jazz scholarship remains far apart from the world of popular music studies. I can't recall a single article on British jazz being submitted to Popular Music, and my own interest in the subject has been, symptomatically, in Britain's jazz fans rather than jazz musicians, in the 1950s jazz scene only as the precursor of the 1960s rock scene, in issues of authenticity not pleasure. Johnson is interested in these themes too but from a player's perspective. The result is a startling rewriting of a story I thought I knew. The nicest irony is that a music most commonly defined as 'traditional' must now be understood as modernist; the most significant revelation is how important women were to the making of this new expressive form; the most salutary lesson is how quickly scholarly clichés lose their grip when we move in close to particular people in particular places.

There are inevitably things Johnson doesn't do. I would like to have known more about the Bell brothers and the Bell Band sound. I don't know how Bruce judges a jazz performance. And I'd like to think that high cultural arguments are subtler than Johnson allows. But he is mighty persuasive and this is a book to inspire the explorer not the dogmatist, a book to make one marvel at people's determination (not least Johnson's) to have fun.

Simon Frith
October 1999

CONTENTS

CONTENTS

PREFACE

This is a book that seeks to give some recognition to the role of jazz in the transition of Australian society and music into the twentieth century. It is prompted by my growing realisation that aspects of the music which I had taken for granted as a musician were strikingly distinctive within the larger context of Australian music, particularly in the first half of this century. Furthermore, the significance of these seemed to be almost wholly unaddressed in studies of Australian culture, and of music in particular. One reason that music itself is relatively under-represented in the former is, ironically, because it is everywhere. Unlike literature or painting, music is present in every area of private and public life. This is so much so that in its more pervasive forms it ceases to be noticed and noted. Music washes over every aspect of Australian life and culture, from political to sporting activity, social conduct such as eating and leisure, secular and religious rituals, domestic and public definitions of identity. Music brings us in and sees us out. From christening, through courting, seduction, marriage, interment ... from cradle to grave there is incidental music. Ruth Finnegan's *The Invisible Musicians* was a benchmark exploration of the pervasiveness of music-making in an anglophone community, and my title is a way of acknowledging the importance of her work. As to why jazz in particular should be relatively inaudible in studies of Australian music, that is a parallel subject of this book.

It is not to be read as a 'history' of Australian jazz. There are other books which provide partial historical overviews, and in which many of the topics I cover receive only a passing mention. On the other hand this study barely refers to some figures who must be regarded as central to any attempt at something calling itself a 'history'. The opening historical orientation stops short in the 1950s, and respectfully foreshadows the later period during which some of the most important events have continued to unfold. The purpose of this collection of prismatic essays is to cast light on a process which occurred during the first half of the twentieth century. The transition to modernity was not simply and mechanically inscribed in musical style, in ways that may be deciphered through formal musicological analysis. Indeed, a focus on stylistic innovation can distract from deeper ideological conservatism. It is a transition of sensibility, of ways of feeling, and how those feelings can be expressed through the social realities that accompanied modernisation—technologies, physical spaces, morals and manners. This connection, between jazz and Australian modernity, has not been addressed at any length before, which is why the points of reference—what is included and what is left out—will not correspond to expectations appropriate to a history of Australian jazz. This is reflected in the titles on the CD, *The Inaudible Music* (Larrikin's Yesterday's Australia Series).

The aspect of our jazz history that receives least attention is the progressive movement of the post-war period. There is some reference to this era in some of the contextualising sections, but the detailed case studies are generally confined to what may be called 'pre-bop' episodes. This does not reflect stylistic preference on my part, nor a judgement about the balance of historical significance. My interest here is in cultural processes taking place primarily in the first half of the century, so the arrival of bop in the late 1940s, and subsequent developments, are necessarily peripheral to the study. With due caution about stylistic labels, I would describe the styles which receive closest attention as traditional and, in the case of Barbara James, Swing. In the final section, I demonstrate that these styles have been the most neglected in jazz policy, education and public discourse. If I attempt to argue for their importance with some vigour, it is not to assert that they are 'superior' in absolute terms to later developments, but to restore a balance. If I refer, for example, to Graeme Bell as the most important figure in our jazz history, I do so not *because* he was a traditionalist, but because of the ground he has broken and the influence he has exercised in a career now extending over sixty years.

At certain points I make distinctions between traditional and modern styles of Australian jazz. This is not because these distinctions are reductively applicable to musical practice; but they have had force as public and critical constructions, sometimes as a historical distinction, sometimes aesthetic. Especially in the post-war period, the traditional/modern binary has governed the way musicians are positioned. In practice, however, every musician transgresses the distinction constantly, so the terms are better seen as a way of denoting two extreme notional positions, from which most musicians shift back and forth on the continuum between. At one extreme we may think of 'traditional' jazz as, among many other things, giving much more weight to techniques of polyphonic collective improvisation, as compared with the greater focus of 'modern' styles on extended solo improvisation. As someone who constantly traverses most of that continuum in his own playing, I am in no position to ascribe to any style absolute superiority. I do argue, however, that each requires the development of different musical and social skills; and that the critical neglect of more traditional styles has led to the atrophy of some of those skills, producing performers who suffer disempowering imbalances as musical and social identities.

If terms like 'traditional' and 'modern' are critical rather than innately musical constructions, the same is true of the term 'jazz' itself. I shall take this up further as part of the discussion of jazz and cultural politics, but I wish to signal the point at the outset. The word 'jazz' has been disputed since it began to be applied to musical practices. Like any generic category, the centre is reasonably solid, but there are arguments at the edges. I cannot imagine anyone denying that the Armstrong Hot Fives,

Charlie Parker's Dial sessions, John Coltrane at the Village Vanguard, are jazz performances; but other stylistic streams intersect the jazz tradition unevenly. In the case of big bands associated with Swing for example—Fletcher Henderson will excite less debate than Glenn Miller, though neither of these could have sounded the way they do without the development known as jazz. I have used the term in such a way as to accommodate a very broad range of meanings, sometimes recognising more purist positions through the term 'jazz-based'.

This is not only a book about Australian jazz and other forms of music, but a book about how we choose to talk about them. Here and throughout I press the point that my taste is eclectic. Apart from the fact that I happen to play jazz primarily, the pleasures I derive from hearing music are not discriminated by genre or style. If I make what appear to be distinctions of value, it is the value of different discourses about music rather than about music itself, and should be distinguished from observations about use and function.

The question of how language itself affects the realities it describes is neither trivial nor merely trendy. In the early seventeenth century Francis Bacon understood that fundamental changes associated with the scientific revolution could not proceed without a renovation of the English language. A generation later the Royal Society, implementing that revolution, initiated linguistic projects that recognised the inadequacy of existing discourses to describe new insights about the universe. Over the last few decades debate has resumed over language, as both a screen and a window to experience.

Nineteenth century ways of talking about cultural forms do not always have the words to register twentieth-century social realities. The issues go to the heart of the question of how certain sections of a community maintain power over others. Jazz has been assigned to every category of expressive form, from art to trash, from highbrow to lowbrow. The question of how we talk about the music, what labels we apply to it, what kind of critical language we use in reviews, record notes, advertising, is central to attempts to determine its cultural value, and even shapes the music that is produced in the name of jazz. The way we talk about an art form is a way of 'naturalising' its position in our culture, and the result is that we often overlook or overvalue its actual importance to social practice. If we always talk flippantly about something, it soon becomes difficult to imagine that it might after all be important. I have had an article on jazz to a commissioning journal rejected on the grounds that it is 'too academic': too exhaustively documented, too sophisticated in its theory. Such a charge is rarely made against scholarly articles about 'classical' music.

Let me provide an illustration of how effectively, yet unconsciously, this process works. A few days before I first drafted this Preface, the composer and musician John Sangster died. Sangster is one of the major figures, not just in jazz, but of Australian music, and this was said during television interviews at a wake held for him in a Sydney pub. But Sangster was a jazz figure, so comment that accorded him serious status in Australia's culture generally finished up on the cutting room floor. Instead, the televised feature on 'Sango', as he was referred to, made much of the roistering anecdotes, the roughhouse camaraderie. The pub became the 'jazz watering hole', subliminally implying that its sub-human habitués drink alcohol the way 'us normal folks' drink water. Those present were asked to pose with their schooners foregrounded. All these things *are* important components of the jazz life, but they dominated the report to the exclusion of any other level of discussion of Sangster's contribution to Australian music. This ensured that Sangster's monumental achievements went unrecognised. Jazz itself was safely boxed in as a picturesque but trivial entertainment that does not compete with art music's position on the high ground.

It is very difficult to know what is the right voice' to give to jazz. The idea that the jazz *milieu* is more vernacular and bohemian than that of classical music obviously has a measure of truth. Those differences have to be recognised in order to maintain the integrity of each. But difference often becomes implicitly hierarchical: one is more important than the other. By the standards by which the cultural value of the arts' is officially measured, jazz is at least as significant in our lives as are the forms of music which enjoy scholarly attention and official support. I hope to show in this book that the music matters. And it is therefore appropriate that it not be excluded from intellectually disciplined cultural analysis.

This is why I have brought together several different 'discursive strategies'—I have discussed jazz in a number of ways. Some sections of this book are relatively dense, since I hope to demonstrate that jazz is an appropriate subject for intellectual rigour, and this sometimes generates a specialist language. If I use a phrase like 'cultural capital', another scholar will recognise a certain tradition of analysis centering on the work of, say, Pierre Bourdieu, and I am saved the trouble of reinventing the wheel. Jazz gives us an analogy. If I take a gig with musicians I have never met before—and this is not uncommon—we don't have to sit down and have a long discussion to find out what we share as a basis for what we are going to play. We can work out very quickly what kind of musical dialogue we can conduct simply by starting out with a blues, and listening to particular phrases. A quote from "West End Blues", or "Billie's Bounce", the use of a particular turnaround or chord substitution, proclaims a shared vocabulary to the musicians, which enables them to build more effectively.

This book therefore talks in several voices. There is straightforward narrative, about what Australian jazz musicians have done here and overseas, including ways in which jazz has helped to form our collective identity in the twentieth century. These are included because most of these stories are not generally known, yet they tell of achievements that would be regarded as central in confirming the importance of other art forms. There is also discussion that refers back to the theoretical literature on culture and music; about the politics of art, by which I mean the connections between art and the way different sections of society maintain power over others. I shall be looking at the way dominant interests construct categories (like 'high art' and 'mass culture') to justify and perpetuate positions of power; at how technology affects our attitudes and valuations of different art forms.

Interpolated among all these sections is another kind of 'discourse' altogether. This is a book about Australian jazz, what it is and what it means; but when you are actually playing it, listening to it, standing on a bandstand, sitting in its venues, that *feeling of* being there is the most powerful part of the experience. It is that moment, in its physical, emotional, cognitive, and often demonic detail, that is the centre of the encounter. I have therefore interspersed the theoretical and narrative accounts with brief first-hand accounts of jazz experience. Some of these refer to places and persons unfamiliar to a non-jazz readership. I don't feel that this is an impediment to communication of the spirit, however, and rather than lumber this book with even more explanatory apparatus, I refer the obsessively curious to a standard jazz glossary (Grove, for example), and my own *Oxford Companion to Australian Jazz* for clarifications. Although these interpolations are the least academically orthodox way of writing about culture, to me they remain the most vivid. In the same way the uncensored, unstructured diary of the common soldier in the trenches communicates the experience of war with a different kind of intensity from the distanced overview of the historian.

The interpolations are just snapshots of gigs or people who have given their lives to gigs. I thank those people for their open-heartedness in allowing my version of events to become public property. These passages were not artfully produced for this book, but come from journals I have kept intermittently since the 1970s. I found that they helped me to recall and frame events in which I had participated, in ways that sometimes gave them meaning. What I have included here is the merest fraction of about five volumes. They do not always show me in a good light, and sometimes I have gone back to them and been appalled at the person who wrote them. Also, notwithstanding the comments made earlier about the report of Sangster's death, I see that booze plays a prominent role in many of these narratives. Well, I guess that's because the music is so often played in such circumstances. Many years ago, when drummer Alan Geddes heard that someone was writing a book about why musicians drank, he said matter-of-factly, 'Because it's there'. I note also that several of the interpolations refer to serious musical disasters. Perhaps that is because it is easier to write about those than about the triumphs. When a performance works well, it is like no other experience I know, though I imagine that the same ineffable completeness is experienced when a sports team or theatre troupe is playing well. When something goes wrong, it is apparent and noteworthy. So I want to say now that I recorded some catastrophes not because they are the norm, but quite the contrary. The overwhelming majority of the 7,000 or so gigs I have done have been a pleasure so fully complete that it seems impossible and superfluous to talk about it. There is no life I would exchange for this.

I have been unwittingly 'rehearsing' this book for decades. Since my first embarrassingly inept gig around thirty years ago, I have been playing, thinking and writing about the music. So too this book is a summary of reflections and statements that have been aired and refined in discussion, printed debate, administrative and educational activity. Every individual who has ever assisted with that process of refinement has my deep thanks. I cannot list them all. However, there are some specific acknowledgements that I wish to make.

I wish to express my appreciation to a number of institutions for their financial, logistical and moral support during the work I conducted on this book. Most notably:

- The University of New South Wales Faculty of Arts Special Research Grants Scheme for regularly funding my ongoing research into Australian popular music and jazz;
- My colleagues who have never, as far as I know, wondered why someone based in their School of English seemed to be spending so much time researching music. They, with academics from other disciplines in my university, also gave me valuable feedback through discussions and staff seminars, bringing to bear the valuable checks and balances of alternative parameters;
- The Schools of Cultural History and English at the University of Turku in Finland, and the Department of Folk Tradition at the University of Tampere in Finland, where vernacular musics are accorded great respect and research support. With generous funding from the Finnish Academy these centres provided opportunities for research and writing, through a Visiting Fellowship and a Visiting Professorship;
- The Institute of Popular Music at the University of Liverpool, for continuing support both formally through a Visiting Fellowship and informally through supportive collegiality;
- The University of Aarhus Denmark, whose invitation to attend as a co-ordinator the *Rock as Research* symposium in April, 1997 at the Magleås Kursuscenter near Copenhagen, enabled me to benefit from the work of a wide range of popular music research proceeding in the Nordic and northern European religions.

If these acknowledgements reflect a high level of interest shown by overseas bodies in popular music research and of 'non-metropolitan' (including Australian) cultures, relative to that of research and arts funding bodies in Australia, I shall simply let that speak for itself.

- The International Association for the Study of Popular Music, and its Australian/New Zealand chapter in particular, for listening, correcting, detailing, and providing a scholarly context which is unique in Australia;

- The National Film and Sound Archive, now ScreenSound Australia, and particularly its Sydney office and its former manager Cornel Platzer, for their support for Australian jazz, their cheerful and unfailing assistance in making materials available for perusal—and their great coffee;

- Currency Press for having faith in a topic which was 'too Australian' for overseas publishers, and 'too trivial' for Australian publishers.

In general, I would like to express my appreciation to Currency for their continuing support for research into hitherto unexplored areas of Australian culture, and for research methodologies which are not dominated by metropolitan designer-labels. Thanks to Katharine Brisbane and Sue Tronser for their reading and suggestions about structure which have, I believe produced a more accessible book. And, to Katharine again who always insisted that, finally, these decisions were mine.

I wish to thank those who have given me permission to adapt some material from articles I have published elsewhere. These are acknowledged in footnotes. In every instance, however, the research I conducted for this particular project has decisively amplified and developed that material.

I am a research magpie, picking up material from everyone. But apart from specific footnoted acknowledgements, I wish to make special mention of Bet Briggs, John Colborne-Veel (former President of the Fellowship of Australian Composers), Kate Dunbar (former President, Sydney Jazz Club), Bill Haesler

(Chair, NSW Jazz Archive), Eric Myers (NSW Jazz Co-ordinator and Editor of *Jazzchord*) and Mike Sutcliffe (Editor, *Australian Record and Music Review*), who put up with phone calls at hours when they were trying to sleep, focussed discussions in pubs when they were trying to enjoy themselves, and that apparently disconcerting question, 'How do you know that?' that becomes a conversational tic among obsessive researchers. I wish to thank all those students, and particularly those enrolled in my courses on Australian jazz and popular music, and on modernity and postmodernity in Australia, who have participated in discussions and pointed me in new directions. Along with my children Sam and Shannon, their 'street' knowledge has often saved me from reinventing the wheel. Ian Collinson is conducting research on literary ethnography under my supervision, but of a kind that often borders on collaboration; he helps to keep me on my toes. Dr John Whiteoak has been a long-time friend, and a fellow researcher whose magnanimity is exemplary. His generosity with his knowledge, time, and archival resources seems to know no limits. He also read through several drafts of this, providing meticulous, constructive and wonderfully informed suggestions. The final draft is much the better for his having done so. Finally, however, I take responsibility for the arguments presented here.

- Thanks to those who have supported and believed in the music and especially those jazz musicians who built the traditions of Australian jazz. If, as I hope, this book seems blessed with a panoramic view, it is because I am standing on their shoulders.

- Finally my heartfelt thanks and appreciation to my partner Gaye Poole. Her knowledge of Australian film and theatre helped to enlarge the compass of my own enquiries. She also helped with proof-reading and indexing. More pervasively, she tolerated and even made space for, the excesses, weaknesses, the profound and often tacky selfishness, that enable me to live the life out of which this book grows.

Bruce Johnson
School of English
University of New South Wales

INTRO
TRADITION: AUSTRALIA—ABE ROMAIN

Sydney, 13/1/91

This morning I went to visit Abe Romain, to pick up some acetate recordings from which to make some transfers for possible inclusion on a CD of Trocadero bands. Abe is 85, and although not quite as chipper as when I interviewed him last in 1988, is basically healthy and with a sharp mind and a detailed and tidy memory. His wife of over sixty years died a few years ago, and his son died of diabetes in 1990. Also afflicted with Alzheimers, he was only about 64. How curious to see your child die of causes associated with senility. Abe had a bypass operation last year and takes medication to prevent the accumulation of pulmonary fluid. Recently he suffered from an attack of shingles. All that presents a picture of decay and that is seriously misleading because, in spite of his age, Abe communicates a sense of vitality, alertness, intelligence. His apartment has the neatness of a space that has been long tended by an occupant who requires order, who has determined a place for everything.

Listening to him talk, I feel honoured and lucky to have the opportunity. Here is a man whose career goes back to the earliest days of jazz in Australia, and who was central to some of its major episodes and venues. This man facing me was taught trumpet by Eddie Frizelle, who came out here with the Palais Royal Californians. He played the Fuller and Tivoli circuits, led bands at the Trocadero and Romanos, accompanied Des Tooley on the recordings made at the most important point of her career, and worked overseas with the big names like Harry Roy.

I'm not talking about the stream of jazz that flowed from the revivalist movement, but the jazz influenced tradition that patterned the history of professional dance and studio music. Among individuals still living, Romain is to that stream something like Graeme Bell is to the other. Although born in New Zealand, he seems to me to be one of the quintessential Sydney people in a way I believe that I never will be. He is Sydney the way Merv Acheson was Sydney, Wally Norman, or Alan Geddes (in spite of being a Lithgow boy). From where I stand it is best described as a large club from which I feel indefinably excluded though without malice or intent. It's just that there is a shared history that makes all the difference, emerging above all in anecdotal reminiscences peppered with local references that, if you were there, constitute a window on a whole place and era, and if you were not, become indecipherable code words: Stones, Sammy Lee, Christies, the Roosevelt, Smith's Oriental, Burt Howell, Jim Gussey. They're part of a mythology that can only be entered by growing up in a place, and to which access is only preserved by staying there. I don't feel a part of any such community, though when someone recently said, 'Who's that?' while Dick Hughes was playing, I began to see how relative it might be.

Anyway, I'm writing this because something moved me while I was talking to Abe, a very strong sense of entering into his past. But also, in Abe himself, the sense of its passing. He's 85. Wife and son gone (no other children, I think). He lives in an apartment in MacLeay Regis, MacLeay Street, Potts Point. The building is perfectly preserved 1938 Sydney. Opulent foyer with thick carpet, mirrors and columns in a rusty coloured marble. Solid, so solid, hushed, protected from the street, intimidating. The original lifts, with bench seats at the rear of the cabin. Original wooden doors throughout, lighting subdued in pearly shades that would have been the latest decor in the inter-war period. Abe told me that the man who built the apartments was not happy with the original plans submitted, but didn't quite know what he wanted until he saw the Rockefeller Apartments in New York. He purchased the plans, or the rights to them, and MacLeay Regis is in almost all respects their duplicate.

He has lived there since 1940. Only one other tenant predates him. And I think that almost nothing has changed since then, with several inevitable exceptions. There's a television, but it sits on the floor of the living room without a stand like something that shouldn't be there, as though it's waiting to be packaged and dispatched somewhere else. There is a big wireless with a large square dial with clock-hand style tuning, in some beautiful wood that looks like the grain of walnut, but blonde. 'I don't use it any more,' he tells me. Off the living room there is a small study with a table and typewriter, lit from a window, but the daylight scarcely penetrates the living room itself and at mid-morning we still had the electric light on.

He invited me into the kitchen to listen to a tape. He listens to cassettes when he is cooking, in particular to Don Goldie who is an abiding favourite. He played the same tape to me last time also. The kitchen tells a story of a different conception of domestic cooking in an Australian city since the 1960s. No spacious bench or table for food preparation, no racks for knives, copper-bottomed pots, sauce pans. It's just wide enough for one person, more like a corridor than a room. The only flat working space was the terrazzo sink, somewhat roughened now, with the original taps. Shallow cupboards, a stool tucked between those and the doorway. A rack of spice bottles was as much of a statement about the 1980s as it was prepared to make. The switch for the toaster was the old white, squared-off plastic or bakelite style. The tiles were 1940s cream with a green border; and I suddenly recognised my grandparents' kitchen decor in Adelaide before I started school.

He played the tape, sitting opposite the narrow bench (yes, I remember now, there was an abbreviated bench, about ten inches deep, opposite the sink). He listened intently to the music he obviously knew well and cared about. He looked vulnerable, but that's only because we probably all do when we don't know we're being watched. He was in profile to me. His eyes flickered absently from cassette player to switch, to this or that object, but his mind was so focussed on the music that he seemed quite unaware of how the rest of his body was behaving. So his face arranged and rearranged itself in those small ways that we don't know we are doing—pursed lips, small muscular reflexes, and pale blue eyes flickering about as he listened to Don Goldie playing 'Bourbon Street Parade', 'I Think I'm Going to Change My Plans' and 'My Honey's Lovin' Arms' (which he had mistakenly referred to as 'Bill Bailey').

The intensity of his concentration made me want to touch him. I had a picture of him, living alone in this third floor time capsule from Kings Cross in the 1940s, wartime Sydney, with everything still in its place. The jar of rubber bands, the scribble pad on the desk, the browned tea-strainer hanging from a hook attached by a rubber suction pad to the tiles above the sink—maybe stuck there decades ago by him or his wife, and now virtually sealed in position. Stuck there while he went out in the evening to lead the band at the Trocadero.

He talked about his early career, about the first gig he did in Sydney, taking a tram out to Balmain to play a George Sorlie tent show. It included a melodrama for which he was handed a sheet on which there were several brief themes which he played, like a loop tape, as directed, as the incidental music for the action. He told of trombonist Eric Ambler who came to that first gig with him, a strong player, strong drinker, who finished as a high official of the Queensland Musicians' Union. But now dead. He showed me photographs of his wife Marjorie as a young woman. A stunner, with vitality bursting out of the photograph. Another photograph at 82, still looking like a woman in her early 50s. He mentioned that the apartments were originally equipped with small fridges that all ran from the same motor somewhere in the building. Everyone had to defrost at the same time.

I've rarely felt so much in touch with that ambience of Sydney in the 1940s. There are different parts of Sydney that seem to have defined their essence during a particular period and to have kept that character, though with diminishing intensity as the spiritless redevelopment continues. Coogee, especially as seen from the hill at the northern end, has the smell of the 1930s for me. Parts of the city around Goulburn and Wentworth Streets still suggest the teens of the century. The Cross, or that end of it around the lower numbers of MacLeay Street, always conjures up the war period, the late 1930s and early 1940s. Partly, I suppose because of the nightlife that entertained the Americans, but also because of those imposing residential apartment buildings that still house some of the people who bought them at that time. There's a city spirit that, strangely, the CBD doesn't possess at all. Sydney's CBD lacks a sense of solid reality. All those gleaming skyscrapers climbing away from human beings, deflecting penetration with mirrored façades, seem depthless, insecure and fragile You really can't take them any more seriously than you can someone wearing mirrorshades. But the McLeay Regis seems to me to embody the idea contained in the words 'city living'.

As Abe walked me to the lift, another tenant, a woman in perhaps her 70s, passed us in the broad, silent, solid wood-panelled corridor. She said, 'Good morning Mr Romain'. There seemed to be something very valuable, grounded, in the milieu from which those words came.

CHAPTER 1
JAZZ AND MODERNITY IN AUSTRALIA

Part 1: Jazz In Australia To The 50s

> It looks as if Ben Fuller has started a craze that will last for a long time.
>
> *Reviewer, Sydney, July 1918*

The history of jazz in Australia cannot be understood simply by imagining a passive reflection of the story of jazz in its birthplace, the United States. There, it appeared first as a wholly intelligible music of local performance, and began dispersing through the country in that form rather than as something technologically processed. The word itself grew out of the living speech of the communities that engendered the music.[1] New Orleans musicians such as Jelly Roll Morton were travelling the country playing the music from the turn of the century, and although he realised that what he was playing was regionally distinctive, it does not seem to have been incomprehensible to other musicians.[2] There was a further substantial migration of his colleagues northward to Chicago before the first jazz recordings were made. In addition a music identifiable as jazz was spontaneously emerging in widely dispersed regional centres other than New Orleans. Thus for many North Americans jazz began as a music of local live performance dominated by provincial musicians. New Orleans jazz musicians arrived in major centres like Chicago and New York, bringing with them rural *gaucheries* that were often greeted derisively by northern urban sophisticates.[3]

The Australian experience was very different. 'Jazz' was a

strange new word with no obvious analogues in English. First it was a rumour from afar about the most up-to-date musical fashion in the 'New World', the country that signified all that was modern, brash, self-confident, the reference point for fashions in mass culture. As a sound, it was first defined by the early American white jazz and hot dance groups which arrived, first as recordings and later as touring groups. At the same time, the word was inextricably entangled with black or 'negroid' primitivism. Although there would be almost no exposure to the 'classic' black bands of New Orleans and Chicago for some decades, nonetheless it was public perception that jazz had emerged from African-American music. Although clearly distinguishable, these notional streams—white hot dance and black jazz—flowed together with other 'new' popular musics having reference to exotic mindscapes like Pacific paradises and oriental cultures, to present themselves as an 'Other', one of the alternatives to the Anglo-Celtic traditions that had dominated colonial popular music.

Jazz entered Australia as a compound of live performance and sophisticated technology. The earliest advertised jazz performance dates from 1918, the band assembled by expatriate American Billy Romaine who had been leading ragtime dance bands in Sydney as early as 1914, and his jazz performances were in theatres with traditions rooted in English music hall and American vaudeville. Australians had been exposed to African-American music during the nineteenth century in the form of touring minstrel shows, and through such informal grassroots contact as on the multi-cultural goldfields.[4] In the twentieth century overseas military service introduced Australians to jazz performance, including two airmen who heard the Original Dixieland Jazz Band in London and teamed up as Leslie and Dare to assemble the Syncopas Jazz Band in Sydney in 1920.[5] It is also likely that Australians heard, for example, the black military band of the 369th United States Infantry ('The Hellfighters') led by James Reese Europe. Although a rather lumbering sixty-piece orchestra it played jazz compositions like 'Memphis Blues', and 'Clarinet Marmalade', scored with heavy syncopation, and relatively complex and intense rhythms.[6] The Hellfighters entertained allied soldiers in France in 1917, so Australians might have been among the audiences in relatively large numbers.

The urban 'mass' consumption of music was expanded with the growth of public dance halls from the teens of the century. Sheet music was another important medium, available at retailers, but the latest song would also often be published in newspapers or professional magazines. The player piano provided a medium for the delivery of music to the untrained and helped to democratise its domestic enjoyment, as did the wireless when it arrived officially in 1923. The technology which above all others enabled the global dispersal of this performance-centred music was the sound recording. Especially outside the major centres like Sydney and Melbourne, recordings were the first exposure to jazz for most Australians.[7] Prior to the beginning of local production in 1925, huge numbers of imported records were 'dumped' in Australia. After 1920 increasing numbers of these were by white jazz groups, particularly of the New York school. Advertisements such as for the Melola record player (*Graphic*, 20 January 1921) specifically presented their products as being 'as effective as a full jazz band', and by 1925 the inaugural edition of *Music Trader* estimated that there were one million phonographs owned in Australia. Radio followed recordings. Noting that in the nineteenth century the level of domestic ownership of pianos had been 'remarkable even by prevailing European standards', Roger Covell suggests that in this remote corner of the world, the instrument was a comforting link with European gentility and civilisation.[8] As radio became a major home entertainment medium in the 1920s, it often literally displaced the family piano.[9] Doubtless this was read as further evidence of the corrupting effect *of* technology, and of jazz also, since dance bands proclaiming jazz influences managed to gain a large share *of* programming time. Jazz was thus frequently encountered as a music mediated by the most up-to-date forms of domestic technology.

The sense of the new was strengthened by the unfamiliar, low fidelity cacophony emanating from the phonograph. Furthermore the earliest jazz recordings heard in Australia were by musicians who were at several removes from the origins of the music, and who could themselves scarcely construe the logic of their sources. It was not until 1920 that a jazz record appeared on an Australian label: two Original Dixieland Jazz Band sides on Zonophone 3296, pressed in England for sale in Australia. Prior to 1914 Germany was an important source of recordings, but from 1914 until 1920 there was almost no American jazz on record heard in Australia. The earliest recordings Australians heard of something like jazz were more likely to be of European origin. 'Down in Jungle Town', recorded by a singer listed as Rastas Brown, was one of the pre—1914 imports. The performance, issued on the Prussian-pressed Globe label, was straight out of blackface music hall, with crude stereotypification and a legitimately projected voice. Australians were at the end of a long chain of Chinese Whispers. The message heard by young ears eagerly crowding around the phonograph in Australian parlours bore little relation to the message being shared between New Orleans musicians and their audiences at picnics, dances, parades, brothels, funerals.

Nor was it decoded as the same message received by other countries outside the United States English ears would unscramble the sounds in very different ways. 'America', popular music, black ethnicity, all meant something distinct, conditioned by a different cultural and musical memory. The sounds were processed through different histories, geographical realities, demographies, class differentiations, mythologies. Even the different routes of access to the United States—via the west coast for Australia and the east coast for England, altered the messages received in each country. In the period following

World War I Australians evolved a range of attitudes to Europe and the United States that corresponded unevenly with those of England. These attitudes were bound up with such issues as national and ethnic identity, modernity, mass culture, technology. They were crucial to the way in which Australians assimilated the music on which all these attitudes converged: jazz.

Many of the implications will be explored in what follows. At the outset, it is necessary to provide a review of jazz in Australia over the first half of the century as a road map on which to situate areas explored in more detail in later chapters.

The Roaring 20s

The earliest documented performance of an Australian jazz band as such is that of singer Belle Sylvia and her Jazz Band in August 1918.[10] Formed by Billy Romaine for the Fuller theatre circuit, the band ushered in the massive jazz vogue in Australia during the twenties. In 1920 the dance band entrepreneur Jim Bendrodt booked Romaine's group to open the Palais Royal in Sydney, thus strengthening the link between jazz and dancing. Jazz also enjoyed exposure in public dance halls in Melbourne, particularly in St Kilda, where the Palais de Danse and Wattle Path enjoyed great popularity. The fashion spread to other major mainland centres, and by 1926, when the population was six million, a Melbourne music company estimated that there were 1,600 jazz bands working in Australia, around twice the number listed as servicing a population of 17.5 million in 1994.[11] The music had made such inroads that even the fastidious South Street competitions in Ballarat capitulated and introduced a much-publicised jazz band category in 1926.

We should not imagine, however, that what these Australian jazz bands were playing sounded much like the music of black American groups of the same period. Nor should we assume that 'jazz' bands all over Australia were similar, any more than bands all over the United States were. Jazz is transmitted less through a fixed text than by aural channels, word-of-mouth descriptions, tentative guesses about what sounds a review might actually be describing. A Sydney-based band of professional dance musicians would have had a different order of competencies and a different level of access to the 'source' from amateurs in a remote rural group, whose only adjustment to the new musical vogue was likely to have been the addition of the word 'Jazz' to the band name and perhaps a bit of onstage clowning.

Until the arrival of the first visiting American jazz bands in 1923, the musical conventions of Australian jazz were likely to have been a combination of local dance and vaudeville traditions, with ragging and related effects based on earlier touring minstrel groups and later associated with vaudeville, cinema and dance music. All this was now augmented with a sometimes Dada-esque, anarchistic sense of the new 'jazz' component. Contemporary reviews describe animal impressions, the banging of kitchenware, revolver shots, drums thrown around the stage—a genial twenties form of the high-energy, in-your-face iconoclasm that announced several phases of popular music. The earliest supporters and opponents of jazz agreed on this: this twentieth-century music was part of a larger post-war interrogation of moral and cultural traditions. It became an anthem for a new age of emancipation that expressed itself in such breaches of Edwardian decorum as short dresses, American slang and immodest energetic dancing. It was meaningfully noted that 'syncopation' began with 'sin'.

The extravagances of local jazz performance diminished with the arrival of the first American jazz bands from 1923, beginning with Frank Ellis' band, brought from the United States by promoter J.C. (Jim) Bendrodt to play in Sydney, followed by a season in Melbourne in 1924. Ellis was followed by Bert Ralton, Ray Tellier and others, many of whom recruited local musicians who went on, like Frank Coughlan and Ern Pettifer, to lead their own groups. These visitors and the Australian groups that emulated them displayed little of the rhythmic complexity and the improvisational boldness which Australian audiences were to hear in 'classic' United States recordings of the 1920s reissued in subsequent decades. Later writers have often preferred the term 'hot dance music' to the style played in the name of jazz in Australia during this phase. The jazz credentials consisted of novelty effects, including the use of mutes and wide *glissandi*; the violation of conventional cadences of 'closure'—unresolved endings—and ventures into whole tone scales; and a frequently bludgeoning emphasis on dotted quavers as a way of signalling peppiness. The emotional range also narrowed as we moved farther away from the source tradition. The recordings which have been canonised as the cornerstones of the classic tradition sustained a dignity and poignancy even when the lyrics might be *risqué*, as on Louis Armstrong's 'Tight Like This' (the Savoy Ballroom Five, 1928). In the 1926 recording of 'How could Red Riding Hood (be so very good?)' made by the Australian Al Hammett's band, the sexual reference is simultaneously more oblique and more prurient, more self-consciously saucy.[12] Jazz was declared to be 'Joy, Animation, Zip, Zest'.[13]

If, however, in comparing the Australian and American versions we ignore the question of context, we form an inadequate appreciation of the achievements of these pioneer Australian (and visiting) jazz musicians. Louis Armstrong and Frank Coughlan were emerging from very different histories, in worlds that were scarcely even aware of each other. Furthermore, as jazz filtered into local consciousness, it had to compete with other music traditions, such as English and Irish popular musics, which further mediated the sound. Even groups presented as jazz bands were still, in practical terms, dance bands first. A night's program at a Palais would include the full range of popular dances, novelty pieces, light classics, but now with a jazz component added. Bert Ralton's band recorded 'straight' material like 'Parade of the Wooden Soldiers' as well as jazz repertoire. Although some dedicated individual musicians like Frank Coughlan and singer Des Tooley formed an attachment to jazz for its own sake, there was probably no professional band in the 1920s that was exclusively a 'jazz band' in the later sense of the word. The general pattern is of professional dance musicians accommodating a new vogue. But having noted that, we should still try to hear the Australian musicians on their own terms.

The imported orchestras in the 1920s helped to increase local jazz interest and knowledge, partly because they enjoyed a disproportionate share of local recording opportunities. Jack Mitchell's *Australian Jazz on Record 1925–80* (Australian Government Printing Service, Canberra, 1988) lists only 58 tracks recorded before 1930, of which 31 were under an American leader, with the dozen by Ray Tellier being the largest individual contribution. A mere six American-led groups made more than half the jazz records in Australia during the 'Jazz Age'. This market dominance both signalled and increased the influence they exercised. According to Frank Coughlan in a 1936 article, the influx of American bands was 'the great turning point' for local practice, resulting in a more constrained approach to the music than was the case in the very early phase from 1918 until the first visitors in 1923.[14]

Even if the results sound tepid in the light of later knowledge, it was still impudent enough to offend the professional establishment. The reasons included the claim that the visitors were taking work from the locals, though in fact the growth of interest generated by the United States bands was also creating more work. The opposition to jazz was more complex than the issue of work opportunities. The control of taste in Australia is exercised from a predominantly conservative centre with a distrust of mass and popular culture. This has been especially so in the case of music, and with particular emphasis in the early twentieth century.[15] Jazz—a discordant music with 'negroid' origins—was aesthetically and morally reprehensible, and that it was earning so much money made it all the more offensive. The worst jeremiads were triumphantly fulfilled in 1928, by members of a visiting black revue troupe called the Coloured Idea. Its band, Sonny Clay's Plantation Orchestra, became a *cause célèbre* when members of the group were surprised by police, with reporters in tow, in a hotel room with local girls in scandalous circumstances. The band was sent back to the United States in disgrace.[16]

The opportunity for local musicians to absorb at first hand what a contemporary reviewer described as the 'completely different' sound of a black jazz band was not repeated until the 1950s.[17] In addition, jazz was further demonised, like rock'n'roll thirty years later, linked in the public mind with sex and drugs. This blow was followed up by the effects of talking pictures and, more emphatically, by the Great Depression from 1929. The insouciance of jazz was inappropriate to parlous times, and the first wave of the music's popularity receded with the Roaring Twenties. Although it suddenly seemed thoroughly dated, it had nonetheless situated itself decisively in the national consciousness, and the somewhat racy and rebellious reputation which it generated during this first phase has been decisive in its subsequent history.

From Depression To War

During the early 1930s mainstream popular music reverted to older forms with sentimental lyrics that replaced fun with hope, heedlessness with stoicism. The Soothing Serenaders sang of constancy in adversity on 'Goodbye My Darling' in 1932. One of the Serenaders was Jack O'Hagan, whose composition 'The Road to Gundagai' resurrected the myth of pastoral innocence predating the woes and complexities of contemporary urban living. Although published in 1922, it is symptomatic of the Depression that it was Peter Dawson's 1931 recording that marked the onset of the song's massive popularity. Some jazz activity continued, however, and in the more than thirty tracks recorded by singer Des Tooley over the period 1929–1933, with musicians that included

Abe Romain, Frank Coughlan and pianist Beryl Newell, we hear some of the most convincing jazz yet played in Australia. The men on these sessions went on to establish major careers. Had the two women, Newell and Tooley, recorded in more propitious times, they would have made a much more audible mark. As a public vogue, however, jazz was dead.

Swing brought a reawakening of interest in all forms of 'hot' or modern American music.[18] As early as 1933, drummer Jim Davidson's big band recorded the spritely 'Shuffle Off To Buffalo' back to back with 'Forty-Second Street'. This release reportedly sold an astonishing 95,000 copies, aided by the band's appearances at the Sydney Palais Royal.[19] The shock and the effects of the Depression were ameliorating, and by 1935 the standard of living again approximated the level of 1920, bringing with it a new growth in public recreations.[20] The much publicised opening of the Sydney Trocadero ballroom in 1936 helped to identify the city, the venue and its bandleader Frank Coughlan, with Swing. The fashion quickly became a national phenomenon, with Jim Davidson's national tours for the Australian Broadcasting Commission from March 1937 spreading the message across the country, inspiring the formation of other bands under such leaders as Perth-born Bob Gibson.

Suddenly, the style known as Swing was the essential ingredient of the dance band repertoire. Bandleaders who had formed their competencies during the era of the Edwardian ballroom and music hall now receded from prominence and a new generation of Young Turks emerged, characterised above all by an intelligent awareness of recent developments in United States popular music. The 'Swing Era', covering the period from 1936 to the end of World War II, was a decisive moment in the re-orientation of our popular music from England to the United States. In the work of Barbara James with the Trocadero orchestras, there is virtually no trace of the declamatory English music hall style which was audible in the so-called jazz singers in Australia during the twenties.[21]

Swing clubs, frequently operating in conjunction with radio stations, re-awakened interest in 'hot' music in general, producing a coterie who studied the lineage of the music on reissued recordings of the earlier black groups of the twenties. During the war years, the foundation of the magazine *Jazz Notes* in Melbourne, the Bell brothers, Graeme and Roger, and Ade Monsbourgh, became a focus for this important movement that would gain momentum in the post-war years. Its members increasingly urged the claim of pre-commercial folk authenticity, and became a musical rallying point for artistic and political groups who opposed what was felt to be the philistine commercialism of Australian culture.

The outbreak of World War II reawakened traditional ties with a bravely besieged England, an imperial nostalgia dramatised in such popular songs as 'A Nightingale Sang in Berkeley Square' (1940) and The White Cliffs of Dover (1941). The loss of many of the more experienced and adventurous young musicians to the services also left older musicians (some called out of retirement) in authority over tyros prematurely recruited into professional dance bands. The mood altered with the entry of the United States into the war in December 1941. Accompanied by the rumbling threat of Japanese invasion, this marked the beginning of the most massive invasion in Australia's history: an estimated one million United States service personnel passed through the country.[22] This influx included musicians, many of whom were at the forefront of Swing; and who quickly drowned out the twitterings of the bluebirds over Dover. Apart from the high profile Navy band led by Artie Shaw, other United States entertainment units stationed around Australia mingled with local musicians. A few surviving acetate recordings, the testimony of Australian musicians and contemporary media coverage, confirm that the American personnel gave 'hot' music—Swing and what was being called dixieland—new impetus. Musicians absent in the services were enjoying the stimulus of new influences, particularly American. Local bands operating in areas where United States servicemen were based in large numbers, such as Brisbane, attempted to adapt to the demand for hotter forms of music.

It is important to recognise the important contribution made by young women in the local assimilation of American popular music at this time. Graeme Bell's banjo player, Jack Varney, recalled that during a wartime visit to Brisbane the streets were full of 'marauding Yanks' and the local girls talked with American accents.[23] Through their liaisons with visiting servicemen, women became the major local mediation of the taste for Swing. In their turn the Americans were liable to exaggerate their own enthusiasm for Swing as a musical way of enhancing their desirable American accent.[24] The American presence indelibly transformed Australian popular culture. In terms of music, the period from 1936 to 1945 culminated in a multitude of conflicting forces within which jazz in various forms was increasingly gaining definition.

The Post-War Decade

Following the war there were virtually no visiting American bands for nearly a decade, and Australian jazz began to develop what many have felt constitutes a distinctive style. The years 1946–50 saw the polarisation of Australian jazz broadly in terms of traditional/modern (a bifurcation which was then imposed retrospectively on Australian jazz history). The 'Australian style' grew out of the traditional jazz movement which developed a sense of national identity through the first Australian Jazz Convention (AJC) held in Melbourne in 1946.[25] Two of the central figures in its organisation were amateur drummer Harry Stein, an official of the Eureka Youth League, an organisation strongly linked with the Communist Party of Australia, and Graeme Bell.[26] Attended by musicians from Sydney, Hobart, Adelaide, Brisbane, Geelong, and of course Melbourne, the AJC provided inspiration for those who participated, as well as a glimpse of their regional stylistic differences. The AJC has continued to be held annually ever since, making it the world's first and oldest annual jazz festival.[27] Although little known to the general public, it now often attracts over a thousand delegates and musicians. In its durability and function it is a unique phenomenon, an extraordinary case study of the way in which music constructs a community. It has been the primary means by which Australian traditional jazz has maintained a national community over the last fifty years.

While Melbourne remained the centre of traditional activity, the movement also initially centred on Dave Dallwitz's Southern Jazz Group (Adelaide), the bands led by Tom Pickering (Hobart), the Port Jackson Jazz Band in Sydney, with less focussed activity in other capitals. Through the 1950s this traditional stream broadened, recruiting a growing number of followers, and articulating philosophical positions which embraced cultural issues in which 'authenticity' became increasingly central. This distinguished them significantly from the immediate post-war modern musicians, whose interests were more exclusively musical, and whose attitudes to the sometimes wilful unprofessionalism of the traditionalists therefore ranged from bewilderment to scorn. The latter argued their positions among themselves in a number of highly influential journals, notably the *Australian Jazz Quarterly* (1946–1957). Both this and the earlier *Jazz Notes* were established by Melbourne solicitor William E. (Bill) Miller, and with the AJC they defined and distinguished traditional jazz in Australia. Perhaps they also help to explain why the development of an 'Australian sound grew out of traditional rather than modern jazz. The politics as well as the sound of jazz in post-war Australia were largely shaped by debates over what the word meant and who owned that meaning.[28]

While sections of the traditional jazz community seemed to be regressing through the history of jazz, a growing modern movement was, in its own terms, progressive.[29] The conventions of Swing had consolidated higher technical (if not always aesthetic) standards of musicianship, but within parameters which now became constraining to adventurous young professionals, who therefore sought new stimulation elsewhere. They found it in bop, a complex and (for its time) dissonant form which presented both technical and theoretical challenges.

The development of bop and its relationship with the traditional stream in post-war Australian jazz was shaped by distinctive local conditions. Australia's first jazz phase, during the 1920s, had drawn its models almost entirely from white jazz and hot dance records. The classic jazz which had been recorded primarily by black New Orleans and Chicago-based musicians in the 1920s did not become generally available in Australia until after the advent of later developments in Swing. Advertisements for recordings by the Hot Five, Bix Beiderbecke and Joe Venuti appeared as early as 1932 (*Australian Dance Band News* [*ADBN*] June 1932), but in 1934 jazz multi-instrumentalist Benny Featherstone, a well-informed commentator, was complaining about the serious shortage of 'hot records' and the absence of visiting bands over the previous five years. (*Australian Music Maker and Dance Band News* [*AMMDBN*] 1 February 1934.) Recent and occasionally earlier 'hot' recordings could be heard with increasing frequency on the radio and at Swing club meetings which proliferated in the late 1930s.[30] The first systematic reissue of the 1920s' corpus, however, did not begin in Australia until May 1941 when EMI duplicated locally the Hot Jazz Classics series inaugurated by American Columbia in the previous year.[31] Material shortages and the recording ban imposed by the American Federation of Musicians (1942–44) had restricted importations and occluded the evolutionary development of bop.

American jazz history thus came to Australia deformed and telescoped. When the dam broke, two widely-separated moments in the development of jazz, loosely termed traditional and modern, arrived in Australia almost simultaneously and under different names. The overwhelming majority of Australian musicians experienced bop as an apparently completed commodity, technologically severed from its social origins. Its new name—'rebop'—disclosed no semantic relationship to 'jazz'. These conditions contributed to its image as a culturally neutral higher exercise in musical problem-solving. Bop created deep division in the jazz world. The whole apparatus of production, distribution and consumption which still dominates Australian jazz today is a legacy of these circumstances. Professionals were suddenly presented with a challenge of which they had barely conceived, and many traditionalists could see no good reason even to think of it as having anything to do with jazz. The result was a bifurcation between traditional and modern. 1946 is generally remembered as the year in which the first examples of bop became available in Australia, in the form of the '52nd Street' album with Dizzy Gillespie.

Pianist/composer Don Banks became the centre of the earliest bop experiments in Melbourne through the late 1940s, along with a group of musicians that included Charlie Blott (drums) and Splinter Reeves (reeds). Apart from after hours in coffee lounges and nightclubs the main performance opportunities were in the jazz concerts which became the leading jazz forum in Australian cities from 1947 through to the late 1950s. In Sydney the music found powerful proselytisers in trumpeters Wally Norman, who wrote perceptively and conducted record sessions on the subject, and the much younger Ron Falson, whose Beboppers performed at Sydney's jazz concerts. Although lacking the poise of the American models, in the historical context it is arguable that these early essays required greater imagination than almost any subsequent explorations in Australian jazz. In both Melbourne and Sydney (bop at this time was virtually confined to these centres) this first phase ended with the decline of the jazz concert phenomenon. In Melbourne, the end came rather abruptly around 1950, partly because of the departure of Don Banks for Europe. In Sydney the movement receded more gradually, but left a residue in the activities of musicians like Falson, Don Burrows (reeds), Terry Wilkinson (piano), which maintained some continuity with the next efflux of modern jazz.

The main public forum for live jazz in the post-war decade was the jazz concert phenomenon, which presented the full range of current jazz activity: boppers, traditionalists, and pioneers of the big band progressive styles based on Stan Kenton and Woody Herman, notably under the leadership of Ralph Mallen (Sydney) and Freddie Thomas (Melbourne). While the old dance halls generally catered to a generation thankful for the re-establishment of familiar peace-time values, post-war youth found something more visceral in the jazz concerts, whose stylistic variety also provided the gladiatorial spectacle of 'Battles of the Bands'. During their heyday the concerts were essential in keeping jazz publicly alive on a national scale, but ultimately the competitive element led to a repetitiveness and exhibitionism, which helped to sap their vitality. Another cyclical factor was the progression of its supporters into a new phase of life; of establishing career and family. Technology also played its part in the decline of the jazz concert era, as the long playing record and television began to provide fresh domestic recreation.

Post Rock, Post TV

The displacement of jazz as the dominant Australian youth music was signalled above all by the advent of rock'n'roll in the mid-1950s. In conjunction with changing international marketing strategies, popular music now entered a radically new phase which situated jazz in a new relationship with mainstream music.[32] Although the present account concludes at this point, Australian jazz went on to acquire unprecedented definition, legitimacy and recognition both locally and internationally. More recently it has been a significant musical register of

Australia's social ambiguities and diversities in the late twentieth century. This later history is sketched in other publications, and while it warrants a full-length study of its own, it is not germane to the present discussion.

Over its whole history, jazz has at different times been located at most points on the continuum from mass to high culture, from folk-form to art-form, from popular to elitist. 'A unique type, it cannot be safely categorized as folk, popular, or art music, though it shares aspects of all three'.[33] It appears to have journeyed farther across the terrain of musical categorisation and politics than any other music of the twentieth century. As such, it is the most sensitive and versatile register of the state of negotiations between hegemonic and subaltern musical cultures, and thus a useful site for the broader examination of the political and aesthetic dynamics of twentieth-century western music.

Part 2: New Music, New World

I died in hell—
(They called it Passchendaele)

Sassoon, 1918

Ain't we got fun

Whiting/Kahn/Egan, 1921

If any music announces the twentieth century, it is jazz. It emerges in the 'New World' around the turn of the century, and becomes an international phenomenon during the closing years of World War I. The year 1917 is pivotal. It is the year that the United States entered the war, and in which, for related reasons, the red light area of New Orleans, Storyville, was closed, accelerating the diaspora of musicians that marked the beginning of the global dispersal of jazz. In January 1917 the New Orleans musicians who made up the Original Dixieland Jazz Band opened at Reisenweber's Restaurant in New York, the city that later became the world's jazz Mecca. In the same month they made what are recognised as the first jazz recordings. Their popularity is one of the signs of the beginnings of a major phenomenon of modernity: mass mediated popular music.

The transition to a new order can be dramatised by reference to specific events. On 17 August 1917, the youthful members of the ODJB, as the band became known, assembled for their fourth recording session. All white males, in their 20s, their names suggest a relatively harmonised American cultural diversity. La Rocca, Edwards, Shields, Sbarbaro, Ragas. They wet their reeds, warmed up their instruments, oiled valves, tuned up, assembled their drums, talked over routines and probably shared a joke and maybe a drink. They then faced the huge bell through which their sounds would be transmitted to wax, and prepared to record the music of the new century. By the end of the session they had put down 'Barnyard Blues', 'Ostrich Walk', 'Tiger Rag', and 'There It Goes Again', of which all but the last were issued, to become among their most popular recordings, part of the Esperanto of the jazz repertoire of that time.

On that same day, in England, *The Times* carried the headline 'YPRES BATTLE RESUMED'. As the ODJB were making these recordings, across the Atlantic hundreds of thousands of young men with equally diverse names were struggling and dying in the mud of Belgium, in the Third Battle of Ypres. It culminated in a battle that took its name from the village that marked the limit of the British advance: Passchendaele. The few miles of ground won through the months of the campaign were lost in a few hours in the German offensive of March/April 1918. Total casualties of Third Ypres were up to three quarters of a million men. Australia's population at that time was less than five million.[34] For many, Passchendaele marked the point beyond which the idealisms of the nineteenth century could no longer sustain the criminal waste of life that was called the Great War. On 16 August the Pope had called in vain for an end to the war: 'Shall then the civilised world be naught but a field of death? And shall Europe, so glorious and flourishing, rush ... toward the abyss, ... to her own suicide?' (quoted, Wolff 1958, p.130). In Russia, a new order emerged in the October revolution. The entry of the United States into the war in that year helped to end it. It was the recordings being made by the ODJB at the same moment which musically signalled the new age—of emancipation, of the rise of mass culture and its technological mediations, of modernity.

Jazz and its predecessor in fashion, ragtime, were symbols of the New World. An article in the Australian journal the *Lone Hand* in 1913, reprinted from the London *Times,* had linked ragtime with American qualities of vigour, feverish activity, 'music of the hustler of the Skyscraper'. Syncopation represented an eagerness, a desire to be beforehand which is eminently characteristic of the nationality of its performers'.[35] Whether embraced by enthusiasts or deplored by opponents, jazz inherited this coding. Throughout the 1920s American jazz bands would be hailed as the pioneers of syncopation, playing 'arrangements and styles two or three years ahead of Australia's music world' (*Everyones* 12 December 1928). The sense of innovation was a threat to conservative sectors of the music industry. *Everyones,* 10 September 1924 reported that the general secretary of the Musicians' Union of Australia had complained to the Minister for Home and Territories about the importation of United States jazz bands, claiming that they were taking work from local musicians. He added that the only reason they were being imported was 'because of the novelty', and that this could lead to the importation of 'coloured musicians'. On the same day the *Sydney Morning Herald*, reporting the same event, made pointed comparisons between the 'classic strains of grand opera', and imported jazz bands, described as 'the latter day American cowbell school of music'. These bands 'were drawing crowds to St Kilda to hear the noise that passes in America for music ... we are in danger of Americanisation'.

The references to skyscrapers, speed and loud noise invoke a primary metaphor of the twentieth century—technology. World War I brought about a uniquely heightened perception of technological noise. In a way that is not apparent in the case of World War II, technologised noise was a conspicuous signal of the moment of the arrival of modernity.[36] R. Murray Schafer has traced connections between modern architecture and urbanisation, and increases in the density of acoustic information.

> The size and shape of interior space will always control the tempo of activities within it ... The modulation speed of Gothic or Renaissance church music is slow; that or the nineteenth and twentieth centuries is much faster because it has been created for smaller rooms or broadcasting studios. This development reached its climax in the highly concentrated, information-packed music of the twelve-tone composers. (Schafer 1977, p.219)

Schafer's observations help to explain why jazz and ragtime, as well as serialism, should be so appropriate to the sense of modernity. The dense and apparently dissonant collective improvisations, the fast tempos and rhythmic displacements of the early recordings, were perceived as 'sonic anaphones' for the dense, disjointed acoustic traffic of technologised contemporary life.[37] When leading English bandleader Jack Hylton's trombonist Lew Davis first heard the visiting United States Original Dixieland Jazz Band, he described it as 'an entirely new sound', the drummer using new traps which he played 'in a very modern way'. In Moscow in the early 1920s, when constructivist Valentin Parnakh presented 'machine dances' recreating the spirit of industrial technology, he used jazz.[38]

The point here is not that the devices associated with jazz and ragtime were in any absolute sense 'new'. In fact, they were not. Apart from non-Western music, improvisation and polyrhythm were also significant Western musical practices until falling into decline.[39] In Australia, improvisation gradually fell out of approved practice over the nineteenth century and, by 1918, as jazz entered the country, it had virtually disappeared from art music.[40] Innovation frequently occurs, however, through the retrieval of dormant traditions.[41] Even though jazz was understood to be rooted in 'primitive' African traditions, nonetheless its profile in relation to the European Enlightenment, its *épater le bourgeoisie* component, coupled it with an emancipatory new-century carnivalesque.

Apart from the timing of its arrival and its alignment with New World energies, the formal properties of jazz reinforced the affinities with the modern. The use of previously inadmissible sounds, as of *objets trouvés,* was a marker of twentieth-century music. Apart from occasionally italicising its outrageousness with revolver shots and kitchen utensils, the standard format of jazz groups emphasised new age instruments not formerly prominent in dance-band settings.[42] Some novelty innovations, like the 'shovelene' (a violin/cornet hybrid) were short lived; but others, like the 'jazz stick' (presumably the drummer's brushes) have taken their place alongside banjo, drum kits and saxophone in the jazz line-up. The jazz instrumentation which displaced the relatively low-decibel stringed dance band produced a raucousness that assaulted genteel musical tradition. The saxophone in particular embodied the musical and moral odium which jazz was frequently felt to display. A writer in the *Graphic* of 21 February 1924 condemned the instrument as an 'atrocity', the 'horrible atavism' of the jazz lover, and the 'incalculable harm' likely to be caused by syncopation.

In addition to specific instrumentation, jazz also foregrounded timbral extensions outside the range of traditional notation. Animal noises were prominent, certainly in diasporic jazz as in the celebrated 'Livery Stable Blues'. In Australia during the 1920s this technique was regarded as standard jazz vocabulary by the adjudicators of the Jazz section of the South Street competition in Ballarat.[43] The use of *glissandi,* smears, muted 'wa-wa' effects, growls, evident on Australian recordings from the earliest period, violated legitimate Eurocentric musical techniques in a way analogous to the modernist painters' interrogation of conventions of fine draughtsmanship. Apart from the obvious case of scat singing, the expressive range of the human voice was also extended in jazz performance, employing broader possibilities than modernist Schoenberg's *sprechgesang.* To some extent this was enabled by the arrival of electric amplification; but this was accessible to all forms of music-making, and so it does not, on its own, account for the importance of jazz in modern experiments in vocalising.[44]

Jazz lyrics, as conceived by Tin Pan Alley in the inter-war period, also offered parallels with the experiments of modernist poetry. Philip Furia's study of the lyricists of American popular music of the period demonstrates how creatively they broke up simple popular song structures, displacing accents and introducing cross rhythms that frequently contested overt sense, introducing ambiguities that reflected contemporary urban consciousness and speech. They also disclose resemblances to the modernist poetry of writers like William Carlos Williams and e.e. cummings, in ways that would be more generally recognised were it not for the intimidating high/popular culture divide.[45] Furia cites Lorenz Hart on the impact of jazz phrasing on this development in popular song: it created new problems for the lyricist by throwing the rhythm 'out of gear' (p. 101). Like the Gershwins and Cole Porter, Hart accepted the challenge of jazz as a way of developing a popular music aesthetic through which the contemporary *milieu* could be sketched with a succinct sophistication and wit that recalled modernist poetry, and exploited one of the pervasive modes of modernity—irony.

Formally and thematically, buoyed by the innovations of

jazz, these lyricists modernised the genre by going beyond the expressive and formal constraints of nineteenth century bourgeois popular song. Furia relates Ira Gershwin's lyric for 'Fascinatin' Rhythm' to collage and cubism; and notes the writer's avowed wish to 'write the way Rouault paints' (p.129). Likewise he documents the collagist—the 'list song'—genre, like Porter's 'You're the Top' from 1934. Popular song also moved beyond the genteel treatment of love that dominated light opera and art music of the nineteenth century. The motifs of overt sexual appetite and exotic eroticism—voodoo, black magic—were presented in conjunction with 'jazz' effects of harmony, timbre and rhythm—what was called, in reference to Duke Ellington's palette, 'jungle music'. Furia's documentation casts light on the link between jazz-based lyrics and the rejection of Enlightenment inhibitions regarding alternative erotics. In songs like 'That Old Black Magic', 'Night and Day', 'Day in Day Out', the narrative embraces a primal sexuality in a way for which there was little post-war equivalent in polite society. Porter's 'Love for Sale' ('... appetising young love for sale ...'), voiced a form of eroticism so taboo that vocal versions remained banned in parts of the United States for decades, if not to the present day.[46]

For a range of formal reasons, then, jazz and related African-American musics were available in the inter-war period as markers of modernity to sub-cultural interests situating themselves at the contemporary edge of fashion. This was especially so in Australia where an aura of innovation surrounded the United States as an alternative to imperial traditions. The Sydney Artists' Balls in the early 1920s were a celebration of *le dernier cri* of fashionable bohemia choreographed to jazz. The music gave its name to modern dancing, colours, décor, costumes, and is linked with other gestures of radical chic, including Cubism. As early as April 1918 the *Australian Musical News* had linked Cubism and Futurism with such modern music tendencies in expressing 'the complexities energy and novelty of present-day conditions of life'. Peter Kirkpatrick cites poetry from the 1920s which incorporated jazz elements as a way of accentuating a mannered modernist fragmentation and impressionism.[47] Richard Haese also notes the overlap between young Melbourne radical painters and the local jazz movement.[48] And although declared *déclassé* by the aesthetic and moral arbiters, the music had a voguish appeal across classes. Even for the charity ball set the name 'jazz' represented high fashion, with jazz dances in aid of such causes as the Lord Mayor's nursing appeal and distressed ex-servicemen and their dependents.[49]

Cultural gatekeepers with a custodial duty to civilised traditions, and who opposed the onset of modernity, agreed that jazz was its music. As director of the Albert Street Conservatorium of Music, Fritz Hart FRCM wrote to *Listener In* of 21 March 1924, approving attempts 'to keep jazz and similar music apart from the better class of music'. The influential artist and cultural conservative Norman Lindsay referred contemptuously to modernism as 'jazz in art'. His brother Lionel, virulently anti-modernist essayist and a trustee of the National Gallery of New South Wales, wrote:

> Modernism in art is a freak, not a natural evolutional growth. Its courses lie in the spirit of the age that separates this century from all others; the age of speed, sensationalism, jazz, and the insensate adoration of money.

J.S. MacDonald, as Director of the National Gallery of Victoria a pillar of the conservative art establishment, also attributed decadent modern art to an array of demons of particular relevance to this inquiry:

> ... a generation revelling in jazz, jitterbugging, the elevation of the dress-model to stardom, the transformation by artifice of women into broadshouldered

> narrow-hipped, bottomless beings committed to ungainly attitudes; the exalting of the discordant and the ugly.[50]

The alliance implied by MacDonald's equally vehement attacks on jazz and modernist painting, was explicit among the targets of his spleen. Graeme Bell, who became arguably Australia's most significant jazz musician, began his career in the 1930s, and was also a painter who studied under Max Meldrum.[51] He has remarked the affinities between the jazz coterie and other radical groups in politics (the Communist Party), painting (the Contemporary Art Society—CAS), and literature (the Angry Penguins). The radical alliance of oppositionality is emphasised by the terms in which it is habitually described, and by its multi-levelled libertarianism.[52] The network was social, artistic, ideological. Jazz musicians were frequent visitors and performers at Heide, the virtually 'open house' outside Melbourne where John and Sunday Reed played host to radical painters and *literati* from the mid-1930s to 1940s. Recently published evidence suggests that in at least some cases the musicians were part of the shifting sexual *ménages*.[53] Since the mid-1980s I have had from the jazz community recollections (which remain confidential here) regarding intimate connections. The general suggestion was publicly affirmed by historian Janine Burke who reports assertions by painter Joy Hester and Sunday Reed that the father of Hester's son Sweeney (1945–1979) was not her husband, the painter Albert Tucker, but a local jazz drummer.[54]

Painters of modern inclinations lent their talents to jazz activities, as in décor by Warwick Armstrong and Tony Underhill for the Uptown Club opened by the Bell band in 1946. Clem Meadmore designed the gallery décor for Graeme Bell's Sydney art gallery, and the catalogue for its inaugural exhibition in 1959. The catalogue cover incorporated an abstract by Tom Gleghorn who was represented in the opening along with other emergent experimentalists including John Coburn, Judy

Cassab, Stan Rapotec. Meadmore had once grouped Jelly Roll Morton with Mondrian, Gropius and Frank Lloyd Wright as modernism's most advanced practitioners.[55] The compliment was returned, as in the titles of Roger Bell's compositions 'Old Man's Beard', inspired by a Sidney Nolan drawing and 'First on the Left, Second on the Right', inspired by one of Tucker's.[56] The founding Chairman of the Adelaide chapter of the Contemporary Art Society, Dave Dallwitz, is also a major architect of the 'Australian' jazz style.[57] The common ground between the painters and *literati* of Australian radicalism was also defined musically through jazz. Chief 'Angry Penguin', and *bête noir* of the Adelaide/Melbourne arts community, Max Harris, identified jazz in the 1930s and 1940s as the music of radical identity.[58] In the 1970s Dave Dallwitz wrote and recorded the *Ern Malley Jazz Suite,* commemorating the hoax that brought the controversies over Australian literary modernism to crisis point in 1944. The record cover bore a painting by Sidney Nolan. To mark the inauguration of the Australian Jazz Convention in 1946, Harris and co-editor Harry Roskolenko devoted a full issue of the *Angry Penguins* broadsheet to the event, filling the issue with jazz articles by Australian and overseas writers, and incorporating the official Convention program.

This convergence of interests is representative of a complicity between jazz, with its emancipative life-styles, and the arts that goes back to the closing years of the Great War. This book seeks to throw light on that relationship in Australia's passage into twentieth-century modernity. More durably than any other music, jazz reflected the complex dynamics of the history of mass mediations of the twentieth century. Of our other forms of popular culture, it ranks close to film in this regard, though arguably jazz has suffered fewer and briefer intervals of quiescence.[59] The investigation is not simply a plea for one music *genre.* Jazz is an instructive case study for other vernacular 'arts' in debates on cultural value. This examination will suggest ways of reading our twentieth-century music which are more appropriate to the social realities of Australian cultural history and practice. Their importance relates to a number of issues of increasing urgency: national identity, gender politics, cultural history and policy, technology and discourses of value in the arts.

FIRST BREAK
RECORDING, UNWINDING

8 August 1977, Sydney

A lot of work. I seem to be with about five bands I think and it's a little out of hand. Lessee, lessee, the Eclipse, Dick Hughes, Tom Baker, Graeme Bell, Ray Price. It is hard to keep up. Several gigs with Ray at schools around Sydney. They're really quite pleasant, and however corny some people say his spiel is, the kids apparently like it. It's probably the only time a lot of them have (or will have) encountered a live concert, and more so, it's probably the closest a lot of them will ever get to jazz. Ted Sly is really good with kids—drummers always seem to go over well with young children, maybe because they're allowed to hit things—and Ted's got the bonus of being very comfortable with them.

The other Thursday night at the Soup Plus, Dick was in fine form, which takes me back to the recording session earlier in the day. When I arrived for it Dick was preparing to record one of the Satie solo pieces. He was vibrant with studio jitters. I sat in the control booth with Horst and Ross. Every time Dick would begin they'd start their stop-watches—click click. Fifteen seconds, half a minute, two minutes ... we knew that the piece was three minutes and thirty-two seconds. Two minutes or so rolled around, then at two minutes fifty: Clunk. 'Fuck'. A pause. 'Rolling'. A new start. Two minutes. Clonk. 'F-u-u-u-ck!!' I couldn't see Dick from where I was sitting in the booth, but I could hear him breathing. Hear the scratch of a match and the mighty gulp of smoke. 'Rolling'. One minute. Clunk. 'Shit! Shit! I can't get this fuckin' thing right'. Another take. Another. We are all on edge. After about ten takes it's going, it's going. Two minutes. Three minutes. Just about there. Just then Don Heap arrives, walks past the window and catches Dick's attention. Clunk. 'Fuck.' I am more tense now than if I were recording myself. Next time there's a break I leave the control booth and walk through the studio into the outer office, where I intercept Don. We chat, have a beer. Finally a call comes to say they've got a take. I go back into the studio. It's hot. Dick is now shirtless, taking frenetic oral gratification in the form of smoke and liquid. Mixing the band recordings we had made earlier, and even recording them, actually took less time. Ross rolled the tape, and we played the four numbers straight through, and that was it.

I left for Bondi to do a late afternoon gig in a shopping mall with Graeme, then straight from there at 8p.m. back to the Soup Plus, where Dick is discovered unwinding with a vengeance. As the night rolls on the music becomes a bit disorganised. There's an utterly anaesthetised customer sitting a couple of feet in front of me. He becomes more and more enthusiastic as the booze goes down, a condition he manifests by shouting continuously in cod spade, 'Who-o-o-o dat walkin' round up dere? Who-o-o-o dat walkin' round up dere?' Once or twice this works as an appropriate interpolation. But its frequency and volume increase. Now he is singing through every chorus. It is very loud. We take a break. He says he likes the music. Good, we say. He asks if he can blow my trumpet. I tell him no.

'Jus' one note.'

'No'.

'Jus' half a note.'

'No.'

'Come on. Why not?'

'Just, No!'

'Jeez, jus' a couple of notes.'

Chris who is playing sax in the band, has been listening and interjects.

'Come on man.' he says. 'It's personal. It's personal. Would you want someone else borrowing your false teeth?'

Surprisingly, this seems to make some impression and the

drunk sits down. He is disconsolate, but, alas, is restored to mania when the band starts again. He sings loudly, but he is no longer listening to the band once he has determined what song it is playing. He bawls his way through a softly articulated break on 'Lazy River'. I am pissed off and somewhat pissed. It was my break! I say, 'For Christ sake shutup!' Nothing penetrates his universe now. I make threatening gestures at him with my trumpet.

No impression. Ultimately, towards the end of the night he finally succumbs to some inner prompting and disappears.

Later I am talking to a visiting English jazz musician who has been sitting clear across the other side of this dimly lit room. He probably saw my gesture, but he couldn't have had a clear view or audible impression of its target.

'You know, you ought to be more tolerant of people like that. They're the ones who come to listen. They're the listening public. You should be pleased by their enthusiasm.'

And so on. Do me a favour, I'm thinking. I don't need homilies on the rights and wrongs of drunks in the audience. And 'listening' is exactly what this guy wasn't doing, and making impossible for everyone else. Why should everyone else in the audience have to suffer so that we can all indulge one dickhead. Chris and I looked at each other and said nothing. This seemed pretty presumptuous to us. It was as though he felt constrained to adopt the role of the experienced old trouper offering a few polished words of advice to an eager bright-eyed young hopeful. Sitting at the back of the room all night is a statement that he probably didn't realise was transparent. Later we failed to take up his invitation to join him for supper across the road, since by midnight Dick was putting on a far more compelling show. Chris had taken over at the piano and the rest of us had packed up. Gradually Dick's conversation with a customer became a counterpoint to the piano. His tone, intonation and finally his subject matter adapted themselves to the cocktail languor of Chris's playing. And it wasn't Dick any more, talking while there happened to be a piano playing. It was Noel Coward receiving sympathetic accompaniment to his reading from one of his own shows. It was the best performance of the night. It just pours out of Dick when the mood is on him.

CHAPTER 2
MODERNITY AND MODERNISM

> Modernism in art is a freak, not a natural, evolutional growth. Its courses lie in the spirit of the age that separates this century from all others; the age of speed, sensationalism, jazz, and the insensate adoration of money.
>
> *Norman Lindsay, 1940*

In subsequent chapters I will explore in greater detail the central role played by jazz in the musical articulation of Australia's modernisation. It will also become clear, however, that jazz has received infinitesimal recognition in accounts of that process, nor of musical modernism in Australia—anomalies themselves instructive regarding Australian cultural dynamics. Before proceeding to particular case studies, we must therefore spend a little time investigating the relationship between modernity and modernism; that is, very loosely, the relationship between the condition of living in the modern era, and the attempts to authoritatively define that condition. To do so will involve entering into a debate which is rarely used to frame discussions of Australian jazz. Yet, as I hope the cumulative effect of what follows will demonstrate, it is necessary to do so in order to approach a full appreciation of the significance of this music in Australian social history.

Marshall Berman defined modernism as one of the twentieth-century 'visions ... that aim to make men and women the subjects as well as the objects of modernization, to give them the power to change the world that is changing them, to make their way through the maelstrom and make it their own'. Taking this as a point of departure for an analysis of the Australian situation, J.F Williams reflects the growing recognition that the fit between the discourse of modernism, and modernity as a repertoire of social practices, has been extremely uneven.[60] Recent interrogations of modernism suggest that its attacks on mass culture, for example, reflected growing alarm among intellectuals about the democratisation of access to contemporary culture; modernism itself was a discursive strategy to regain control over such access.[61] To pursue this it is useful to refer to the case of painting which, in Australia, produced a more robust public debate over modernism than music. It also happens that the progressive figures in Australian painting frequently demonstrated affinities with the jazz movement.

A representative architect of the modernist paradigm was Clement Greenberg, two of whose essays, 'Avant-Garde and Kitsch' (1939) and 'Towards a Newer Laocoon' (1940), in the words of T.J. Clark 'set out the main lines of a theory and history of culture since 1850'.[62] Tracing a history of the modernist avant-garde, Greenberg centralises the 'text', the formal properties of the image—thus consciously turning away from the social context of the artwork. This reflects the same despair at contemporary mass culture and its threat to approved aesthetics that animated pessimistic intellectuals from both Right and Left. Greenberg observes with relief that:

> ... the avant-garde arts in the last fifty years achieved a 'purity' and a radical delimitation of their fields of activity for which there is no previous example in the history of culture. The arts lie safe now, each within its 'legitimate' boundaries, and free trade has been replaced by autarchy. (pp.41–2)

Greenberg's formalism became the basis for authoritative apologias of modernism, and took charge of the discourse with a confidence untroubled by anything that might be heard from the producers of modernist images, or the consumers of mass culture.

Models associated with this approach have come under critical scrutiny since the 1970s for a range of reasons.[63] The works privileged by this account do not in fact present a very wide vista of the distinctive experience and character of modernity. To begin with there is a great deal which lies outside the sanctioned modernist field that exhibits the approved formal properties in striking abundance and detail.[64] Modernism conceived primarily in terms of a new and distinct, internally coherent set of formal languages, cannot provide an account of modernity. In an age of mass reproduction and mediation of images, meaning cannot be finished and sealed, inviolate, in the image or object itself. The central issue in the shift to modernity is not so much in the content of the culture in circulation, but in how it was circulated.

Technologised culture, mass-produced and mass-marketed, changed the ways images and their meanings were produced, reproduced, circulated and used in society. Likewise access to cultural images was now given to those hitherto excluded by class, race, place, gender. Jay Winter notes, for example, that in nineteenth-century Europe women were the major consumers in the growing market for mass-mediated culture.[65] This democratisation has increased further with twentieth-century developments in the technology of mass mediation and in parallel with other forms of political and social enfranchisement. All levels of society now have access to an immeasurably greater range of artistic images and practices (visual and acoustic) than even the most privileged of earlier centuries. And in the circulation and consumption of these images, their meanings are constantly renegotiated.

Academic discussion of these changing power relations often seems abstract; nonetheless they recognisably shape every aspect of modern life. The nervous tremors produced by the appropriation of art music in advertising, and by its popularisation as in the best-selling records of 'The Three Tenors', are reminders of how sensitive is the question of the ownership of culture and its meaning in an era of mass reproduction. Irrespective of what Carl Orff's *Carmina Burana* might sound like, and its formal resemblances or otherwise to its thirteenth-century model, its public meaning has now been taken over by mass-marketing. Among other things it has served as soundtrack music for a film about King Arthur, an advertising jingle for a brand of instant coffee, and more recently it became a techno theme. At no point was any uncontestable 'high art' meaning which it might be held to possess, robust enough to withstand these public appropriations. It required the distinctly unaesthetic intervention of copyright legislation to defend its formal and semiotic identity. Even this will not prevent its appropriation in an infinite variety of private meanings, for example as the soundtrack of a custom-produced or home video of a special event.[66] Mass mediations have largely assumed control of the public meaning and value of culture. If we turn away from this profound lesson, whether out of nervousness, disgust, nostalgia or snobbery, we cannot construct an account of modernity.

This process of re-appropriation proclaims the limits of simplistic notions of high and low culture which have flowed from debates regarding modernism, and which fastidiously situate artefacts in one or the other category. In recent critiques of modernism, that mysterious space known as 'mass culture' acquires a different resonance. It is not to be confused with related concepts such as 'low', 'popular', 'folk', which attempt to objectify 'the people'. Such constructs are, as Bourdieu remarks, very largely sites of struggle among intellectuals who situate themselves outside the designated field.[67] The benchmark essay is Walter Benjamin's inescapable 'The work of art in the age of mechanical reproduction'.[68] In terms simply of the cultural artefacts which are produced (film, radio, recording), it is arguable that the 'centre' of the production of meaning and value can no longer be constituted by a privileged intellectual élite, and defined through class, demography, geography. The centre is now the mass mediations themselves. 'Mass' does not refer to a distinct social group and the content of their culture, but to the level and extent at which culture is mediated and distributed, closer to the sense it assumes in the phrase 'mass production'. It is thus almost inescapable, 'just another way of saying culture under developed capitalism'.[69]

It also identifies a very fluid space. Richard Ohmann traces the origins of mass culture to the early nineteenth century and attributes to it:

> ... the homogenization, the over-riding of local and subcultural distinctions, that has [sic] accompanied the expansion of the media in this century ... mass culture in societies like this one includes voluntary experiences, produced by a relatively small number of specialists, for millions across the nation to share, in a similar or identical form, either simultaneously or nearly so; with dependable frequency; mass culture shapes habitual audiences, around common needs or interests, and is made for profit.[70]

He contrasts with this a set of cultural practices through which the homogenising effects of mass culture may be contested. They include:

> ... street games, gossip, square dancing, joke-telling, poker, jogging, smoking marijuana, even Mardi Gras in New Orleans—all those activities that people generate themselves, more or less independently of the market, on their own schedules, and in their own way. Mass culture comes at us from a distance, produced by strangers, (p. 15)

It is, however, increasingly recognised that there is a complex two-way traffic between the two zones which he opposes so neatly. The throwaway phrase 'more or less' elides the extent to which the sites of resistance listed can appropriate the materials of mass culture to reconstruct them and assign them new meanings which are self-empowering. Street rap, cutting and mixing, are just the most topically obvious examples. But even someone listening to a CD in the living room has more power to reconstruct, reject, resituate, recode the music than a dutifully silent and regimented audience in a concert hall. A fixation on the product in the analysis of culture (which characterised the classic theorisations of mass culture such as those of Adorno and Horkheimer), overlooks the extent to which the *processes* involved in consumption are characterised by creative re-articulations of the mass-produced and mediated product.[71]

This idea of creative consumption has sometimes been used to romanticise mass culture as an unambiguous site of heroic emancipation. This is as dangerous a simplification as demonisation, and for the same fundamental reason. Both positions refuse to let the 'object' speak on its own terms.

> To liberal, Frankfurt and dominant ideology theories of the high culture/ popular cultural divide, the same single objection can be made—they assume ordinary people are fools.[72]

Having declined to ask the 'masses' or 'the people', whoever they are, what they think of culture, how they read it and use it, the proponents of such theories have interpreted silence in whatever way it suited them. If, for example, they deem the product simple-minded, so too must be the consumer. There is no particular evidence that consumption of so-called low culture is, in its own terms, any more or less finely discriminated than consumption of high art. Varnedoe and Gopnik, explicitly adopting the word 'popular' as a substitute for 'mass', revisit the high/low binary

> ... to examine the transformations through which modern painters and sculptors have made new poetic languages by reimagining the possibilities in forms of popular culture. (Varnedoe and Gopnik 1991, p.19)

Why is it axiomatic to distinguish absolutely this form of 'consumption', which is called 'reimagining the possibilities', from other forms? Or: how do we know that the demotic consumers (who, incidentally, are discriminating enough to reject most films and pop records produced by the 'culture industry'), are not also 'reimagining the possibilities' in the way they use commodities? The answer is that we have very little information on which to take this for granted. The pessimistic and patronising bulletins about the benighted 'masses' which are regularly issued from modernist and postmodernist commentators are based on their conviction that only they can see through the shallow surface of contemporary culture. Until they check with the patient, these diagnoses are of little other than career value.[73] This is why the immediate future of cultural studies must lie in such mechanisms of consultation as are evident in relatively recent music ethnography.[74] I have tried to recognise this *terra incognita* in my discussions of particular popular cultural products and practices, by using circumspection in reading the message of, for example, recordings and film, and by trying as far as possible to listen to the voices of the 'object', such as Barbara James'.

In any event, the idea that the academies can control the definitions of the experience of modernity simply by continuing to occupy the cultural high ground, shows a profound ignorance of one of the central features of modernity—the fascination exercised by the products and processes of mass culture. Frequently missing in the modernist paradigm was a recognition of the quotidian manifestations of modernity on a popular scale. The most immediate and pervasive experience of modernity was not through the work of self-consciously modernist writers and composers, but through emancipative changes in everyday life at a 'mass' level. Culture was a mass clamour, in the midst of which the voices of Ezra Pound, T.S. Eliot, Virginia Woolf were extremely faint. The experience of the modern converged upon and manifested itself in mental and physical spaces regarded as negligible by the intellectual elites, even while they shared those spaces.

These spaces were trivialised in the authoritative post World War I discourses of cultural value by which Eurocentric intellectuals appropriated the experience of modernity and controlled the meaning of 'modern'.

> Modernism is an ideology which systematically misrepresents the real relations between the meaning of art and its practices and how and why works of art are and were *produced.*[75]

Its effect was to regulate the flow of the cultures of the modern into the category of meaningful experience and discourse, deciding what had significance in the new order and, perhaps more importantly, to exclude that which might threaten the existing intellectual hegemony. This is why, even as it proudly proclaimed the imperative articulated by Pound as 'make it new', the deeper foundation of establishment modernism was a romanticism in conflict with many overtly radical modernist mannerisms. The bloc which retained control of the meaning of modernity was compelled to exclude those aspects of the modern (mass culture, especially) which threatened the model of cultural politics by which the superiority of the intellectual was maintained. This is above all the case in relation to the ownership of cultural meaning and value. The articulators of modernism took for granted that the meanings of cultural objects and practices are defined by an intellectual élite, and that no valid meanings or communications can occur outside their cognisance.

However unreliable this account of modernity, it was nonetheless a discourse which had the power to create a modernist movement in the imaginations of Australians, and like all maps it made something distant appear real, to be imagined, desired or feared, and to govern conduct and attitudes accordingly. Notwithstanding recent critiques, the ideology of modernism remains robust in public and institutional cultural discourses, as I shall illustrate in the final section of this book.

Modernity and Modernism in Australia

The incongruities between modernity and modernism proliferate even further when applied to the case of Australia, with its distinctive geographic and socio-cultural positions. Anne-Marie Willis is one among many scholars to observe the complicity of modernism in debates about national identity, and in her comment that 'national culture is seen as an important component of national identity', there is latent a fundamental contradiction in the idea of 'Australian modernism'.[76] The two terms are competitive, the first having a regional pull, the second an internationalist vector. One asserts distinctiveness from a metropolitan centre, the other assets sameness.

The tension emerged with particular clarity in the exhibition of paintings called *The Field*, presenting Colour Field work as exemplified by, among others, Sydney Ball. It opened at the new National Gallery of Victoria (NGV) in August 1968, to mixed receptions. In his preview, Patrick McCaughey claimed that these artists of avant-garde modernism had transcended regionalism and had entered an international discourse, 'Responding not to the dilemma, "What does it mean to be an Australian painter?" but to "What does it mean to be a painter?"' At the same time he asserted that this was the first genuinely modernist movement in Australia. Traversed by other dynamics including local and state rivalries, this is the *reductio ad absurdum of* the equation of modernism with internationalism, implying that no articulation of modernity can accommodate Australian regional identity, that Australia, indeed, has no validly expressible experience of the twentieth century on its own terms. If, as Heathcote asserts, this moment marks the long-overdue institutionalisation of the idea of innovation at the NGV in the influential opinion of McCaughey and his supporters, it is also the institutionalisation of a definition of modernism that writes out of existence nearly all of the individual and collective experience of modernity in Australia, including of all previous painters. It is Australian modernism largely purged of Australian modernity.[77]

Such ambiguities will always be present in any cultural dynamic, but they protrude with particular grotesquerie in the attempt to fit the drapery of Eurocentric modernism over the Australian experience of modernity. There are many contours in the twentieth-century profile of Australian society that cannot be comfortably accommodated to European models.[78] The impact of World War I on Australian society exhibited crucial differences from its effect on Europe. These included the conservatism of authoritative post-war mythologies, which diverted post-war Euro-modernist momentum towards a nostalgic nationalism that invoked imagined rural values of the 1890s. The suspicion in bush mythology of urban life was resistant to one of the primary sites of European modernism. This itself is a provocative irony, given the role of urban voices in constructing the rural myth.[79]

To try to read Australian modernity by unreflective reference to European discourses also overlooks a major feature of global modernity: the shift away from Eurocentric and nineteenth-century cultural formations, including the particular forms of the élitism which they took for granted as centres of cultural gravity. In short, modernisation decisively, though not un-problematically, overlapped with Americanisation.[80]

In Australia, apart from the geographical factor, the shift is associated with the emergence of a new model of cultural dynamics based on factors such as class, relations of production and consumption and mass media. The assumption that in the formation of culture, and the account of that formation, the traditional sites of these processes and debates are still the 'centres' is, as I have suggested, a failure to grasp a crucial feature of modernity. That is, that the centre from which public discourse was controlled was shifting from an intellectual élite to some other cultural space. The evidence is, however, that the established power blocs—patriarchal, inward or anglo-centric—overestimated the pliancy of mass culture to their standards of taste, civilisation, excellence, and the redemptive power of their own idealism in steering the young away from vulgarity to the sites of higher culture. If they wagged an Arnoldian finger at it, it would behave itself or go away.

The alternative hypothesis is that modernism—insofar as it denotes the sense of modernity—made its earliest inroads into Australia at an *ad hoc* popular level rather than through the systematic discourses of high art. Anne-Marie Willis suggests that early Australian consumer culture was a more open channel for the infiltration of modernist images into the public consciousness than were the high art forms.[81] Mary Eagle has noted the emergence of pictorial representations of modernity in practices which, because they were conducted outside the patriarchal discourses of 'serious' art, were not officially recognised for what they were.[82] She is writing about the work of cartoonists, interior decorators, magazine illustrators who, precisely because they were 'popular', were deemed to have nothing important to say about reality. Peter Kirkpatrick has also observed the connection between popular cultural practices, modernism and (in something of an aside) jazz. While 'cubism' was still a dirty word in high art circles, its images were adorning the paraphernalia of urban popular recreation through Art Deco design.[83]

The sites at which these images were consumed are suggested in Mary Mackay's report of Norman Lindsay's dismissive attitude towards Thea Proctor's modernist paintings. They were too trivial for a London art show, but 'all right' for the modern life-style journal *Home*. 'Fashion', writes Mackay, 'was positioned as a very important signifier of the modern'.[84] Sydney Ure Smith's association with 'fine art' is a commonplace of Australian art history, but his editorship of *Home* is less often noted, and he himself observed the anomaly of the prejudices against the modern in serious art held by people who embraced it in domestic decor (Eagle 1978, pp.80,84). The primary environments in which modernity was embraced were not those which provided institutional legitimacy, but in domestic and recreational spaces. In a discussion centred on the United States, Martin Pumphrey wrote:

> Any adequate reading of the modern period ... must take account of the fact that debates over women's public freedom, over fashion and femininity, cosmetics and home cleaning were as essential to the fabrication of modernity as cubism, Dada or futurism, as symbolism, fragmented form or the stream-of-consciousness narrative. (Pumphrey 1987, p. 181)

This being so, it should not be surprising that early modernism was gendered. Cultural authority is inevitably resistant to any innovation that threatens its power base. Such innovation was therefore likely to be practised on the margins of the high-art landscape. In terms of gender, that means women. The association between cultural corruption and femininity is perennial in patriarchal mythology, and has particular inflections in relation to the advent of modernity.[85] In her study of the place of women in the popular imagination of England in the 1920s, Billie Melman has shown that the whole disruptive project of modernity was traced to the 'new woman'. From the threat to patriarchy to the rising tide of international socialism, it was all summarised in the passage of the Representation of the People Equal Franchise Bill in 1928.[86] Women's emancipation was the threatening face of the twentieth century, reflected in their shift from the home to the public sphere and in the 'massive body of erotic literature written by women for a female audience (Melman 1998, pp.104, 150).

The industrialisation and urbanisation of the West throughout the nineteenth century also saw cultural authorities come to regard many popular recreations as manifestations of vice.[87] This connection had particular resonance in Australia, where, because of its settlement as a remote penal colony, the danger of being outflanked by the criminal and the savage encouraged the authorities' civilising mission, producing a generalised suspicion of demotic energy. Geoffrey Bolton distinguishes the pattern in government at the foundation of the colony from those in England and the United States by its 'positive discouragement of grass-roots enterprise'. Similarly, Hilary Carey reports that the government saw the early clergy as more akin to prison chaplains than providers of pastoral care for the colony as a whole. The clergy for their part assumed that all convicts, both male and female, were 'dead to all religious sentiment'.[88]

In Australia the relationship between cultural control and the unruliness of popular social practice, was tautened as modern technology democratised access to the material embodiments of culture. Images that represented the highest ideals of a society based on privilege, class, wealth, became available to every living room. The appurtenances of life—fabrics, furniture, domestic comforts—which had once defined the balances of cultural and economic power, now became common property. As ownership of culture could no longer be monopolised, it became necessary to refine stratagems of control. Initially the tactic was opposition to the rising tide of modernity. The custodians of Australian culture, the Norman Lindsays, the J.S. MacDonalds, condemned and trivialised pleasures and gratifications spreading beyond their control. The tone began with composed superciliousness, modulating to strident anger as it became clear that theirs was a lost cause.

By 1939 MacDonald had lost the plot, declaring an exhibition of contemporary European art held in Melbourne in 1939 to be the work of degenerates and perverts, filth that would pollute the gallery.[89] The floodtide of modernity was rising from the cultural lowlands and threatening to engulf the high ground. As it did so, opposition became increasingly desperate, notably in the deranged stridency of Lionel Lindsay's *Addled Art* (1942). Prime Minister Menzies' Academy of Art can be seen as beginning the last phase in the tactic of opposition by damming; it finally withdrew behind the levees of the National Gallery of Victoria. As late as 1953 one of its trustees, Mr Justice Scholl, responded to suggestions that the NGV should purchase more contemporary works:

> I can never see why we should use public money to place every eccentricity of modern art in our gallery ... Modern art is a revolt against the camera and should be allied to industrial design. It is neither pleasant in subject nor accurate in presentation. Moderns will not spend time to become real craftsmen. (quoted Heathcote 1995, p.40)

Following a brief resurgence of conservatism during the Great Depression, modernism continued its ascendancy.[90] The new generation of legislators shared with their predecessors the objective of controlling the discourse of the arts, but instinctively recognised that a new tactic was necessary—appropriation rather than resistance. Four years before MacDonald's comments, Mary Evatt, returning from Europe with her husband, the barrister and parliamentarian H.V. Evatt, was quoted in the *Women's Weekly* on her impressions of the works of the 'modern masters' she had been 'privileged' to see. 'In essence', she said, 'they stand for what is best in the masterpieces of the past.' She referred to their 'colour and design', the 'inspiration' they derived from the 'Primitives' (thus capitalised) and 'superb' ancient sculpture; 'impeccable' draughtsmanship:

> My husband was lucky enough to see much of Picasso's new work. In the last two years he has painted more than a hundred pictures. He is one of the greatest personalities in Paris. (quoted Williams 1995, p.216)

Modernism has now produced a sanctioned version of the modern. Evatt's words reflect the appropriation of modernity into unthreateningly familiar paradigms. Picasso's revolutionary assault on a naturalist tradition informed by representational draughtsmanship had nothing to do with his canonisation by Evatt. He is redeemed simply by a member of the establishment-elect pronouncing that his draughtsmanship is 'impeccable'. During a visit to Europe, which only those of her class could enjoy, Mary Evatt (through her husband) was able to take ownership of Picasso in a way that could not be disputed by the stay-at-homes. The statement re-establishes the gulf between those who own the meaning of culture and the others, *hoi polloi,* who really don't understand.

'Modernism' became the approved version of what mattered in modernity. It is noteworthy that everyday, popular culture was prominent in the inventories of modernity by those who opposed it, but then all but vanished in the accounts of those who defined and embraced modernisms. That is, it was equally unwelcome to both elites, attacked by the earlier group, excised by their successors. The mass culture that is one of the markers of modernity, is banished from institutionalised modernism, a manoeuvre paralleled by a process of masculinisation. Williams cites a 1935 *Australian Women's Weekly* article which enthused about the new emphasis in the Julian Ashton art school:

> There is a new school in painting among these youngsters in art, whose members are as modern as the 'maddest' of the Continental schools. This is the Crowley-Fizelle school. Fizelle will be remembered not so long since as a painter of high talent who was developing along conventional lines. Of a sudden he said goodbye to all that and set about a new technique, a new viewpoint, a new colouring, and a new everything. (quoted Williams 1995, p.213)

Apart from Williams' extrapolations from this statement, there is a further point to be made. The discussion is not just about evidence of modernity as a life-style—the modern woman, the modern kitchen, modern fashion—but the sacralisation of modernity as art. In the process the spotlight now narrows to a leading established institution (the Julian Ashton school was founded in 1890), singling out a painter who is a male teacher, as central to 'new' styles, and it implicitly locates the source of the style in Europe. There is not the slightest glimpse of a substantial tradition of over two decades of modern design and painting in Australia, largely sustained by women. It was institutionally unsupported—indeed trivialised—mediated through the popular press and domestic décor, and drew much of its subject matter from local and everyday experience (as in Grace Cossington-Smith's now celebrated *The Sock Knitter* of 1915).[91]

The modern has suddenly sprung into existence at the 'top', in a patriarchal educational institution for high art. The *Rebels and Precursors* exhibition of 1962 at the NGV gave public legitimacy to modernism, but implied that the movement had 'only emerged and matured during World War II'. Apart from writing out the work of the 1920s and 30s, this also enhanced the masculinisation of modernism—Joy Hester, for example, was not included in the exhibition. When the *Bulletin* listed the thirteen most commercially successful modernists of the early 1960s, all were male.[92] Modernity has become modernism and, in the process, has shed all the vulgar (and feminine) baggage which would compromise its dignity as 'art'.

These are richly ambiguous dynamics, which confound simple binaries like conservative/radical. Modernism was also traversed by politics of gender, generation, class and geography. The way someone situated her/himself in relation to the struggle for control of the modern might depend on gender one moment, on locality or class the next. But the significant revolutionary thrust in the everyday manifestations of modernity was not manifested as heroic opposition. It lay in subversive indifference to the whole institutionalised debate over the artistic legitimacies. Whichever side one took—academy or Contemporary Art Society—that debate itself was part of the exclusionary conservatism threatened by mass-mediated modernity. To campaign for the acceptance of an expressive form into the institutional discourse is a noble cause, but it also accepts the authority of the latter. Not to care is more threatening. The transition to modernity was largely characterised by the decision that it just didn't matter, the action was elsewhere: in the commonplace, the vulgar, unselfconscious ordinariness of mass culture.

The avant-gardists of the Colour Field movement were ideologically still at one with an Enlightenment dialectic summarised by Heathcote as 'a belief in the artist as an heroic being, in the creative act as an unmediated expressive emission, and in the work of art as a transcendental object with a single implicit meaning'. These modernists were 'embarked on a quest for a lost absolute'. Rather than turn towards contemporary mass society, they closed the shutters and comforted themselves by ransacking the attic of recent art history, 'recycling a sequence of idioms from the golden age of modernity', going back as far as Russian and European experiments of the 1920s. 'Late modernism had become the age of *déjà vu*'.[93]

An alternative response was to look unwaveringly at contemporary society, as in Melbourne artist Robert Rooney's representations of the mundane richness of everyday life, to aestheticise rather than to anaesthetise the relationship with the abundant ordinary (Heathcote, 1995, p.213). Aesthetics were thus bought belatedly into greater recognition of the conditions of modernity. There is some irony, then, in the fact such developments came to be categorised as postmodernism, when they seem really to reflect a closer convergence of arts discourse with modernity itself. By this logic, postmodernism reflects not a cultural vanguard, but a rearguard, a delayed recognition of the implications for artistic practice of twentieth-century mass culture. Modernism attempts to maintain control of cultural value by writing large tracts of modernity out of aesthetics, postmodernism is the attempt to do so by writing it in, under strict conditions.[94]

The history of modernism as it unfolded in relation to Australian painting provides a model which helps give some intelligibility to other areas of Australian cultural history, and from it we can abstract some general patterns which will throw light on music in particular.

In noting Rooney's engagement with everyday mass culture, it should be remembered that people who have enjoyed the designation 'artist' have defied the high/low divide since the onset of modernity. The early avant-gardists themselves were clearly fascinated by the products of mass culture. Braque and Picasso had set the agenda in avant-garde painting precisely by incorporating industrial stencilling, scraps of newspaper and synthetic materials into their work. The *Blaue Reiter Almanac* produced by Kandinsky and Franz Marc in 1911 sought to embrace the contemporary in all its forms: 'We must show that something is happening *everywhere*.'[95] The significant change is not in what people are doing in relation to mass culture, but what the guardians of value are saying about it. That is, which phase is dominant at any moment: resistance or appropriation?

Of course these distinctions are by no means absolute. There is for example two-way traffic between artistic debate and artistic practice. Any aesthetic which gives or withholds approval from a position of power is going to encourage works of art made to order. Whether by design, instinct, or something between osmosis and coincidence, the Colour Field painters produced work that was ideologically congenial to the discourses of modernism. It is in this sense that I suggest they most fit the description 'modernist painting': it is not that they reflect the unregulated social realities of modernity, but rather the version approved by modernism. Hence their *déjà vu* quality: they are produced in accordance with an ideology that has produced a canon. In the same way, Australian music, and jazz in particular, has come to include a stream that is constructed with the criteria of government funding bodies in mind.[96] This is not necessarily a derogatory observation: we have to express ourselves in relation to some cultural imperative, and aesthetically it remains to be demonstrated why public money is any better or worse than private capital.

The Colour Field exhibition and the work by Rooney were proceeding in the same decade, and reflect a moment which is analogous to the tactical shift from resistance to appropriation that generated an approved form of modernism. J.S. MacDonald's resistance to modernism was grounded in the institutionalised resistance to modernity and to mass culture. The enthusiasm for the 'Cowley-Fizelle School', and Mary Evatt's praise of Picasso signal the overlapping phase of appropriation, in which modernism became an acceptable version of modernity, decently cleansed of mass culture. A similar transitional moment is apparent in the coincidence of Colour Field and the movement represented by Rooney's work in the 1960s, but in this instance, a transition from 'Modernism' to 'Postmodernism'. The institutionalisation of modernism is in fact a conservative gesture, while what became known as postmodernism was recognising the need to appropriate mass culture if it were to have any chance of controlling its meanings.

The thread of continuity through all this remains the

insistence that the ill-defined demographic called the 'masses' have nothing meaningful to say, that they cannot produce meaningful culture, that they cannot be relied upon to engage with mass culture with any discrimination, depth, or self-empowering intelligence. The ideological substrate is thus continuous with the anxieties experienced by intellectuals since the rise of mass culture over two centuries or so and which found expression in romanticism, modernism and most recently forms of postmodernism. Each proudly foregrounds rupture, emancipation from a preceding repressive regime, but each is a refinement of the same strategy: the attempt to retain cultural power in the face of its democratic material devolution.

Music and Modernity in Australia

I have documented the growing institutionalisation of modernism, to the point at which, by the 1950s and 1960s (depending on which expressive form we are considering), it defined the authorised perspective on our cultural modernisation. More recently, as I indicated at a number of points in the foregoing, the ideology of modernism has come under increasing critical scrutiny. That scrutiny has changed the way we read contemporary and recent cultural practices, and has also led to refreshingly revisionist histories of Australian painting. In broad terms, however, such revisionism in relation to music historiography has scarcely begun, and certainly has made negligible impact in the public arena.

In the remainder of this chapter I wish to show that the history of institutionalised music discourse follows a parallel trajectory, in which jazz was implicated because it was the pre-eminent music of modernity. As musical experience exploded beyond the control of an élite (defined by class, gender, race, economics, but legitimated by moral and aesthetic 'ideas'), it became necessary to implement strategies to regain the cultural authority which had formerly been enforceable through the ownership of the musical product. If everyone now had music, 'taste', projected broadly through the construction of high and low culture (on which both moral and aesthetic converged) fenced off one part from the other, providing the lever in successive stages of maintaining control: resistance, appropriation—raise the fence or move the fence. At some levels expressive life went on heedlessly, making meanings without reference to the critical arbiters. At other levels there were adjustments made to expressive practices, above all by those who sought institutional approval. These obligingly produced art to order, and offered themselves as exemplary confirmations of the approved artistic paradigms: individual genius, scorn of commercial success, conveniently unworldly.

In its liminal position, shifting back and forth across the musical terrain, jazz has reflected these dynamics more than any other music. It has thus produced street music, museum music, concert music. With cheerful opportunism it has engaged with popular commerce; it has also produced its art-music pastiches as votive offerings to high culture. The former are generally dismissed as negligible, the latter receive approval as examples of what the simple natives can do when they try. As a consequence those forms of jazz activity which, out of indifference or ignorance, have remained outside the jurisdiction of art music have simply failed to register in the cultural ledger. And yet it is here that jazz has made the most profound contribution to Australia's culture and music.

That Rooney was associated with jazz-based improvisational projects is one of many connections that contribute to a discussion of the parallels between painting and music in the construction of Australian modernity.[97] The historiography of modernism in Australian music parallels that of modernism in general, but is intensified because of the entrenched conservatism in music scholarship which prevailed until the emergence of 'New Musicology' in the 1970s. Steven Paul Scher speaks for many when he writes that in general, 'of all humanistic disciplines, the study of music has been perhaps least receptive to novel critical approaches'.[98] One consequence is that, as in painting, the canon of 'modernist' music excluded most of the music of modernity. Summarising the field, Richard Middleton wrote: 'Musicology ... is clearly a science which, above all others, should study popular music. With a few exceptions, it has not done so'.[99]

Joseph Kerman sweepingly identifies two phases of modernism in music: the first concluding just before World War I, with, for example, Stravinsky and Schoenberg's *Pierrot Lunaire* and the second starting directly after World War II in the work of Pierre Boulez, Stockhausen, John Cage.[100] Brown identifies a series of polarities in the language of nineteenth century music, which contrasts with much of the most characteristic music of this [the twentieth] century'; the first major interrogation of that mode of proceeding was conducted by Schoenberg.[101] Schwartz and Godfrey identify the development of modern music in the emergence of micro-tonality, dissonance and the weakening of tonality; the expansion of instrumentation and musical coloration; the questioning of goal-oriented narratives; a new interest in music composition as process and in its performance conditions.[102] Jazz unquestionably exemplifies most, and arguably all, of these. Yet while it (and other popular musics such as so-called folk) is referred to, it is only as an *influence* on the modern composers, such as Stockhausen, Carter, Babbit, Martino (pp.59, 61, 85, 88). At precisely those moments where one could expect jazz to surface, it remains conspicuously silent. In discussing the expansion of admissible sounds in modern music, Schwartz and Godfrey mention Antheil's xylophones, doorbells, automobile horns, in his *Ballet mécanique* (1923), and Varèse's bells, sirens, temple blocks in the 1933 work *Ionisation* (p.109). Although these are markers of modernism, no reference is made to the jazz, jug and spasm bands of the 1920s and earlier, in which instruments such as the jug, kazoo, comb and paper, suitcase, woodblocks, cowbells, and temple blocks were commonplace.

In Australia, the jazz band leader Linn Smith was augmenting his tonal textures by plucking the strings of the piano with his right hand while playing the keyboard with his left (Whiteoak 1999, p. 182). The fact that this probably appeared to be in a spirit of fun does not in itself alter the fact that the formal gesture anticipates those of later musical modernists. Abe Romain (who joined Smith in the late 1920s) described the use of 'loop' scores which predated similar devices used to accompany experimental practices in the 1950s; these in turn look back to procedures used in earlier theatre entertainment.[103] Yet the closest which that seminal development in modern music, jazz, can get to the discourse of modern music is as an influence on it, but not an example of it. One explanation recalls the discussion of modernism in general: post-diaspora jazz is also an example of mass culture. As in the case of the Greenberg model, musical modernism thus arises largely as an outraged protest against that phenomenon (Middleton 1990, pp.13–14). Again, 'Modernism' is an attempt to purge modernity of one its most significant characteristics.

The difficulties that beset Euro-modernism in music are exacerbated in the case of Australia for reasons operating in Australian modernism in general. Williams observes the disappearance of young men from the 'making of music, art and literature' in Australia during World War I, paralleling a feminising of such activities at a time when cultural discourse was controlled by a conservative, imperial-minded, anti-modern patriarchy. It coincided with a huge chasm between high and mass culture. The latter was embodied in American life-style and entertainment technology, and represented cultural degradation (J.F. Williams 1995, pp.6–7). Waterhouse among others has also noted the antipathy among intellectuals to American culture, particularly as in its popular manifestations, films and comics, from the 1920s to the 1940s.[104]

The chasm between high and low was particularly wide in

music scholarship. Roger Covell's account of Australian music cited John Antill's *Corroboree* as the first public notice of 'music truly belonging to the twentieth century ... being written in Australia'.[105] As its orchestral music dates from 1946, by this account no Australian music had signalled the arrival of the twentieth century until it was half gone. By 1960, most Australian composers were still writing in styles that were already 'stale' in other countries fifty years earlier (p. 158). This represents the same occlusion of demotic activity as in painting, and a parallel case of the late modernist *déjà vu* reported above by Heathcote. The significant advent of modernism in Australian music is conceived in Eurocentric formalist terms, and signalled in the work of Richard Meale and Peter Sculthorpe in the 1960s. Yet in the search for Australian 'music truly belonging to the twentieth century' a clue is waiting to be found in representatives of the 'forward wing' of Australian music. Among these Covell identifies Raymond Hanson, whose experience in organising and writing for jazz bands in wartime Australia is cited as a reason to expect metrical innovation (p.161). Again, however, jazz is not part of the field designated by the label 'Australian music', but some kind of presumably non-musical activity hovering outside. It must be stressed that my observations are not a particular reflection upon Covell's pioneering historiography. The same selective vision is evident in other music scholarship post-war, as in the accounts of Don Banks below. These draw attention to a pervasive reluctance on the part of institutional music discourse in Australia to give serious consideration to 'music' in terms broader than 'art music'. At the sites where the cultural importance of music is established—academies, conservatoria, concert halls—those practices which are the most widespread sources of twentieth-century music experience have been largely ostracised.

There is welcome evidence of a growing shift away from this paradigm. Papers presented at recent Musicological Society of Australia conferences; the local growth of the International

Association for the Study of Popular Music; the journal *Perfect Beat,* and the 1996 *Register of Theses on Australian Music,* produced by Melbourne's Centre for Studies in Australian Music; all these disclose a growing appreciation of popular, multicultural and vernacular musics. There is a long way to go, however, before the implications of current and as yet largely unpublished scholarly research impinge on authoritative public discourse. As recently as August 1993 the composer Carl Vine, delivering one of the inaugural Eugene Goossens Lectures at the Sydney Opera House, pondering 'where the 21st century may lead' in terms of music, dismissed popular music as having nothing at all to offer of any interest to his subject.[106]

This is a view which takes for granted that there is a 'leading edge' of music as a register of contemporary civilisation, and it is to be found in 'art music' of a kind which had little significant presence in Australia until the 1960s. Yet the evidence assembled in Chapter One indicates that the sense of modernity was heard in Australian music from at least as early as 1918, when the first jazz performances were advertised as such in this country. Internationally the importance of jazz as a major musical embodiment of the modern has been noted if not studied, both by a number of art music performers and composers of the early twentieth century and by subsequent historians of modernism.[107] Because Australian cultural discourse deferred to Eurocentric and 'top-down' models of cultural influence, however, it has been very slow to recognise the arrival of modernist sensibilities except as propagated by high art European sources.[108] In the meantime, major twentieth-century developments in African-American music had been directly crossing the Pacific and influencing local grassroots practices since the 1920s. As we have seen, jazz was the musical code for modernity and exhibited significant 'modernist' formal properties. But the music was also popular, American and as we shall see, often feminised. As far as the Australian music establishment in general was concerned it was therefore beneath attention. Musical modernism largely ignored musical modernity.

Don Banks: Jazz Musician

The resulting schizophrenia may be briefly illustrated if we revisit the convergence between jazz and modernism in painting and literature in the 1930s and 1940s. A striking number of the pioneers of modernist experimentalism spent their early careers in jazz or related popular musics. In the immediate post-war period examples include Keith Humble, Malcolm Williamson, Don Banks, followed by composers such as Eric Gross, Barry Conyngham, Nigel Westlake and Martin Wesley-Smith. But up to the late 1950s jazz was still generally excluded from academic musical discourse. Thus, the musical careers of emergent modernists were seen as having no very significant activity outside art music. Any popular music activity was just dabbling, and in fact, not really 'music' activity at all, but an influence on their music.[109]

The example of Don Banks provides a pertinent illustration also because of his involvement in the Bell/CAS/Angry Penguins vector. Don Banks is regarded as an influential figure in the modernist wing of Australian music. His significant career is almost invariably dated from his departure for the United Kingdom in 1950. Before this, in accordance with the self-abasing cultural lag perspective, this lively minded twenty-seven year old experienced a conventional and uninspiring education in music. He arrived in Britain as a naïf *tabula rasa* awaiting the up-to-the-minute enlightenment which had been denied him in Australia—where, it is incidentally noted, he dabbled in jazz.[110] Murdoch cites his *Piano Sonatina* as 'the only work of his to achieve public performance before he left for Europe' (Murdoch 1972, p.16).

Yet evidence from outside the established scholarship is that this period was both formative for Banks and influential on others, particularly in experimental innovation. In Melbourne during the 1940s his eclectic curiosity enabled him to act as a two-way channel between insights absorbed from a jazz scene undergoing one of its most volatile periods, and a conservatorium ethos that, among the post war 'rehab' students, was far from conventional.[111] Far from being musically quiescent, Banks was so central to modern jazz experimentation that his departure was one of the most important factors in the termination of the first phase of bop in Melbourne.[112] From 1943–1950 Banks participated in at least eight recording sessions, producing a total of 23 tracks.[113] There is also evidence of other recording sessions: for example in December 1941 four tracks were apparently recorded, including 'Don Banks Boogie'.[114]

Apart from the fragility of the claim that this period was negligible musically, this blocking out of his activity has deprived historians of 'serious music of the opportunity to study aspects of Banks' musical development towards subsequent work more dear to their interests. Approaching Banks from the direction of jazz, John Whiteoak has observed that the jazz recordings reveal the early emergence of third stream characteristics and broadened the composer's receptivity to post-romantic composers well before he received the imprint of his British experience.[115] Banks himself later recalled that the practice of jazz improvisation opened up exploratory opportunities no longer available to him in the Western art music tradition, and asserted with unequivocal vigour that by the time he left Melbourne, Australia had already left an indelible impression' on him.[116]

Banks was also active in more traditional areas of jazz, as a boogie soloist and with the Graeme Bell group. He is present on recordings that are milestones in both traditional and modern jazz, including leading, composing and recording what is arguably the first bop recording ever made in this country. In October 1941 Banks participated in an event which Richard Haese has called 'a landmark in Australian art' (Haese 1981, p.72). Denied hanging space by the National Gallery, the Contemporary Art

Society staged its exhibition in the cosmopolitan, secular setting of the Hotel Australia in Bourke Street. With its connections to the Communist Party, and the Angry Penguins literary group, the CAS exhibition represented all that was progressive and modern in Australian culture.

The catalogue for the exhibition invoked allied movements in another art form—specifically, music—and included an essay on the music appropriate to its modernist profile: jazz. The exhibition was planned to incorporate two nights of concerts to complement the aggressively modernist complexion of the event. One was to have been 'serious' music, the other a jazz concert. As it turned out, the 'classical' composers and performers appear not to have lent their support to this avant-garde moment.[117] The jazz night however, with Graeme Bell's band and Don Banks as a solo pianist, provided an appropriate and heady ambience:

> Long haired intellectuals, swing fiends, hot mommas and truckin' jazz boys rubbed shoulders on friendly terms. While swingsters hollered 'Go to Town' and jittered in the aisles, the intelligentsia learnedly discussed differences between rhythms of hot jazz and pigment of Picasso.[118]

This not to say that people like Max Harris were unalleviated cultural democrats: they were still committed to a literature of élitist mystification. But when it came to making a musical alliance that was considered modern, they found themselves with a band playing American-sourced popular music, a form largely derided or ignored by the music establishment. Their complaints were directed at the same 'shortcomings' the academic painters and critics alleged in modernist painting—lack of craft, lack of formal logic, undisciplined expressiveness. It is not surprising then that, while painters were seeking to establish links with other cultural activities which might strengthen the cause of modernism, they found themselves in the company of innovative popular musicians (ie, at this time, jazz musicians) rather than classical musicians. The following chapters examine particular case studies in this relationship between jazz and Australian modernity.

SECOND BREAK
INTERACTIONS—AUDIENCES RESPOND TO THE BAND

3 August 1981, Metropolitan Hotel, Bathurst

Awakened at 5.20 by the sound of a blowfly, buzzing punctuated by clicks as it collided stupidly with the wall; the hotel is of a kind, but a kind that has character. Spartan dilapidated. The walls of the room have several holes gouged or chipped in the plaster, showing the brick underneath. The wardrobe doors hang crooked and the carpet is speckled with stains and cigarette burns. There's one window, rough white painted frames, streaks of the paint edging onto the glass panes. A circular fabric patch advertising the Western Plains Zoo has been stuck onto the glass—someone else at some other time stayed in this room, in this bed. It's one of those rather mysterious, dark pubs, preferable to motels: from the outside a symmetrical and right-angled facade, but inside the corridors take inexplicable curves, the floor of the passageways suddenly rise in a short ramp for no evident reason.

It is raining. I'm in an upstairs room, and can hear the sound of it on the roof. And from outside in the grey damp morning air comes the sound of a pigeon huddling for shelter under the eaves.

Playing as part of the promotion for the car race they have here. It includes playing at various points in the streets of Bathurst. One spot was acoustically lovely, in the doorway of an optician. A band playing in a street is hardly inconspicuous. Apart from the loud noise it makes, it constitutes a minor physical obstacle on the footpath. In addition, we looked outrageous—gaudy Guy Mitchell blue and red spray jackets and baseball caps, sartorial advertisements for a cigarette company that also sponsors a team of cars. And with the band a couple of striking blondes, tall, slim, scantily dressed, handing out free packets of fags. Not exactly a gathering you could accidentally fail to notice, especially as the light rain kept the pedestrians on the footpath seeking the shelter of awnings. A gig like this is meant to call attention to itself, and I find that the best way to play it is to bear that in mind. It's no good playing soft, pretending you're not conspicuous, avoiding eye contact. Say hello to people, smile, talk to them.

It's also a really instructive exercise in audience responses, and how Australians—and probably most Western city folk—are conditioned to deal with music and musicians. Some people (and more on the whole in the country) stop, smile, tap their feet, clap, come up to the band and say how much they like it and want to know where you'll be next. Others walk past, acknowledging the band with a smile. Some acknowledge the band by trying to summon up a clear message of contempt or ridicule. These are mostly adolescents and young adults still trying to get some leverage on life. This is an interesting power game, because I've realised that if you feel confident about what you're doing, simply standing there looking unashamedly ridiculous, playing loudly and obviously unembarrassed about it, it gives you a powerful moral advantage. The attempt to send a message of scorn is always so timid that it remains ineffectual. Some people walk past without breaking their step, pretending not to have noticed you; but a few yards further on they suddenly discover something in a shop window that occupies their attention very closely indeed. Or, and this is very common, especially if they are with a group of friends, having passed the band they pause after a few yards, stop, and suddenly become interested in something behind them, way back up the street. They mutter to each other, then crane their necks around to look back from whence they've come, as though one of their group has straggled and become separated. They always look over the shoulder away from the band, and try in general to remain with their backs to the music; thus affirming clearly that they have not paused in order to witness this extraordinary phenomenon but have stopped more or less in the normal course of a morning's shopping. They tend to light cigarettes, ever glancing back down the street, sometimes turning their heads so far as to accidentally look at a member of the band. When they finish their cigarettes, they often by tacit consensus return the way they have come, pausing to repeat the pantomime at the same distance from the band, but in the other direction. Their indecisiveness is massive.

But the saddest person is also one of the most common. It is usually an older person—30s to 50s—settled but still working at it. He/she has picked up the unmistakable signals that Something Is Going On from quite a distance away. The first response is an ambivalent blend of curiosity and resentment. The resentment is really interesting. Standing in the street just blowing, there's not much else to do but watch and think; and I think the resentment comes from several things. First, that the pattern of existence they have come to accept should be made to seem banal by this chaotic and vivid alternative. More importantly or consciously, that the tenets of law-abiding responsibility and prosaic order should be subverted, so to speak, by these larrikin harlequins, these over-paid indolents, these violators of 9–5 sober working habits, these good-for-nothings troubled by no conscience; and who (even worse) probably lead as a matter of course, the kind of life he visualises in his sticky and ashamed fantasies. Yes—look: those women, tall, stylish, red-lipped—I bet they all go off together after this and drink and sleep with the musicians WHILE IT IS YET DAYLIGHT!! While I am slogging out the dull day, entering figures in a column, tapping away at a keyboard, responsibly devoting my life to the bread and butter needs of the family, those ... those outrages to decency will be cavorting between the thighs of those blondes. Perhaps two women to each musician. Perhaps ... unspeakable depravities. And to really cap it off, they are being listened to with respectful and pleasurable attention. People like me are actually encouraging them.

He's wrong. I've played a lot of motor events—rallies, motor shows, races. Carby-groupies are only interested in petrol-heads. Product promotion musos and girls always have just an amiable working relationship, and the girls are usually more interested in the Nazi style of the motor-cycle cops, with their boots, tight pants and Starsky-&-Hutch strut. Just how inaccurate is this fantasy about the off-stage life of musicians, is beside the point. What matters, to the particular audient I'm talking about, is what he fantasises, and it is of profound psychological importance that he NOT NOTICE THE BAND. He can't avoid it by crossing the street, he has got too close, and this concedes their existence. No, he must walk on the coals and emerge apparently unmarked. And, apparently, he does. Eyes fixed with determination, head rivetted firmly to the front, he strides within a couple of feet of a five piece band in full roar, saying, 'I don't recognise the existence of this situation'. The armadillo rigidity is very fragile, however. If he/she falters for so much as a flicker, the armour is destroyed. When there is nothing else to do with your eyes but watch the people passing by, games become inevitable. One woman walked past the band. I picked her out a long way up the street, saw her register the hazard up ahead, saw her checking the controls, counting down to the ordeal, plugging leaks, battening down hatches. I watched her. The light didn't flow from her to me, but the other way round. I isolated her with my eye, caught her in it like a bomber in a searchlight. She got adjacent to me, her eyes flickering minutely, she came right opposite us, and broke. Her head came off automatic pilot, the eyebeam was too much, the irritant had to be scratched. She turned and I caught her right in the eye, a momentary destabilising connection. Her head swivelled back to eyes front with the breathtaking reversal of a superball. She put her hand up to do something to her hair, fingered it compulsively. She actually lost her balance momentarily, colliding gently with one of the stationary watchers. All that had happened is she had made eye-contact with a street musician. But it was as though she had unexpectedly identified a rapist smiling at her from a line-up. Probably went home and told off the kids, and that night responded to her husband by asking if that was all he ever thought of.

Everybody with any responsiveness to the existence of Others is also responsive to personal territory. Because of its extrovertedness, a band will generally create a larger territorial space for itself than the sum total of that of its separate members. In the street, those who respond most positively also give it more space. The band tends to find itself at the centre of a semi-circle having a radius of about fifteen feet. It is mostly children at the edge.

While the band was playing to one of these ragged edged circles, gradually a small fragment of that edge detached itself, as though washed free by the flow of the music. It moved towards the musicians and came to rest in a more or less central point in that strangely generated space surrounding the band. A small boy, maybe three years old. Something in his face and dress made it hard to tell his age. Was there a trace of Downes Syndrome in the blandly spherical head? Even so, he had been dressed with such love that it hurt to think about those detailed devotions. He wore a school cap on his head, and a fussy little suit. Together they gave him the appearance of a dwarf schoolboy. The incongruous impression of age was reinforced by the seriousness of his expression: little furrows in his forehead and a look of urgent and unsmiling concern. And without changing his expression he entered into a funny rickety little dance, all jerkiness and stiffness, like a clockwork toy. It continued throughout the music, as though he was locked tarantella-like into its lines of force, the little legs wilful but graceless, jerking his small body back and forth while his eyes looked up at the band with puzzled seriousness. Alone in the sacred centre, this forlorn yet loved little boy receiving one of those early imprints that will very likely float beneath his thoughts for the rest of his life, perhaps to surface as the last thing he farewells, his 'Rosebud'.

I was really pleased that I was a musician just then.

CHAPTER 3
JAZZ, MASS CULTURE AND GENDER IN AUSTRALIA

And agile maidens, dainty and dapper,
Sleeker of head than the orb of the plum,
Each with her chosen whipper-snapper,
Forth to the fox-trot nightly come;
And above the chatter of midnight meals
The cornet bleats and the saxo squeals
And the sandalled hoofs of the fearless flapper
Follow the beat of the furious drum.

C L Graves 'in the style of Swinburne' c. 1926

The story of the 1941 exhibition suggests why jazz is peripheral to accounts of musical modernity in Australia. The carnivalesque tone of the newspaper report, its imagery of cultural miscegenation and misrule, gives the clue. Jazz was also a manifestation of a pre-eminent phenomenon of modernity which destabilised elitist regimes, particularly one as conservative as Australian music in the 1940s.

Jazz, that is, was the musical version of twentieth-century mass mediated popular culture. Australian modernity may first be identified in the convergence of such forces as the non-European (American), the popular, the mass-mediated (cinema, recording, broadcasting) and the young, all foreshadowing a possible future characterised by the cultural enfranchisement of the 'masses'. The age of mechanical reproduction made both old and new visual and acoustic images democratically accessible, thus destabilising the balance of cultural power hitherto maintained through the control of cultural capital. To try to preserve that balance, then, the meaning of culture itself would have to be transformed: if the masses were suddenly going to come into possession of certain expressive images and processes, then it became necessary to move those images and processes outside the realm of culture. Film—especially United States film—was not to be incorporated into the realm of 'true' culture.[119] Nor mass-produced texts, like life-style journals. Nor music that impertinently bypassed the sacrosanct and carefully monitored sites of storage and consumption (the score, the concert hall): popular music and especially modern popular music. Jazz.

Jazz became a major popular innovation of the 1920s, denoting not just the music, but the style of an era to which it ultimately gave its name: 'the jazz age'. When the daughter of painter Frederick McCubbin, Kathleen Mangan, published her memoirs in 1984, the title summarised the stages of her youth: *Daisy Chains, War, then Jazz.* At the same time, however, jazz was attacked from the ramparts of high culture. The reception accorded jazz in Australia thus reflected the negotiations between hegemonic and subaltern cultures, following patterns which were also evident in other areas invaded by jazz, particularly Anglo-European. In 1920 the French *Revue Musicale* spoke for a trans-national arts community when it declared:

> Jazz is cynically the orchestra of brutes with unopposable thumbs and still prehensile toes, in the forest of Voodoo. It is entirely excess ... the monkey is left to his own devices, without morals, without discipline, thrown back to the groves of instinct, showing his meat still more obscene. These slaves must be subjugated, or there will be no more master.

These attacks proceeded along the usual parallel tracks of aesthetics and morality. Jazz was both ugly and evil. Its perceived origins in African-American traditions confirmed the paradoxical atavism of contemporary mass culture; the modern was also the site of the barbarous. The final sentence of the extract above, however, reminds us that power relations are at stake here. The moral argument, that jazz would cause conspicuous depravity among its followers, was both a matter of relativities (what is 'depravity'?), and even in accepted terms of the day, there is no evidence that jazz produced any more or less inhumanity than other forms of music. A love of art music did not prevent a holocaust; popular music never caused one. And the aesthetic condemnation of any new expressive form—on the grounds of ugliness—is perennial in cultural cycles, simply reminding us that the ugliness of today's innovation is the beauty of tomorrows tradition.

The charge that jazz would lead to destruction was thus part of the larger action fought against modernity by an intellectual establishment that had always experienced acute discomfort with popular cultures that were not of its own making and controlling. Promotion for Australia's (and the world's) earliest 'jazz festival' in Australia capitalised on the ambiguous space across which high and low negotiated.[120] Advertising for the 'Jazz Week at the Globe Theatre' in Sydney in 1919 asked the question 'Does the JAZZ lead to Destruction?' (see p. 58). The newspaper publicity campaign featured a caricatural construction, Mr McWowse ('Mc'!—so much implied even in this detail), who initially declared that, yes it did, and therefore he and Mrs McWowse would have nothing to do with the event. The organisers thumbed their noses at McWowse and invited readers to do likewise, and come along to the 'Jazzy Fun', which would feature dancers, music, 'whirlwind frolic', and a 'comedy drama' film *The Whirl of Life* starring the internationally famous exhibition dancers Vernon and Irene Castle. The appeal was thus not only to a love of 'fun', but to a violation of moral decorum at the level of popular recreation. As the week proceeded, the advertising narrative suggested that the moral guardians indeed had something to fear. Each day McWowse's moral fibre unravelled a little more, and by the end of the week, he defiantly announced that he no longer gave a 'dash for the congregation' (a most telling way of characterising the establishment), and that he now embraced jazz and the road to destruction.[121] It is a narrative of the triumph of contemporary mass culture. And jazz is the narrative site.

Of all musical idioms, jazz-influenced popular music was most deeply implicated in the construction of Australian modernity. As suggested earlier its profile was quintessentially modern. Apart from sound recordings jazz was also strongly allied with that other major technological medium of modernity, film. The Globe Theatre jazz week provided the opportunity to 'learn to jazz from the movies'. *Does the Jazz Lead to Destruction?* was actually the title of the locally-made movie that became the centrepiece of the week-long event. Jazz was frequently referred to in film narratives of modernity, including the Australian films *Why Jesse* (aka *Mabel Learned to Jazz*) in 1919, and *Greenhide* and *Should a Girl Propose,* both made in 1926, perhaps the peak year of local jazz popularity in the 1920s. These are discussed further below. Diane Collins cites the campaign by the Feminist Club and the Imperial Film Club in 1933 to promote British alternatives to unwholesome American films with their 'jazz music'.[122]

The case of the Feminist Club, however, reminds us again of the ambiguities in Australian modernity, as class intersects gender. Part of the alarm experienced by this highly vocal group was doubtless prompted by the fact that it was the sisters themselves who were most exposed to the dangers of American popular culture. A royal commission into the moving picture industry in 1927 received evidence that about 70% of Australian film audiences were women. This had been well understood by distributors since before the war. In 1912 the Australian film exhibitor J.D. Williams had recognised that women were the largest potential audience for film. Only one in ten married women worked, compulsory children's education freed mothers for parts of the day, and labour-saving devices reduced the amount of time spent on housework. Williams employed women ushers, provided child-minding facilities and 'retiring rooms', played matinees for women and children, and promoted visits to the cinema in conjunction with shopping excursions.[123] This affected censorship decisions in ways that bear significantly on the whole connection between conservative patriarchy and mass culture. The figure of the bushranger will play a role in the following discussion, and it is therefore relevant that a ban on bushranging themes in film did not extend to stage presentations. In justifying the banning of an attempt to make a film based on *Robbery Under Arms* in 1918, the censor expressed the opinion that no reasonable objection could be made to a play on the subject:

> ... in which case the audience is composed almost exclusively of adults; in the moving picture proposition we are immediately faced with an entirely different set of circumstances—here the audiences are comprised largely of women, young children, and impressionable boys.
> (quoted Pike and Cooper 1980, 135–6).

The connections we have observed above between women and socially emancipated modernity were especially strong in Australia. A Feminist Club, for example, had been established in New South Wales as early as 1914 to push for equal opportunity and wages. Well above the conservative post World War I substrate of Australian society, the 1920s continued to nourish versions of feminism. The magazine called *Herself in Australia's Affairs* promoted both social and environmental reform, and equated the spirit of Australia with 'the Woman's Touch'.[124] It was the connection between woman and postwar emancipation which opened the sites of fashion, leisure, domesticity—feminised spaces—to modernity, while high culture, dominated by a conservative patriarchy, remained closed.

In the previous chapter a connection between modernity and everyday social and domestic experience was noted. As long ago as 1978 Mary Eagle recognised the role of gender in the Australian art world:

> ... *serious* art had the function of promoting Australia through a sort of natural description. National qualities were the masculine ones of 'breadth', hardihood , strength and virility . Modernism, embracing 'all the arts that pertain to living', was more for women. By the end of the twenties modern art appeared to have been absorbed into the decorative arts, leaving serious national expression to the painters of important people and Australian scenery.[125]

The experience of modernity emerged in Australian painting in representations which were outside the dominant masculinist discourse of 'serious' art. 'Modernism signified the city, progress and technology. It was the painting of women [that is, paintings *by* women] that brought modernism to Australia in the first decades of this century' (Hoorn 1992, p.9). This was true thematically as well as formally. The pressures on the male artist to deal with the big themes (spatially and temporally) in a heroic style were not such powerful compulsions upon women, who were free to devise ways to represent 'miniature' experiences like knitting, flower displays, domestic interiors. It is the difference between locating significant reality in the epic or the quotidian, but in portraying the realm of the everyday, such work confirmed its own status as 'décor' rather than art, as in Norman Lindsay's trivialisation of the work of Thea Proctor.[126] She in turn spoke of the prejudice against 'modern art' in Australia partly because of a perceived association with 'design': 'As soon as one uses the word 'design'... people who call the modern 'jazz art' become suspicious'.[127] Proctor's reference to 'jazz art', like Lindsay's quoted earlier, leads us via the broader terrain of 'modernity', to music practices.

Jazz and Gender

As long as the 'modern' remained menacing, it also remained largely female. This gendering of cultural corruption in Australia, which can be traced back to the colonial authorities, gained new momentum in early twentieth-century Australia, when it was explicitly articulated through popular music.[128] The connection between femininity and corruption has a strong tradition in music, as documented in the extensive literature on music, gender and gender transgression.[129] The period of World War I had seen a much more overt objectification of female sexuality in popular song, a shift from ethereal innocence to voluptuousness, though at the popular level this was more a male scopic pleasure than an ideological threat.[130] In the wake of the war, jazz became the pre-eminent musical expression of women's emancipation. At first glance, this might appear to be an unlikely proposition given the subsequent masculinisation of jazz performance, in which the stereotypical role of women has been as feminine adornments singing about their victimisation and subordination in love. It is therefore useful to move some furniture around to make space for the next stage of the discussion.

I shall take up the question of the gender balance among musicians below, but first wish to make the point that in the word 'jazz' there is inscribed a more complex model of the producer/consumer (performer/audience) binary than in the case of the mainstream art music tradition. In any case that distinction is ambiguous in all musics which are primarily brought into being in the moment of public performance, that is, involving a significant level of improvisation.[131] But the distinction has a particularly acute ambiguity in the case of jazz in Australia in the 1920s. The practice to which the word referred was not exclusively one of instrumental and singing performance, but also a particular kind of dance. Although public dancing went back to the earliest period of European settlement, the arrival of jazz happened to coincide with a sudden burgeoning of purpose-built public dance halls.[132] They were regarded in many quarters as morally dubious for reasons traditionally associated with venues for popular culture. In the early days of the colony, even convicts regarded their female counterparts as excessively devoted to dressing up and going to 'dancing houses'. Venues such as 'dancing rooms' in pubs had been noted as places frequented by prostitutes, a reputation not at all dissipated by the fact that as public dance halls proliferated in the early twentieth century it was common (in two senses) for women to attend them unchaperoned and unaccompanied.[133]

The association of these venues with contemporary emancipation was strengthened as they also became the site for the enactment of 'doctrines of heterosexual modernity' promulgated through film.[134] The unease about the collapse of cultural regulation which seemed to be reflected in jazz was thus fortified by the fact that the dance halls, with their unregulated social dynamic compared to concert halls, quickly became the musics primary public venues. But there is more to this than the mutual reinforcement of social odium. The notion of 'dance' both in general terms and as it was evolving in the 1920s, made it particularly hospitable as a site of emancipated femininity. Of all public expressive practices, dancing is perhaps one of the two most democratic.[135] This is almost certainly one of the reasons for its enormous popularity during the hardship *of* the Great Depression.[136] For the same reasons it is also potentially among the most unruly *of* expressive forms in that it needs no expensive equipment or hard-won competencies—only a body that will do as its owner tells it. Or—and here is an even greater threat to the deeply rooted imperative of cognitive control—as it tells its 'owner' what to do. When the Graeme Bell band promoted jazz for dancing in London, this provoked outrage among the local guardians of the jazz movement, at the same time as it provided an outlet for the most abandoned dance practices by London youth.[137] The pure physicality of dance provides the possibility for the most unmediated, unregulated display of subjectivity. The dancer is the dance.

Now we must imagine these politics of the dance also framing jazz. 'Jazz' has been so securely categorised as a musical product or genre, that it is puzzling to encounter its Australian usage in the 1920s. A question like 'Does the jazz lead to destruction?' now sounds like the quaint grammar of a non-native speaker. The Jazz Week at the Globe offered patrons the opportunity to 'learn to jazz', and two exhibition dancers, George Irving and Ethel Bennetto, 'will show you the Walking Waltz, the Jazz, and the Tickle Toe'. The poster for the film *Should a Girl Propose?* describes the modern girl as one who 'jazzes'. It is only when we realise that jazz was understood to be interchangeably a musical form (noun) *and* a dance (verb), that these odd grammatical constructions become explicable. 'The jazz is a dance', reported *Table Talk* in August 1919: like 'the waltz', 'the tango', 'the quickstep'. A woman 'jazzes', as she also waltzes, foxtrots. This semiotic archaeology has implications that go far beyond the solving of a grammatical puzzle, however. It meant that the word 'jazz' carried with it all the semantic and ideological luggage of 'dancing'.

'The Jazz' was imagined and practised as a dance—a process in which active participation is the actual condition of its consumption. To a greater extent than is already the case in improvised music in performance, 'the jazz' was seen to be something done by what we would now think of primarily as its audience. You didn't dance to jazz that was being made exclusively by people who were separate by virtue of instrumental ownership, competence and the space defined by a stage. You 'jazzed'. Although the earliest Australian performances seem to have been on a formal stage, by 1919 jazz had certainly dissolved that implied distinction by situating itself in the public mind as a dance.[138] Jazz was thus inextricable from perhaps the most popular and distinctive social recreation of the 1920s: dancing. Kathleen Mangan summarised the spirit of the period as she recalled it in 1984:

> By the mid-twenties I had quickly caught up with trends and the age in which we lived. Bobbed hair had given way to the Eton crop, waistlines had descended below the hips, and skirts had receded above the knees. It was fashionable to play tennis and golf, go to bridge and poker parties, and attend smart cocktail parties where we consumed gin mixed with vermouth, white-cargoes (gin and bitters with icecream) and various other heady and ghastly mixtures. If you belonged to the really smart set you learned to smoke cigarettes in an elegant, long holder and tottered around in spike-heeled shoes. And of course you danced: in the afternoons, in the evenings, at night, in dimly lit cabarets you danced until the small hours, and your feet ached and you could scarcely hold your head up. (Mangan 1984, p.195)

This catalogue of style markers has passed into 1920s mythology, and is reproduced in Australian films such as *Greenhide,* discussed in further detail below. Its heroine Margery dances, but she dances joyously alone, reinforcing the proposition that dancing is also, in Australia, a feminised activity. Women were in the overwhelming majority among owners of dancing schools, judging panels and administrative bodies. It became a matter for public concern that working women were spending so much money on dancing attire that they were going without lunches to pay for it.[139] Women dancing alone, or with each other, was not an exceptionable public spectacle, especially given their male partners' masculinist reluctance to participate. Men dancing alone or with each other in most Australian public places would risk ridicule at best, and at worst ejection and assault or arrest.

Dancing in the 1920s was thus not only available to be appropriated in more active and democratic ways than other embodiments of mass culture such as film (the object of relatively physically passive spectacle for the audience), but in addition the re-creative domain of dance was especially open to women. The archetypal jazz identity was female, described in London's *Daily Mail* in 1920 as 'the frivolous, scantily clad "jazzing flapper", irresponsible and undisciplined' (quoted Melman, 1988, p.19). And the posture in which she is most immediately recognisable is the abandoned expansiveness of the quintessential dance of 'The Jazz Age', the Charleston. The European 'Cubist and Dadaist dancer, Nina Paync' established her reputation dancing to jazz.[140] Kay Ferres has shown how the moral panic associated with jazz was largely generated by its powerful connection with emancipated female sexuality, particularly expressed through 'jazzing'—that is, dancing. Ferres quotes, among others, Dulcie Deamer, speaking for herself and other Australian women:... we *do* jazz in order to experience a mild—very mild—sex adventure, and to allow our repressed polyandrous instinct to get a breath of fresh air'.[141] This sexual dimension was, to use Stuart Hall's coinage, a significant zone of contestation' for a larger project: jazzing was a site for the re-invention of women throughout the 1920s in ways that sought to expand the possibilities available to them. The ambiguities of this zone are signalled in a number of linkages between women and jazz. The Melbourne clothing company Buckley and Nunn advertised the 'Jazz Corset' for the modern young woman, a coupling which pulls in two different directions both physically and semantically.[142] Not just dance, but jazz specifically was in important ways feminised.

We can push the thesis further. Even seen from the later more restricted perspective of jazz as performed music, jazz was less masculinised than it later became. In playing, as well as otherwise participating in the music, women were far more prominent than later reconstructions of jazz history suggest. Australia's earliest jazz groups largely consisted of Edwardian dance band musicians who were simply trying to keep abreast of their profession, and thus reflected pre-existing gender and class profiles. But although the evidence of photographs, recordings and recollections confirms that men were more central in the profession, the same evidence also suggests that more women led and played in jazz bands than any time since, until perhaps the 1990s, and that this was not much cause for remark in itself.

The cover of the Australian sheet music of the 1920s composition 'Flappers in the Sky' depicts a biplane bearing the transgressive name *Sky Pirate*, with a group of flappers aboard. The currency of the female aviator as one of the popular images of the modern emancipated woman (see Melman 1988, p.95) is indicated in the song's lyric, with its references to modern girls' 'ambitions soaring', while 'man, mere man it seems will have to risk his very life/ By planeing right out through the clouds/ When he wants to find a wife'. The same emancipative message is proclaimed on the cover, portraying the conduct of the women. One is flying while others, dressed in men's flying suits are insouciantly drinking, smoking, applying make-up, and one strums a poorly-drawn guitar or banjo (see p. 4).[143] That a woman would be playing an instrument associated with 1920s popular music is thus as much a part of the emancipated repertoire as all the other activities depicted. When seasoned theatre entrepreneur Ben Fuller formed the country's first 'jazz band' for his theatre circuit, it is unlikely that his shrewd instinct for popular entertainment was dormant when he picked a woman, the singer Belle Sylvia, to lead it and when she left replaced her with another, Maybelle Morgan.[144]

From the viewpoint of the later masculinisation of jazz, it is surprising to find how many women were identified as members of jazz bands in professional dance-band journals. Instrumental jazz instruction by women was also frequently advertised. Music was part of a woman's education in gentility; in using jazz to break out of that mould, many woman exploited the very skills inculcated to fortify it. A surprising number were recognised as exponents of the new African-American musics. In spite of the prominence of men in the music industry, John Hasse has noted that most ragtime in the United States was played in domestic spaces by amateur musicians, and that most of these were women.[145] The association is also to be found in Australia. Whiteoak has studied the importance of women and the domestic piano in the early history of improvisation in Australia. Likewise in the professional domain. The silent cinema 'sustained the highest level of improvisatory practice in the immediate pre-jazz period', and the greater proportion of improvisational cinema pianists and organists were women.[146]

This is a provocative statistic, given that cinema attendance in Australia had outstripped church attendance by 1919. In New South Wales, by 1921 there were more cinema attendances than all other forms of theatre combined.[147] The significance of this goes well beyond quantification, to the question of who controls the meanings of a cultural form. By 1928, as the silent era drew to a close, annual cinema attendances in Australia had reached in excess of 110 million.[148] The acoustic dimension of this pervasive entertainment—the musical accompaniment—was the only way in which the technology of flat moving images produced elsewhere (that is, away from the audience), was expressively integrated into the specific performance space—the local cinema. The accompanist was the commentator upon, participant in, and mediator of, a message whose formal content was in other ways fixed. The audiences—also mostly women—of course reconstructed the film in the act of imaginatively consuming it, but the cinema pianist co-produced the film as a public practice. And this adaptation of the product to local conditions was most likely to be conducted by a woman. Similarly, as discussed in further detail in Chapter Six, in Australia women singers assimilated American jazz models earlier and more convincingly than men, for reasons to do with technology and gender politics.

This is not to make the demonstrably absurd suggestion that women were able to dominate in the male preserve of professional music. The sheet music of 'Flappers in the Sky' was 'as performed by' Dud Stewart and his (all male) 'Magic Melody Makers'. The case of the film *Greenhide* below confirms again that the 'imaginary' of women's social emancipation is frequently articulated within a framing patriarchal discourse: a truism so well established that the sentence feels like an embarrassing *cliché* even as I have to write it. Nonetheless in the earliest history of jazz in Australia, and before it began to acquire any artistic *cachet*, there were surprising numbers of women active in the area, as makers and participants. The subsequent masculinisation of jazz by a patriarchy led to two things—the exclusion of women from active roles, and the writing out of women from its history.

Greenhide: Jazzing And The Modern Woman

I now turn to a case study which discloses the play of these various intersecting cultural forces as they negotiate to produce outcomes involving jazz. These in turn disclose the ambiguities in the relationships between such forces as gender, mass culture, technology, and modernisation. As in the case of Barbara James in a later section, the example is chosen because it representatively summarises a cultural moment, but with distinctive clarity.

It should come as no surprise that these connections between modernity, jazz, 1920s 'feminism' and mass culture, are apparent in early Australian silent film. *Greenhide* belongs to an identifiable film genre which reflects a growing interest in the changing position of women in post-war Australia. A plot formula in these films is to place a young woman at a point of tension between traditional roles and contemporary possibilities, involving such notional binaries as female emancipation against conservative patriarchy, country against city, tradition against modernity, purity against decadence. They raise contemporary issues that include private sexuality and public conduct, and in ways that range from the tragic to the comic. In various combinations they exploit increased social mobility (*Cupid Camouflaged*, 1918; *Sunshine Sally*, 1922) the temptations of city life (*Satan in Sydney* and *What Happened to Jean*, 1918; *The Menace*, 1928) the dangers attendant on the relaxation of sexual mores (*Know Thy Child*, 1921; *Circumstance*, 1922; *Should a Doctor Tell*, 1923). These cut across sensitive areas, as reflected by the banning in New South Wales of Raymond Longford's 1918 feature *The Woman Suffers*. A common reference point in these was the fashionable lifestyle awaiting (as threat or promise) the young girl in the city: a constant round of dancing, jazz parties and cabaret revelling (*Joe*, 1924; *The Price*, 1924; *Painted Daughters*, 1925; *Should a Girl Propose*, 1926; *Caught in the Net*, 1928).[149]

Greenhide (1926) was directed by Charles Chauvel. It was his second feature, following *The Moth of Moonbi* in the same year. It exemplifies again the contemporary fixation on the complicit themes of modernity, gender, country/city. The two films are mirror images of these issues.[150] *Moonbi* is about Dell Ferris, an innocent young country girl who 'longed for the life, liberty and happiness that she had read of in books'.[151] Drawn to the bright lights of the city in pursuit of this dream, she is taken in hand by a 'butterfly girl' Margery Daw eager to supervise the spending of Dell's £500 inheritance.[152] After the money is frittered away, Dell returns, 'back where she belonged ... the only place of sanctuary and forgetfulness left for a moth with singed wings'. Unfortunately, the extant footage held by ScreenSound Australia includes little depiction of the fashionable urban lifestyle that consumed Dell's capital. A scene on a cruise yacht, however, does reaffirm the importance of dance in this *milieu*.

Two couples foxtrot on the deck, and Dell is propositioned by a rakish bachelor with the words, 'Why try to understand the present—life is so short and full of good times—come let us dance.'

Although also incomplete, the print of *Greenhide* held by ScreenSound includes sequences which have a rich and complex relevance to the arguments articulated in this chapter. This film tells the story of Margery,[153] the daughter of Sam Paton, who lives in urban splendour in Brisbane (servants, huge grounds) and owns a cattle station called Walloon in Queensland's Dawson Valley 'out west'. The station manager is Gavin, nicknamed Greenhide for his toughness. Margery is an independent-minded young woman, evidently enjoying a relatively unconstrained social life, 'Sam's only child, spoilt and motherless—living in a girl's dream land of intangible things—things which are not, but which perhaps might be'. By writing to Gavin, signing her father's name, she initiates an indefinite visit for herself to the station. When Gavin's reply to her father alerts the latter to the scheme, he reprimands her for going behind his back, but decides that the best way to teach her a lesson is to agree to her proposal. The film then explores the consequences of Margery's transgressive gesture. In examining one section of this film, I bear in mind that its issues are of course played out in larger contexts than will be discussed here. The scopic medium of silent film, the music that would have accompanied it, the film industry itself, the male directorial control, the audience—especially its female section that would be invited to identify with the heroine—all of these are part of the way in which the film's meanings are negotiated. Without overlooking the existence of these, I wish to concentrate attention on one scene as a point of convergence of the arguments I have been putting about jazz and modernity.

Following eleven minutes of *mise-en-scène* sequences, the audience is presented with a scene located in the extensive grounds of the Paton home. It is daytime, and Margery is hosting a party for a large number of her female friends. Chauvel's challenge is to construct her as a liberated young modern woman exclusively through visual images and subtitles. As Margery sits at a table talking gaily to her friends, the subtitles indicate an interest in horse-racing, and tell us she has recently lost money on a horse that was beaten by a nose. Clearly she thus enjoys the freedoms of secularity, leisure and affluence. She is a frivolous but stylish risk-taker. Given that particular odium was attached to women gambling on horses at that time, Chauvel's use of horse-racing as a vehicle for this message is effective.[154] As the guests talk, they smoke with an ostentation that shouts 'Modern Women'. The shooting script describes Margery as 'Pretty and coquettish, although artificial almost to the extent of being ultra-modern' (Shot 13), and evokes the ambience with explicit reference to characters out of the 'jazz hall' (Shot 68).[155]

The stereotype is then reinforced in a sequence that now seems structurally clumsy and even formally grotesque, but which has deep significance in relation to the connections under discussion. The closeups of party conversation have been intercut with wider shots of the party crowd seated at tables and a band playing for the guests. This, I believe, is the earliest surviving movie footage of an Australian jazz band, and given the constraints of silent film, it is instructive to see how Chauvel communicates its nature, meaning and function through exclusively visual means. In the musical synopsis prepared by Chauvel, he suggests the song 'That Certain Party' be played by the cinema pianist at this point. This song, by Gus Kahn and Walter Donaldson, dates from 1925. Apart from imported recordings, the song would have been active in the public awareness by virtue of its having been recorded in Sydney only months before the release of *Greenhide* in November 1926. The Sydney recording was by the Palais Royal Californians, a visiting United States orchestra (with some Australians recruited for their year's stay), highly publicised as representing the latest in American jazz or hot dance music.[156] The band in *Greenhide* is identified on the bass drum skin as the 'Crystal Palace Orchestra'. It has standard jazz instrumentation: two saxophonists (one alto, the other doubling on tenor and soprano), trumpeter (with mute—often associated with novelty timbres), banjoist, drummer with a full set of traps, and a Stroh violin, its megaphone attachment a reminder of the increasing volume of 'hot' dance music in the 1920s. As jazz markers there are also the extravagantly grotesque movements of the musicians, suggestive of musical abandonment and hijinks. Apart from its importance in setting the atmosphere of chic socialising, this band is then used to provide a significant frame for the further definition of Margery's character.

The party footage is intercut with material that sets the narrative in motion. A maid appears bearing a telegram for Sam Paton, discovered mulching the pruned roses in the well-tended garden (a significant contrast with his daughter's use of the space). His tie and cardigan and general demeanour distinguish him from the weskitted, open-collared gardener (a class scenario to which the maid's air of slight simple-mindedness also contributes). Paton reads Gavin's reply: 'Don't want women on Walloon'. Angry at what he regards as Margery's underhandedness and Gavin's defiance, he walks to that section of the grounds where his daughter is holding her party, summons her imperiously, reprimands her, and sets the subsequent events in motion.

In the meantime the intercut scenes continue to convey the party atmosphere and in particular to reveal Margery's character. Rising from her seat, she goes and dances in front of the band. Flickering through the veil of silent movie technology and the passage of seventy years, this is a curiously disturbing scene, invested at the time with meanings which are not easy to retrieve, and overlaid now with meanings that Chauvel and the actress Elsie Sylvaney (later Elsa Chauvel) could not have foreseen. Because of this, there is a danger of overlooking the complex relationship between the filmic images and the largely female cinema audiences of the period, especially without the acoustic mediation of the musical accompaniment. Cunningham's detailed analysis leads him to characterise the narrative as 'primarily concerned with playing out a repertoire of stock generic motifs'.[157] In relation to cinema history, this is a just appraisal, but the power of 'stock motifs' is based on tight cultural shorthand, and it is this that is my concern. While I 'read' this particular scene with caution, certain clear meanings do seem to be deliberately embedded in it. Margery begins with the standard steps of the Charleston, but then modulates into a less determinate improvised dance.[158] The sequence of just over one minute is longer than the strict demands of the narrative require, and therefore draws our attention as a moment of character revelation (see p. 70).

Of all the cues provided by Chauvel in this party scene, Margery's 'jazzing' is the most sustained and conspicuously foregrounded signal of her standing as a potentially liberating imaginary for the woman in the audience. Margery is a model for the visualisation of emancipative female social roles and practices. Her actions constitute an entry into male spaces: smoking, horse racing, the rebellious plan to move from the decadent, feminised city to the masculine 'elemental' bush. In this semiotic field, and in a silent medium, her jazzing is more eloquent than any other visual signal. She literally enters the frame of the all-male band in a figure/ground configuration in which a woman becomes the 'soloist'[159]. And as a dance that solo is an aggressive transgression of the male (leader)/female (follower) paradigm of couple-dancing that had so powerfully modelled the bourgeois Romantic conception of the molecular social unit—the heterosexual couple 'cut off, turned inwards'.[160] Like the flapper herself, Margery's jazzing is both significantly female and non-feminine: a dance, but one that is improvised, solo, abjuring nineteenth century notions of womanly lightness, modesty, grace, dependency.

In trying to establish the authority of jazz in musical

modernity via issues of gender and mass culture, I have also tried to acknowledge the ambiguities of those relationships. The image of the flapper triumphantly dragging Australia out of the nineteenth century is no more accurate than any other simplistic mythology. The 'picture' becomes less schematic and more interesting if we take this examination a little further.

Given the semiotic density I have ascribed to Margery's jazzing, it is of considerable consequence that it should be interrupted by the arrival of her father, cutting through the sound of the band with a one word title, the imperious diminutive 'MARG!'. Her unconstrained dance abruptly ceases. She becomes small, her gestures chastened, her demeanour suddenly submissive, and even the font size of her titles reduced: 'Yes daddie dear'. There follows the exchange already summarised, concluding in Sam's declaration that she and Gavin will be taught a lesson—she will go to the country. Still submissive, nonetheless Margery is delighted: 'Oh! Daddie, how wonderful!' Patriarchal authority remains intact here, but to ambiguous effect, since Margery has succeeded in her plan. However, we should conclude by noting that similar ambiguities are disclosed in the way in which the young woman visualises her emancipatory adventure. Her friends gather around her as she announces, 'I'm going "West", my dears!' The camera now shows the collective excitement and delight as she looks forward to the adventure, the footage alternating with the following titles, transcribed verbatim:

> I'm going to meet Daddies caveman, and to live Big-
> Vital—and Elemental Life! I'll know what it is to be
> swung to the saddle by big brown arms—to be kissed
> during a wild stampede of Daddie's cattle.
> Or to be sheiked by a real live Bushranger.

The shooting script is a little bolder: 'Or to be sheiked by a real live Bushranger or two'.

The bushranger reference is a reminder that film was a

significant medium through which pre-modern rural mythology was maintained in the popular consciousness of early Twentieth-century Australia. By 1926 Australian audiences had seen scores of locally produced bush narrative films. They incorporated formulaic devices and stereotypes that converge in the imagery and plot of *Greenhide*, including cattle station and bushranging epics. The bushranger film was so clearly identifiable as a film genre that romanticised criminality, as to have been banned in New South Wales from 1912. The loss of that significant market led to a hiatus in the genre, but the image survived in variations such as goldfields or convict narratives, or 'frame-up' scenarios (*The Gentleman Bushranger*, 1921). The ban seems to have been relaxed by 1920, when both *The Kelly Gang* and *Robbery Under Arms* were shown in NSW.[161] Margery also invokes the image of 'The Sheik which climaxcs (yes, I know) her erotic inventory. The flapper is already a complex figure, simultaneously gendered yet androgynous. This ambiguity is compounded when coupled with the 'Sheik' mythology, which incorporates the image of woman as an ambivalently passive rape victim. Yet while the 'Sheik' fantasy might situate a woman in a sexually submissive role, at the same time it was hardly likely to increase her level of satisfaction with the traditional role of Edwardian wife whose only approved locus is the home. What these two tropes signify both singly and in conjunction, is a deep dislocation of the position of women, a heightened awareness of sexual and erotic possibilities, and the consequent sense of the destabilisation of Anglo-European patriarchy.

The image of the Sheik here is of course inter-textual, emerging from the modern sexuality of the best selling novel and the film which refined one of the enduring erotic mythologies of twentieth-century mass culture (with the usual paradoxes of modernity, given its pre-industrial scenario). The reference assumes on the part of the young Australian female audience an easy familiarity with contemporary mass culture. Shot 14 of the shooting script tells us that the book Margery is reading in the opening domestic scene is none other than *The Sheik*—the 'love-in-the-desert' novel by E.M. Hull (*nom de plume* for Edith Maude Winstanley) published in 1919. It was the basis for the 1921 film starring Rudolph Valentino. That the young women in the audience would have immediately recognised the literary and cinematic reference is a reasonable assumption given that the film's six-month run at the Sydney Globe in 1922 was a world record.[162] It is notable in this connection that both film and the 'bestseller' novel were addressed to women in particular.[163] Australian women eagerly devoured contemporary mass culture.

The film concludes with Margery drawn back into her rightful place, as imagined by Chauvel. Although she has initiated her own liberating invasion of a male space, the trajectory is clearly foreshadowed in a letter Margery later writes to her city friend:

> Dear Maisie,
> I really believe I am beginning to like this grim country and I think Daddies Caveman is going to prove much nicer if I can stay long enough to find out. My dear, he is such a tough thing—quite a danger to be dreaded—a mystery to be solved—and the very game of solving the mystery I think will be most delightful. Love to all the girls, ever your pal, Marg.

Maisie's guess on reading the letter, 'My dears, she'll be darning the Brutes socks soon', is shortly confirmed. Both Chauvel's larger *oeuvre* and the publicity he wrote for this movie leave us in no doubt of his commitment to the masculinist mythology of the bush.[164]

Thus, while Margery provides a focus for the arguments developed in this chapter, she reminds us that those arguments locate instructive ambiguities in the constellation of mass culture, gender politics, and jazz itself. Mass and popular cultural forms like film and jazz are significant in the articulation of emancipated modernity in Australia. This cuts across discourses of modernism based on high culture (from the right) and on the 'culture industry' (from the left). But in Chauvel's film the flapper is recuperated into the enfolding masculinist discourse, and it is important not to replace one simplistic essentialism with its opposite. Cultural politics are, of course, multi-layered and dialectical. It remains true, however, that in the struggle for women's emancipation from a conservative patriarchy, mass culture, jazz music and jazz dance are the sites of modernity, the means through which a liberated future is imagined and acted out. When she goes to the west, the semi-private talisman she takes with her is a 'jazz garter'.[165] Whatever the conflicting ideological forces eddying around Margery during the film, she seems to come closest to breaking free into a liberated imaginary of modernity through 'jazzing'.

THIRD BREAK
INTERACTIONS—THE BAND RESPONDS TO THE AUDIENCE

13 May 1981, Sydney

On the piss far too much, and last night Alan and I had separately determined to stay off it for the night. That is odd, because my recollection of events is fragmentary. I woke up this morning and my memory of last night had that dream-like grotesqueness and discreteness that originates in grog. Merv seemed more than usually pissed, and Dick became so as the night wore on. About halfway through the gig the table immediately in front of the band was occupied by a party of about six people, male and female. All of them seemed innocuous enough, just having a harmless good time. But one bloke was evidently getting more pissed than the others, drinking his own bottle of champagne, but to no effervescent effect. He began to mumble to himself, though still in a harmless enough manner. By the second last bracket his mutterings began to compete in volume with Dick's vocals, and seemed to resolve themselves gradually into a string of introspected lyrics. All this time he remained apart from the fellowship of the table, staring more or less straight in front of him at his glass. Gradually his monologues became sporadically louder, though still I seemed to be the only person noticing this, maybe because I was in the frontline and not drinking.

As a prelude to the final song of the bracket, Dick announced a 'special request', which was to be 'Caravan'. To the solitary champagnist, the idea of a 'special request' was rather akin to an electric shock on a rat. The mumbler called out quite articulately for Gershwin's 'The Man I Love'. Dick responded, he said something like 'Next bracket'.

More loudly and aggressively: 'Do you know "The Man I love"?'

Dick: 'I've not met him yet'.

This riposte of course established that a certain amount of banter was now in train. The customer's style, however, was rather less than rapier-like. Dick endeavoured to maintain his version of a jocular and urbane demeanour. The customer was dressed in the style of Peter Allen but showing an age which contested the aspirations of the outfit: balding, late 30s, a man trying to husband the ragged remnants of his youth, a man who suddenly knows he is getting old. He now maintains a sequence of very loud interruptions. He will not be silenced by Dick. It's not clear what he is actually saying, but it is very loud, and a tone of indignation is creeping in.

At the point at which Dick says, 'We shall effect a compromise,' he stands up, picks up his empty champers bottle and smashes it on the edge of the table, bursting into a tirade the gist of which seems to be, 'How can you compromise the Integrity of the Blues etc'. Much shouting, much use of 'fucking'. An outburst that suggested that he and only he understood artistic authenticity, that everyone else was selling out/commercial/etc. Presumably he had arrived at this insight during his introspective champagne drinking and it had begun to exercise him.

Dick managed to bellow 'Caravan' while our merry-maker hurled trays, bottles, ice-buckets, around his vicinity. Mal Morgan is sitting in for the bracket and sets up a roaring drum intro for 'Caravan'. To his credit, he stayed at his post. I didn't. I shifted myself and my instruments down the passage beside the bar out of the line of fire. When I returned to the edge of the stage I observed Merv holding the guy by the throat. My view suggested that Merv wasn't quite having things all his own way, but he actually subdued the bloke, and when I returned after my second trip to put instruments into safe-keeping, I returned to see him frog-marching the disturbance very vigorously up the stairs to the street, followed by Dick flapping. All this time, Mal had been manfully belting out a drum intro to 'Caravan'.

Since the danger of missiles seemed to have passed, I gutlessly returned to the bandstand, and mastering the agitation which makes me incapable of constructive action at the spectacle of violence, I finally delivered 'Caravan', assisted by Mal Rees who returned to play bass at about the same time. The ruckus was over but Dick wouldn't leave it at that. Phoned the police and became incredulously indignant at their indifference. He kept alluding to it during announcements: Merv had been the 'hero of the night'. In a sense Merv was, being the only person in the whole room with whatever it takes to confront the outrage. When he returned he complained, in the manner of someone who has been swindled, that he couldn't kick the guy properly when he was on the floor because he kept moving out of the way.

Finally Dick refused to return to the bandstand until he had circulated among all the tables, like a case of alcoholic remorse that requires phone calls to all the witnesses of one's behaviour to re-establish standing. We finally started without him at 10.15. Alan went to the bandstand and began to play drums, thus signifying. Mal and I joined him to play a blues, and at that point Dick bardically reconstructed the affair, recasting it into a vocal blues, placing it at a safe distance with clear boundaries.

I took my money and left. On the way back to the car I noticed that the window of the optical store next to the Soup Plus had a huge hole in it. There was a black shoe lying on the floor of the display area just inside the hole.

CHAPTER 4
THE MICROPHONE: SOUND TECHNOLOGY AND MUSICAL MODERNITY

> ... really, the whole art of modern singing depends on the microphone.
>
> *Al Bowlly AMM&DBN April 1935*

In the interactions between the character Margery and the female cinema audience, *Greenhide* demonstrated the convergence of jazz, entertainment technology and women primarily as constructions and consumers of mass culture. The encounter was both emancipatory and recuperative in relation to the conservative hegemony. A similar case study presents women as active producers of Australian modernity through music, disclosing again popular culture, the technology of mass mediation, and gender as agents in the articulation of a sense of modernity. The popular culture is jazz, the technology is the microphone, the gender is female and the emphasis is on performance practices.

Just as the masculinisation of jazz in the post-war period erased the earlier role of women, this discussion uncovers a parallel pattern and questions the assumption that the technology of popular music is inevitably the realm of the masculine. Recording and performance technologies are generally regarded as a *milieu* of men operating with sophisticated toys for production (recording technicians), performance (above all the electric guitar, the high volume, phallic emblem of 'cock rock') and even consumption (the hi-fi enthusiast is stereotypically male).[166] In its earliest manifestations, however, women were crucial in the adaptation of aspects of media technology to the expression of the modern sensibility. The case of the 1930s jazz singer will suggest that what is often described as a female subjectivity (whether manifested as femininity in a woman or as 'effeminacy' in a man), is given greater public expression through technology, which that subjectivity also explores with conspicuous freedom. Further, it is popular music that provides the vehicle for this innovation, in ways unavailable to art music because of the terms on which the latter maintained its cultural authority.

While the cultural determinations of expressivity are now axiomatic, they can often mask the complexity of the processes by which meanings are created and exchanged—a field of inquiry which is fundamental to cultural theory. The process of communicating meanings through music is more complex than the question of the character of the utterance, which draws on a symbolic discourse shaped by both social and personal histories. But the reading of that utterance also draws on what is ideally an overlapping, but never an identical discourse. As one obvious example, connotations change from individual to individual and group to group ('Listen. They're playing our song').[167]

The next two chapters are implicitly framed by two considerations relating to meaning and affect in vocal performance. One of these is the issue of bio-acoustics: that certain expressive transactions are shaped biologically rather than culturally. We cannot effectively scream for help in a soft, low register voice, nor whisper tenderly into the ear of a partner using vocal techniques that are used, unaided, to fill a concert hall. Film composers in particular recognise that certain sounds awaken anxiety partly because the ear cannot focus directionally on sounds at the extreme limits of aural intelligibility, and they can also produce physiological damage. There is an optimum pitch and tenor for a range of vocal gestures in everyday life for reasons that are biological rather than cultural. The more closely these are approximated in song performance, the less distance there may be between gesture and meaning—a kind of vocal 'naturalism'. On the continuum of vocal practices, the line separating speech from song is culturally determined. That does not undermine the fact, however, that some kinds of singing resemble conversation more than others. Recognition of this ranges from, for example, Giulio Caccini in the sixteenth century, to *sprechgesang*, which was revived in the twentieth and is one of the defining features of hip hop.[168]

A second point to be borne in mind is that, even to the extent that expressiveness is culturally determined, we have to ask the question, 'Where is this culture? How is it embodied, processed and conduited?' To deny that this occurs in and through the material conditions of life is to topple back into a naive idealism which cultural studies has comprehensively repudiated. And technology is a pervasive presence in those material conditions. Particularly in the context of the twentieth century, technology is inextricably entwined with cultural processes, and indeed it is the implications of this relationship that have become the central concern of the policies, practices and academic discourses of contemporary culture and popular music. Far from denying cultural determinations, positing a link between technology and musical expressiveness is emphatically to 'culturalise' rather than 'naturalise' the latter.

The partnership between music and modern technology can be dated from the development of sound recording in the late nineteenth century, originally imagined as a 'talking machine' that would function as an office dictaphone. The consummation of that marriage has generally been seen as the ten recordings made by Enrico Caruso in Milan in March 1902—the beginning of a recording career that would earn him over two million dollars by the time of his death in 1921.[169] Responses to the alliance have not always been favourable however, with objections that it is unnatural, alienating, and compromises aesthetic integrity.[170] There is a class and political dimension to these suspicions. Early marketing of the gramophone had to contend with a middle-class gentility that regarded technology as vulgar, as in an English advertisement in 1907 for a model designed as elegant furniture, which would appeal to an 'educated class ... and those that did not desire that their next door neighbours should be acquainted with the fact that there is a talking machine in the adjoining house'.[171]

Vulgarisation was also linked with Americanisation. The *Gramophone* editor, Compton Mackenzie, described the new fidelity produced by electrical recording as 'abominable', complaining about the 'exaggeration of sibilants' and the 'harshness': 'I don't want to hear symphonies with an American accent. I don't want to hear blue-nosed violins and Yankee clarinets'.[172] Ronald Pearsall suggests that the radio and record player became means by which distinctions between high and low culture were exacerbated and given wider currency, and Waterhouse implicates radio in the same process in Australia.[173] The ambiguous relationship between music and modern technology is masked by the common but simplistic model of a capitalist takeover of popular music through technological mediations. It is now well recognised that technological change has actually been a source of resistance to the centralised control of popular music, with musicians and consumers showing great ingenuity in reappropriating technology for their own purposes.[174] At the Contemporary Music Summit called by representatives of the Australian popular music industry in Canberra on 27 April 1995, record producers, copyright lawyers, merchandisers, broadcasters and agents gathered to discuss the 'crisis' caused by developments in communications technology such as the Internet. Towards the end of the forum several musicians spoke from the floor, all expressing the view that the Net constituted a positive intervention in their careers, enabling direct access to their fans. Their views were summarised by a young techno producer/musician addressing the legal panel on stage, who declared that the only crisis was that, 'We don't need you any more'.[175] Ironically it is the creative use of mass technology which is one of the greatest threats to the market-controlled commodification of music, and to the simplistic and exclusionary neo-Romantic myth of the creative genius separated from the consumer. Creative responsiveness to sound technology is thus also implicated in the cultural politics of modernity.

When the American Lee De Forest patented his triode tube as the Audion in 1906, the way was opened for electrically-amplified and recorded music. Central to both was the microphone. Most commentary on its impact has focussed on major sound delivery technologies, notably radio and recordings.[176] Peter Copeland categorises that impact in two ways: 'natural' results reproduce the original with as high a degree of fidelity as possible, and 'unnatural' results involve something added by technology to the original sounds. Electrical recording enhanced 'natural' outcomes, including through stereophonic sound, in which Leopold Stokowski is often cited as one of the major pioneers, with recordings made as early as April 1932.[177] While recording his score for Eisenstein's first sound film, *Alexander Nevsky*, released in 1938, Sergei Prokofiev saw possibilities in the microphone as a source, rather than just medium, of musical content, and that 'crackle produced by overload' might have its uses.[178] In this second more interventionist sense, electronic technologies have been explored by experimental art music composers. Schwartz and Godfrey's review of the impact of electronics on music traces the beginning of electronic music from the invention of magnetic tape recorders in 1935, and the pioneering of its possibilities to the work of American-based art music composers in the 1950s.[179] When Jean-Michel Jarre reviewed the work of avant-garde composer Pierre Schaeffer during the 1940s, he described him as 'The first man to consider music in terms of sound, not notes, harmonies, and chords'.[180]

All this overlooks at least two decades of active experimentation by jazz musicians with sound textures enhanced by the technology of the microphone. From the beginnings of recorded music, there is evidence of its more comfortable relationship with popular music forms such as music hall repertoire, while classical music was forced into serious compromises.[181] Throughout the twentieth century, popular music has engaged energetically with new sound technologies, as in the deliberate use of speaker feedback in performance. Steve Jones quotes Grammy Award recording-mixer Bruce Swedien, reflecting on experience going back to the late 1950s:

> When I started recording classical music ... I soon began to feel as if I were taking dictation, or something ... the most that I could do ... was to recreate the original sound field. On the other hand, in pop music ... the only thing that limits the sound image that we create is our own imagination.[182]

The relatively rigid, text-centred and non-interactive performance conventions of the mainstream of art music, accustomed to regimenting the performance space to its demands rather than the reverse, produced a general resistance to a technology that required the musicians and composers to make the adjustments. The attack on popular music from the left, as in Adorno's critiques, is paradoxically based on a combination of a form of romanticism and commodity fetishism. Art music sacralised the 'product' as enshrined in the text, and Adorno assumed it held the same authority for the jazz singer. But far from passively submitting to the mass-cultural product (as art music did before its high cultural 'product'), popular music singers and audiences actively reshaped, re-created, the music in and through performance and recording, and their technologies.[183]

Certainly, the examples cited above of art musicians' interest in the possibilities of sound technology can be more than matched by earlier jazz musicians. Copeland observes that pop (and film) musics are the most conspicuous sites of 'unnatural' innovations. When articulating a related distinction through the terms 'dissemination' and 'insemination', Eisenberg illustrates the latter with the 'classic' jazz recordings by Louis Armstrong and Jelly Roll Morton which were virtually shaped in recording studios rather than in public performance.[184] Duke Ellington was one of the earliest composers to enlarge the 'natural' and 'unnatural' possibilities of recording technology. His extended 1931 composition *Creole Rhapsody* was structured to occupy two sides of a 10-inch 78rpm disc. Stokowski's early essays in stereo recording were just one example of continuing experimentation by RCA Victor in the United States and HMV in England from 1929, which included stereophonic recordings of the BBC Symphony Orchestra under Elgar and the D'Oyly Carte Company, but also popular and jazz repertoire from Leo Reisman, Paul Whiteman, Hoagy Carmichael, Fred Waring's Pennsylvanians, Gertrude Lawrence, Noel Coward and, a couple of months before Stokowski's stereo recordings, Duke Ellington. Ellington is only one among a number who, like Stokowski, experimented with different placements of the musicians. What is striking, however, is that unlike textually constrained art music performances the flexible jazz tradition enabled Ellington to compose/arrange around the possibilities of stereo. In 'Creole Love Call' (3 February 1932),

> ... as the clarinets play the melody, Ellington has the brass come in one at a time, doing what composers call a 'terracing effect'. First, one horn enters slightly on the right; then another comes in slightly on the left; then the rest enter, filling in the gaps. It is a stunning moment, causing one to wonder at how well worked-out was the whole stereo concept by this early date.[185]

Whether or not these recordings were the outcome of a conscious attempt to produce stereo, or by-products of experimentation in LP recordings, they place Ellington at the centre of innovative recording technology, and with a distinctive interest in its 'unnatural' possibilities.[186] As early as the 1920s he was interested in extending the use of electronics beyond enhancing 'natural' results and applying it to the acoustic content. Ellington wrote for the microphone.

> Duke discovered sooner than most how to place microphones to best effect and how to use sounds that the microphones themselves created While recording 'Black Beauty' in 1927, he found that the microphones responded to some notes with mike tones, or sympathetic vibrations, which he thereafter planned for and used in compositions like 'Mood Indigo'.[187]

In general this is in strong contrast to the case of the concert hall tradition, for which recording technology became a way of preserving both the Romantic sanctity of the 'text' and the myth of the transparency of the medium. Jazz was an example of popular music that assimilated the interventionist potential of technology much earlier, and in ways that showed a greater realisation of the corporeal possibilities than that shown by art music composers. They, with exceptions such as Cage, generally regarded technology as a possibility for new kinds of cognitively driven regimentation of sound.[188]

These observations contextualise the impact on Australian music of a particular technological medium. The most immediate effect of electrical recording using the microphone was to enhance 'natural' results—increased fidelity—through quadrupling the frequency range and permitting the reproduction of previously unregistered details such as sibilants. By 1950, the whole range of sound available to the human ear could be stored and reproduced on sound recordings.[189] Its indirect impact on the production of 'unnatural' results was also most evident in record production processes such as overdubbing and splicing. My focus here, however, is upon the influence of the microphone on performance practices, both live and recorded.

Popular musicians, and in particular jazz and jazz-based performers, exploited the performance possibilities of the early microphone partly because they had to, in increasingly large venues with less regulated acoustic ambience: dancers, conversation, the clink of dinnerware. 'Art music' singers enjoyed the benefit of static audiences in fastidiously regimented performance conditions. But popular music singers also enjoyed the freedoms of the marginalised to move into cultural low-rent territories shunned by the aesthetic power blocs, and no one more so than women who were also relatively unconstrained by masculinist notions of public power and propriety.

During the earliest years of jazz in the United States, the country was demographically rural, in the sense that most of the population lived outside urban centres. The shift to a predominantly urban population registered by the 1920 census was accentuated by the rapid expansion of northern cities like New York and Chicago, both of which also succeeded New Orleans as major jazz centres. The diaspora of New Orleans jazz musicians was also, therefore, a movement both historically and geographically into the urban *milieu* of the twentieth century; and brought musicians into very different kinds of enclosed performance spaces. Many of the New Orleans jazz venues had been built to serve local community groups such as lodges, unions, social clubs or as neighbourhood drinking houses. Pete Lala's in New Orleans was a single-fronted one-storey building with a bar room in front and a dance hall in the rear. It flourished from 1906 to 1917 and it was one of the venues where King Oliver led a band. By contrast, New York's Cotton Club, where Duke Ellington's band began its celebrated residency in 1927, was in a two-storey building constructed in 1918 for social recreation. The ground floor incorporated a theatre for film and vaudeville, and the floor above was a designed as a dance hall. Following its refurbishment as a dance and supper club after mobster Owney Madden took it over in 1922, it seated 700. While jazz continued to thrive in small local bars and clubs, as on New

York's 52nd Street, the urban centres in the north also produced the massive purpose-built dance hall and nightclub.[190]

From the end of World War I the stage was set for the rise of the big bands. New York's Savoy Ballroom, opened in 1936, occupied the second floor of a building that extended the entire block between 140th and 141st Streets. It presented major pioneers of the big bands, including those of Ellington, Cab Calloway, Fletcher Henderson, and Chic Webb with Ella Fitzgerald.[191] The size of such spaces, and the ambient noise of huge crowds socialising, necessitated an increase in the volume and definition of the music. This was achieved partly by physical augmentation of the band through the proliferation of the horns, and experimentation with voicing and section arrangements. The augmentation of front line sections overshadowed instruments with a narrower dynamic range, such as the guitar, the bass, and the human voice. There had been some increase in the size of music venues in earlier centuries, but in the absence of electrical amplification this had necessitated the modification of vocal techniques.[192] The arrival of electrical amplification provided a new means by which the human voice could bring itself up to a competitive volume. Rudy Vallee assumed credit for introducing the microphone into vocal performance, recalling that in 1930 he linked a carbon microphone to a home-made amplifier for use in performance.[193]

The most obvious use of amplification was to increase volume, but the advent of rock in the mid-1950s also saw the masculinisation of this technology, applied both to the guitar and the microphone. The pioneer Australian rocker Johnny O'Keefe developed this connection, using the microphone as a metaphor of male sexual aggressiveness:

> Of course in those days to be a rock 'n' roll singer you had to roll on the floor and kick your legs up in the air. You couldn't hear much of what was going on. It didn't matter how you sang the song; it mattered what you

> did. If you moved the microphone between your legs and tried to root it, the kids would scream.[194]

By the time rock had gone on to achieve ascendancy the original connections between the microphone and the performance space had receded so far that phallic thrust and full volume have become a band reflex, irrespective of the size and character of the venue.

I therefore now return to the beginnings of amplification technology in Australia where the developments in the United States were broadly duplicated. Apart from similar changes in performance conditions, dance bands needed to appear to be up-to-date with American models. Despite the fact that the microphone introduced 'a crucial dividing line in music and theatre', little research has been conducted on the advent of the microphone in Australian music performance.[195] The first electrical recording made in Australia was in 1926—significantly by Jimmy Elkins' orchestra, described in 1927 as 'the best jazz band in Australia'.[196] Bands were often broadcast from dance halls in the early 1930s, as in the case of Jim Davidson broadcasting over 2UE from Sydney's Palais Royal.[197] This was accompanied by a high level of public interest in the possibilities of broadcasting, stimulated and reflected particularly in the changes introduced by the Australian Broadcasting Commission Act in May 1932.[198] This and related changes appeared to open up broadcasting to increasing dance band exposure, as noted by prominent bandleader Al Hammett, who declared that 'in broadcasting lies a big percentage of our work in the future'. It was reported in December 1933 that 2GB in Sydney was the first B-Class station to engage a dance band for a weekly broadcast.[199] Close monitoring by the dance band profession from February 1933 to February 1934 drew attention to the deficiencies in sound engineering of programs emanating from Melbourne's 3LO, and culminated in the refitting of its studios. The leader of the 3LO dance band, Cecil Fraser, began to demand 'microphone sense' in his musicians, praising his vocalist Marjorie Stedeford in the following terms: 'Using only half voice at a distance of nine inches from the microphone, Marjorie has succeeded in solving the problem of perfect diction.' (see p. 80)[200] In an article on sound amplification in modern music the managing director of Radioette Manufacturing Company suggested that the new audience expectations of dance-hall acoustics were created by radio (a prefiguration of a more contemporary situation in opera houses, as reported below).[201]

Fascination with sound reproduction technology was also stimulated by the advent of the sound motion picture. Most of the 'outstanding hits' of 1933 had been featured in movies, including Noel Coward's 'Twentieth Century Blues' (*Cavalcade*), Jim Davidson's 'Shuffle off to Buffalo and Forty-Second Street', and even the unlikely 'Who's Afraid of the Big Bad Wolf' (*Silly Symphonies*), which produced a boom in sales of sheet music. Movies also provided a medium for new dance crazes such as the Carioca (*Flying Down to Rio*), and *AMM&DBN* began to carry frequent lists of songs that would be featured in coming films.[202]

It is not surprising, then, that dance musicians became increasingly conscious of performance acoustics, particularly given the tension between the size of many of the halls and a softer approach to the music in the early 1930s. This problem was aggravated by the rise at this time of the band vocalist, as opposed to a musician who could occasionally double as a singer. When 'Jack Coughlin' [sic] was hired as the singer for Keith Collins' band at the Sydney Palais in 1932, it was reported as the first time that an Australian band 'has featured a permanent vocalist'. By 1936 a writer declared that except for 'diehards', hearing 'a band without a vocal is like eating an egg without salt' (*AMM&DBN* June 1936, p.5). This development coincided with the emergence of the 'crooner' and a shift in gender balance as more women were recruited as singers. In the 1 February 1933 issue of the *ADBN an* article called 'The Ladies of the Band' noting the rise of the vocalist, observed: 'Women singers have, however, not been encouraged. It is remarkable therefore that Melbourne should now have three such performers' (p.10). It was subsequently noted that an increasing number of 'girls' were now employed as vocalists in jazz-based and dance bands, an observation fortified by recordings and press coverage.[203]

Changes in Australian popular music conditions sharpened critical awareness of performance acoustics. When Sydney's Palais Royal was built in the 1920s, special care was taken in the design of the bandstand so that the music would be projected adequately into a room that reputedly could hold 5,500 people moving and talking. But when two members of Keith Collins' band left during his season at the Palais, concerns arose on behalf of the depleted group that, 'as the hall is one of the biggest in thc Southern Hemisphere, they will have their work cut out to produce enough volume to fill it'.[204] Such anxieties increased with the arrival of vocalists, and especially when the popular style called simultaneously for bigger bands and a less forced vocal approach.[205] On Jim Davidson's opening night for his Melbourne Palais de Danse season in 1933 he had ten instrumentalists as well as his solo vocalist John Warren, performing to a capacity audience. The dilemma, of whether to play loudly enough to be heard by the audience or softly enough not to overwhelm the singer, was reflected in the comments of one reviewer: '... when John Warren, who has a most delightful voice, was singing to a very small accompaniment, dancers at the end of the room were practically unable to pick up the beat. (*AMM&DBN* 1 December 1933, p.7).

The mechanism originally evolved to address such problems was the megaphone. The Stroh violin adopted this principle in response to the increasing volume of twentieth-century dance music, but in the increasingly cavernous dance halls even the horns needed some assistance. In 1933 an advertisement for the 'claritone', a megaphone for the clarinet, was carried in *AMM&DBN*, and in the same issue a writer recommended enhancing trombone solos with a megaphone (1 November 1933, pp.16, 20). In the same year it was reported that a fire broke out in a Melbourne dance hall when one of the megaphones was positioned too close to a radiator during the band's performance. Even for a 1933 newsreel in which the sound was electronically mediated, bandleader Cec Morrison's singers used megaphones as visual markers of the band's up-to-dateness. As late as 1934, Brisbane's music retailers Drouyn & Drouyn, were still advertising a substantial range of megaphones.[206]

Anyone holding stocks of megaphones by this time, however, must have been planning a clearance sale. We can document the shift to electrical amplification as the standard in live performance in Australia over the period 1933–34. In June 1933, under the headline 'Innovation at Romanos' it was announced that this premier nightclub/restaurant in Sydney had recently installed:

> ... a microphone and a set of loud speakers for reproducing the vocal chorus sung by members of the band. The voices of both Dick Slade and Abe Romaine [sic] sounded particularly well when heard by a representative of the Music Maker (*AMM&DBN* 1 June 1933, p.l5).

Over the next twelve months amplification was added to a growing number of existing venues. At Melbourne's Earls Court, 'Syd Simpson, who has a weak voice, takes many of the solos, but wisely uses the microphone, which enables him to be heard all over the room'. This was supposedly a key to the 'big success' of the engagement and other cabaret venues followed suit. In Melbourne the Rex, when eclipsed by the New Embassy and its new sound system, responded by installing 'a first class amplifying system. This news is of vital importance ... Four speakers will be placed at strategic spots, and will carry the music to the dancers. The dance band will play very quietly, more to the microphone than to the dancers.' By 1934 two of the country's biggest and most popular dance halls had begun experimenting with electrical amplification. Melbourne's Palais de Danse, where Jim Davidson's band had been so indistinct behind the vocalist, was enlarged for the opening of Ern Pettifer's season. The renovations included a new amplification system, though it was presenting teething problems: on the first night the crooner Lloyd Lamble and the female singer Freda Haddad were indistinct and the rhythm section over-amplified. Meanwhile Jim Davidson had returned to Sydney to open at the Palais Royal, where a new sound system also took some breaking in:

> To assist John Warren with the vocals, a sound system has been installed, but as the speakers are placed high up on top of the bandstand one has to dance well out on the floor to hear him at all. He sings very softly into the microphone with the result that those near the stand can see him and not hear him and those out on the floor can hear him but not see him, a fault which will be rectified by the management almost immediately.

This proved optimistic; not until September was it reported that the system had been 'recently perfected'. By 1934 electrical amplification had become part of the design of a 'state-of-the-art' dance hall. Sydney's Albert Palais opened on Easter Saturday of that year, featuring the latest in neon and a:

> ... specially designed sound system ... to enable the vocal choruses and instrumental solos to be featured. This is a wonderful asset to the band and in a very short time every dance hall or cabaret with any pretensions at all will have a similar system installed.

Another reviewer wrote: 'The amplifying system is the best heard in any dance hall in Sydney, and a good example of the material assistance that the microphone gives to a band'. Thus far, systems were hard-wired into particular venues, limiting the use which any given band could make of it. In 1934, however, it was announced that J. Stanley Johnston would be marketing a portable sound system, the 'Orchestrola', for use anywhere by a band:

> The complete unit provides for a broadcast type microphone with collapsible stand, a high-gain wide range amplifier, and a sturdy loudspeaker, and is complete with all connecting leads, flex, etc. It is only necessary to set up microphone stand, switch on amplifier, and adjust volume to the required level and you are ready to go.

The technology became even more personalised by November, with an advertisement announcing the Bridgewater Amplivox, a portable system for the individual vocalist: 'All real crooners need voice reinforcement and this instrument gives Perfect Reproduction and Tone'. (see p. 105)[207]

The technology of electrical amplification was therefore available to anything capable of making a sound. But its most transforming effects were bought about by the two 'instruments' in most danger of being overwhelmed by the rise in the acoustic level of popular music: the human voice and the guitar. The effect of electrical amplification was registered on both of these over the same period, and the vocalist's microphone and the electric guitar were in general use in Australian popular music by the mid-1930s.[208]

The link between amplification and classical music in Australia seems not to have been made until February 1940, when the ABC's subscription concerts at the New South Wales Conservatorium of Music were first relayed by loudspeaker to the three-thousand overflow crowd on the lawns outside.[209] Nonetheless, sixty years later the electric guitar has still scarcely registered in the classical or art music realm, and apart from radical exceptions, microphones have only relatively recently come into use for operatic singers, and are still regarded with suspicion.[210] This resistance is confirmed by all the evidence I have scanned.

Nevertheless, the situation is extremely complex, to the point that there is a separate study here in itself. In March 1998 I asked Susan Falk, one of Sydney's leading singing teachers, about current attitudes towards the use of the microphone among operatic singers. They viewed it 'with great distrust', she responded. There was a suspicion of any intervention that might affect their 'control of the final sound'. A discussion with David Connor (March 1998) the Manager of Sound at the Sydney Opera House, confirmed this, and offered a fascinating insight. It was not a 'first principle' to mike up opera singers, he said, who liked to think they could work without it. But there were circumstances under which a mike was used. These included cases where a singer was at less than her/his best because of illness; and light opera and operetta (as for example Gilbert & Sullivan) performed in English, which required the words to be understood.[211] In such circumstances, sometimes the speech was amplified but not the singing, and vice versa. The audience was unaware of it, and the opera company was likely to deny it. Connor reported that in Europe there was increasing electronic enhancement of sound, and predicted that this would spread to Australia. The reasons are richly provocative in relation to changes in the cultural dynamics of music: audiences had become accustomed to a higher level and quality of sound because of developments in domestic sound technology. Recordings played at home, said Connor, could increasingly put the listener acoustically inside the orchestra, an experience which could not be duplicated in the opera house. Audience expectations of sound were altering, and it was his belief that local opera performance would have to respond to this, as had been the case overseas.

An examination of the early responses to the microphone will illuminate the anomalies I have sketched. It will also reveal that the post-war masculinisation of the microphone has reversed the original gendering, rather in the same way and for the same reasons that the gendering of modernity in painting was also transformed.

The amplification of the human voice in performance and recording expanded the dynamic range available to the singer. He or she could fill a large dance hall without having to operate close to full volume and indeed could still project close to a whisper. The styles of public popular singing which are distinctive to the twentieth century grew directly out of this technology, and one of the first to be given its own name was 'crooning'. One of its major exponents was England-based Al Bowlly, whose work had been frequently remarked in Australia during the early 1930s.[212] Some of his observations on crooning appeared in issues of *AMM&DBN* in 1934. Bowlly recognised the importance of the microphone, 'the simple electrical device which gave rise to the whole art of crooning', which was 'quiet singing into a microphone, in the modern dance-band style'.[213]

To appreciate the impact of this 'modern' singing style, it is necessary to sketch some features of pre-microphone vocalising. These included precision of pitch and articulation and massive projection, since the singer could not drop beneath a volume considerably higher than normal conversation. Popular musics in formal performance venues obviously developed conventions and mannerisms of their own. Music hall, light opera, vaudeville, and even parlour singing, however, took these standards as a template. By this model, singing was ideally the product of formal training and physical power, the latter obviously a masculine quality. Richard Foster, eminent singer and vocal teacher at the Sydney Conservatorium, recalled advice given to him by Allan James Foley (Signor Foli) in 1899:

> You'll need more beef on those bones of yours, my lad, if you intend to become a singer ... you've got to be as strong as a horse ... Go in for gymnastics, do plenty of deep breathing, and build yourself up as much as you can. (Roland Foster, *Come Listen To My Song*. London, Sydney: Collins 1949, p.34)

Al Jolson emerged from a pre-microphone tradition, and always referred back to the acoustic traditions of American vaudeville.

> His style of performance and projection and his technique of vocal production were geared to reaching the balcony. His methods were set. He could no more shift to a crooning style than could an opera singer.[214]

Although the first person to talk on the movie screen, and regarded as a major figure in twentieth-century popular music, Jolson in fact represented the tail end of a tradition that was being overtaken by the mass mediated culture of modernity. Finishing his last radio show for the Chevrolet Hour in 1932, he said: 'This radio business is not for Jolie ... It's a sad day when Jolie needs a mike to sing into'. He threw the mike to the floor, and sang to the studio audience without it.[215]

The microphone challenged the models exemplified in singers of Jolson's *milieu*: that is, singers raised in the acoustic tradition. Cutting across other generic demarcations, it is a category that includes many of the early blues singers such as Ma Rainey and Bessie Smith. Evan Eisenberg summarises the transition:

> When we come to the voice we find, in the 1920s, a tradition of projection developed in opera houses and vaudeville palaces and encouraged by acoustic recording; and in a quieter tradition surviving in folk music and barely surviving in chamber music. Electric recording brought about a great, creative

> flowering of this second tradition of popular music and in jazz as Billie Holiday, Bing Crosby, and Fred Astaire taught singers to make themselves objects of the microphone.[216]

In alliance with African-American popular music, the microphone provided alternative possibilities for vocal production, and in doing so it created authoritative public space for previously unheard voices—the untrained, the small voice, the head singer. Al Bowlly sketched some of the implications:

> The microphone brought into being, and sometimes into very prominent being, a whole host of singers who otherwise would never have been heard.
>
> Their efforts vary between 'a low moaning sound, as of animals in pain' to 'the soft singing of a mother to her child'.[217]
>
> Singers, instrumentalists and recording artists of all kinds were urged to 'take it easy'.
>
> ... even if one sang quite softly the 'mike' picked it up with just as much strength as if one shouted at it. And with an infinitely more pleasant effect. Vocalists explored this new idea of 'whispering vocalism'.
>
> There is hardly a person, of either sex, or almost any age, who cannot sing in some sort of way.[218]

The microphone not only gave voice to those previously silenced; it frequently refused to mediate the hitherto dominant voices when they were projected according to established standards of excellence:

> The robust tenors, whose redness of face was in direct ratio to their height of note, became something of a problem. The microphone has an unpleasant habit of 'blasting,' which is a jarring, shivering sound,

> when the volume forced into it is too much for the delicate amplifying apparatus. Thus it was that, at first, until they grew to understand it better, the recorders found difficulty in coping with the vocalists who were ignorant of King Mike. And the singers, having been taught to sing in a certain way found it very difficult to do otherwise. Their training had always been based upon the requirements of filling large halls and theatres. Volume, especially on top notes, had too often been their fetish. This does not mean to say, of course, that all 'legitimate' singers are bellowers, or that none of them can control their voices to softness. But it was just that their style of singing was, in those early days, unmicrophonic. (Bowlly, 1 May 1934)

Not surprisingly, responses to the new technology from 'legitimate' sectors included contempt and suspicion, and rarely incorporated a creative curiosity about its 'unnatural' possibilities. The microphone negated all the craft which confirmed the professional skills of those committed to orthodox traditions. Simon Frith has documented attempts by the BBC to suppress crooning, 'this particularly odious form of singing' (Frith 1986, p.263). Jolson reportedly dismissed the microphone as being for 'weak-voiced singers', a view shared by art music discourse which regarded its use as 'a demonstration of vocal infirmity, inadequacy or impotence' (Pleasants 1974, pp. 61, 39).

Clearly, when a good voice was also a strong voice, this is aligned towards gender politics. Frith documents the belief among BBC officials that crooners were effeminate (Frith 1986, p.263). Al Bowlly paraphrased the description given by its opponents as 'emasculated moaning' (1 May 1934, p.40), and discussing such criticism, he writes in a way that gives further resonance to his earlier comments about the sound of animals in pain or a mother singing to a child:

> Before we go any further I would like to deal with this attitude, because until the reader really understands the reasons for it, and the answer to it, he is likely to suffer from some kind of inferiority complex—to feel that the ambition to become a singer in the modern microphone is something *shameful and unmanly.* (1 March 1934; my italics)

While it is likely that antipodean responses in general to the intrusion of technology into music were less motivated by anti-American and class animosities, nonetheless, as John Rickard documents, there was hostility on the part of the musical establishment to current developments in what was regarded as jazz, that were specifically related to the effects of the microphone on singing styles. As early as 1930, Thorold Waters, editor of *Australian Musical News*, quoted an overseas article lamenting the havoc unleashed by the microphone, producing the crooners 'reed-like, husky tone and a vibrato of 'soft, cloudy vagueness', [which] broke all the rules of good singing'. In his 1943 memoir, W. Arundel Orchard, former Director of the NSW Conservatorium of Music, complained about the music that had emerged from the wireless:

> I refer particularly to that abomination known as crooning, with its nauseating chromatic slides and verbal twaddle ... It is neither music nor singing, merely a compound of revolting noises which should be rigidly excluded.[219]

Initially sections of the popular music establishment in Australia reflected this attitude, though more in the form of a passing snipe. It was reported that Al Hammett had booked a new singer, George Foster, for his 2GB band, 'and, thank heaven, he is not a crooner'. One of Bing Crosby's recordings was praised for showing him to be more than a crooner, a category fit only for the 'discard'. In some cases it reflected a general opposition to the rise of the vocalist in general, suggested in Brisbane pianist Ninie Hennessy's complaint that a song 'is often spoiled by the inevitable crooner. He will have his chorus'.[220]

In Wellington, New Zealand, in 1936, crooning was the subject of a radio debate between Stanley Oliver (head of Wellington's Harmonic Society) and Arthur Pearce, who had recently begun broadcasting jazz. Pearce was perhaps the most highly informed jazz enthusiast in New Zealand and had strong links during this period to the Australian popular music scene. During extended visits to Sydney in the late 1930s he gave lectures and wrote for *AMM&DBN*, and as a pianist he led a group of Trocadero musicians on a number of significant recordings under the band name the Seven Pearce Arrows.[221] The Wellington debate provides a well-focussed parallel with the Australian dynamic. Laurie Lewis' biography of Pearce carries a full transcription of the debate, from which the following extracts are taken.[222]

Oliver, opposing crooning, defined it as:

> ... that soft high pitched vocalism, set to sentimental words, employed by men who sing what I believe are called 'vocals' in the music of dance orchestras ... [to many it is] a strange perversion of good taste ... Crooning is a type of vocalism of one colour only and, to my ears, that colour is rarely a pleasing one. It lacks all traces of masculine characteristic. It is entirely devoid of all virile utterance. In real emotional expressive equality it is inconsequential. Its vocal value is practically nil. Its essentially cramped ultra nasality causes the performer (I was on the point of saying singer but I changed my mind) to emit distorted and often unlovely vowel sounds. (p.53)

Defending the style, Pearce makes it very clear that it is a style of singing more appropriate to the microphone and modern dance music than that of the 'legitimate singer with the hale and hearty voice of the concert platform ... [in crooning] The voice of the most masculine of men was modified and softened' (p.55). He corrects Oliver's misconception that crooning is the product of a high-pitched voice (p.63). This is of particular interest. Oliver is so persuaded that masculinity is linked to high volume that he mishears softness as a high 'woman's' register.

There are three points emerging from these data. First, the microphone produced a feminisation of music. It was seen as an inappropriate medium for masculinity; women were under less pressure to triumph in the physiological disciplines and crafts associated with male mastery. Second, the microphone altered the expressive dimensions available to the public singer. Bowlly discusses this in terms of acoustics. He refers to the relative ease with which singers can project using a microphone:

> ... in this absence of effort they found several virtues. Firstly, that it suited the microphone so well; secondly, that it gave a new timbre to their voices by making audible harmonics and upper partials which had never previously been heard; thirdly, that it enabled them to enunciate with far greater clarity than before; fourthly, that it gave to their voices an almost stereoscopic effect; fifthly, that it eliminated most of the danger of blasting. (1 May 1934, p.38)

The third point was that these 'virtues' go beyond the achievements of high fidelity and greater dynamic range. They enabled the direct presentation of experiences using the vocal techniques by which they were articulated in everyday life. Intimacy, tenderness, anxiety, coyness, all found their way into earlier public singing traditions, but in the large concert venues for opera and music hall, such inward and private experiences required extravagantly stylised conventions. Softness, nuance and ambiguities integral to expressivity in day-to-day social practice, could not be directly replicated on an operatic stage. The 'natural' voice of private intimacy was not the low-larynx projection required to fill an opera house unassisted by electrical amplification. Such emotions required stylised mediations: high register, coloratura, histrionic gestures—artistic conventions transparent only to a narrow section of the community. In an age in which cinema can register the expressive power of a flicker of an eye, extravagant gestures are in danger of becoming bombast. The point has been graphically illustrated by the performances of stage actors in early talkies. The impact of the microphone on vocal conventions was similar in effect.

The microphone alone, of course, did not determine these changes in vocal projection, but achieved them in concert with all the other circumstances associated with its use in modern performance. It enabled a shift towards public projection which more comfortably approximates the unforced modes of everyday speech than the highly developed techniques associated with pre-microphone theatrical projection. The development of classical singing as it is now understood involved a 'well-documented change from the earlier speech-related singing that probably characterised the high status form in earlier periods'. Modern classical singing calls into play physiological procedures that differ from those of ordinary speech, including, for example, vibrato. Some, like the lowering of the larynx, enhance projection and resonance but also constrain differentiation of vowel sounds, and with a lower jaw and more open mouth 'further modify vowels relative to speech'. This throws light on the discussion above of microphone use in operatic performance. A higher larynx position is characteristic of more intimate vocal communication, a difference which also resonates with anglophone class distinctions, since high/low larynx speech appears to correspond to differences between high and low class English pronunciation. This becomes of particular relevance when we remember the shift of popular singing to North American accents in which those particular class markers are erased. With the microphone this shift enabled 'speech-like voice production' which constituted a crucial distinction between jazz and 'high status classical singing (with its laryngeal constraints on accent and tone colour) and ... between jazz and its predecessors'.[223]

This is not to disparage the high status voice, but to recognise its boundaries. The arguments that seek to affirm the absolute superiority of classical singing cannot operate both ways: either great operatic vocalising is different from everyday vocalisation or it is not. A 'stage whisper' is exactly that: a highly stylised and disciplined convention through which what is being heard by a theatre full of people may be agreed to represent rather than replicate something intended to be heard by only one person whose ear is millimetres from the speaker. If the techniques of producing this representation from an unamplified stage for an audience of thousands, are asserted to be identical to that used to produce it in everyday circumstances, this paradoxically devalues the disciplines by which high status singing technique answers its own criteria of excellence. What is all that training for? What are the textbooks about? The assertion that operatic vocalisation is identical to everyday vocalisation with a microphone is so at odds with the evidence of our ears, with the intent of hundreds of years of professional tradition and pedagogy, with the known physiology of voice production, and with the literature on the subject, that it is a remarkable testimony to the quixotic intractability of ideology.

Like John Potter, Henry Pleasants has traced the decline of the opera tradition into nineteenth century mannerisms which ruptured its affinities with the 'melodic and dramatic properties of the Italian language'. Discussing the vocal techniques of popular song, Pleasants cites Giulio Caccini's commendation of singing 'without tying the man's self to the ordinary measures of time, making often the value of the notes less by half, and sometimes more, according to the conceit of the words'.[224] If we change the word 'conceit' to one of its modern equivalents, 'sense', and de-gender the subject, we have a description of Louis Armstrong, Frank Sinatra, Mildred Bailey, Billie Holiday, the early Ella Fitzgerald. This reconciliation of public singing with the everyday timbres of contemporary speech was achieved by popular singers exploiting the microphone, while art music vocalising has been generally tethered to a pre-technological performance repertoire and its expressive vocabulary:

> ... unencumbered by a stagnant and aging repertoire, or by nineteenth-century concepts of vocalism conditioned by the requirements of that repertoire, the arrival of radio and the public address system has opened the way to, had indeed demanded, a less forceful, more intimate, more natural kind of vocal production and vocal communication. (Pleasants 1974, pp.133–4)

With the microphone the shades of feeling being inscribed in popular song could be presented publicly without being dwarfed by the magnitude of their own acoustic projection. Pre-twentieth century heroics could be replaced by the democratic sagas of the modern quotidian. In the debate with Pearce, Stanley Oliver claimed that the lyrics of a crooner's repertoire are banal, illustrating his lament with what is in fact, the whole point: the lyrics are about ordinary heterosexual love.[225] The voice could articulate contemporary experience at its optimum intonation, while the mike took care of its dissemination. Private anguish could fill the room with a whisper. Feelings that cannot be shouted could now be heard, and the muted conversation of modern domesticity achieve a public voice. Frith has aptly paralleled the effect of the microphone with that of another decisive modern technology: the cinema close-up.[226] Twentieth-century popular music is not only a phenomenon of mass mediation, it is also a site at which mass consciousness is mythologised; and again the microphone connects the two trajectories. As Frith points out, the crooners ability to evoke 'intimate, personal relationships with fans' worked particularly well in the domestic spaces infiltrated by radio and recordings (Frith 1987, p.61).

There are other connections between the microphone and the culture of modernity. The new technology also drew attention away from the composer to the performer, signalling a major shift from high-art traditions, in diminishing the power of the score and score-reading skills. In this way it reconstituted music as something accessible to people hitherto silenced or excluded by a lack of education.[227] The fidelity of the microphone enhanced the mass dissemination of the individualised voice, with its distinctive grain, its ambiguities and subtleties of timbre, pitch, melisma: Bowlly spoke of the importance of the 'singer's ... personality in his rendering' (*AMM&DBN* 1 April 1935, p.27). In doing so it gave expressive authority and mass cultural presence to the modern quotidian. The microphone thus achieved two otherwise competing objectives: it extended the demographic penetration of 'mass culture', but also created the illusion of intimate, private communication, in a way that acoustic vocal traditions could never achieve without accepting amplification in performance.

We can draw many of these issues together with a citation from Pleasants, which provides a direct link to the next stage of this discussion. Under the heading 'New Radio Rules', *Billboard,* 1 April 1922, is described:

> ... a new and very sensitive instrument which catches the buzzing and whispering usually heard in the background. Someone even has said that the new instrument will record the swish of a powder puff as it passes over the nose of some fair lady. (quoted Pleasants 1974, p.25)

This otherwise innocuous announcement resonates with a number of points which I now wish to develop. The new technology, he says, will pick up everyday sounds which until now have been inaudible, or 'in the background'. Significantly, he chooses as his paradigm of such repressed 'voices' the extraneous noises of femininity and its everyday fashion.

As in other countries, Australia's dominant vocal aesthetics scorned the microphone as unmasculine and artistically dubious. It was thus more likely to be those musicians marginalised by, for example, genre, race, class or gender, who would explore the modern technology and its expressive capabilities in the most unconstrained way. In Australia, musically, this meant new forms of popular music, which in turn meant its mass-mediated African-American influenced styles. In the 1920s these were broadly referred to as jazz, and in the 1930s, Swing. Here again, our attention is directed towards women. If some might argue that Frank Sinatra, a (male) dominant figure in the evolution of microphone singing, is not a jazz singer, it is worth recalling that he cited among his major influences Billie Holiday, Mabel Mercer and jazz and Swing trombonist Tommy Dorsey, who 'taught me everything I know about phrasing' (cited, Pleasants 1974, p. 185).

Apart from the 'effeminate' style, the vocal 'closeup', the microphone also provided a channel for new vocal sounds. Roland Butter linked scat singing with crooning as part of the modern style, now developed 'to such a degree that no known method of writing is adequate for the purpose of transferring it to paper' (*AMM&DBN* 1 July 1935, p.29). Discussing the possibilities of microphone singing, at different moments Bowlly talked about 'a new timbre', 'low moaning', 'animal sounds'.

To explore this it is useful to invoke a distinction articulated by the writer Andrew Chester among others. In a published debate with Richard Merton, Chester challenged the assertion that rock is simple and classical music is complex. This is a distinction 'constructed on the basis of the specific mode of complexity of classical music itself', and Chester articulates a counter-distinction through the terms 'extensional/intensional':

> Western classical music is the apodigm of the *extensional* form of musical construction. Theme and variations, counterpoint, tonality (as used in classical composition) are devices that build diachronically and synchronically outwards from basic musical atoms. The complex is created by combination of the simple, which remains discrete and unchanged in the complex unity. Thus a basic principle of classical music is rigorous adherence to standard timbres, not only for the various orchestral instruments, but even for the most flexible of all instruments, the human voice. Room for interpretation of the written notation is in fact marginal.

Against this Chester proposes intensional development as a criterion more (though not exclusively) appropriate to rock, jazz and 'many non-European musics':

> In this mode of construction the basic musical units ... are not combined through space and time as simple elements in complex structures. The simple entity is that constituted by the parameters of melody, harmony and beat, while the complex is built up by modulation of the basic notes, and by inflexion of the basic beat.[228]

The distinction being drawn by Chester should be familiar, though the dominance of traditional music notation makes it impossible to produce an adequate symbolic language for intensionality. The simplest way of summarising the musical effects comprehended by the term is to say that it includes those least amenable to notation.[229]

One of the most striking developments in modern western vocal music has been the expansion of its intensional dimensions. This exploration has been conducted virtually exclusively by popular musicians. The abrasively guttural texture which has become *de rigueur* in so many forms of pop singing, and of which Tom Waits' work is an exaggeration, can be traced back to a timbre most famously exemplified in the voices of Louis Armstrong, Ray Charles and Little Richard. It can also be heard in the black gospel tradition of southern states' *sprechgesang*. This has often been combined with wordless vocalising, ranging from scat singing to the 'moaning' or 'animal noises' described by Bowlly. Louis Armstrong is regarded as introducing the former to recorded music, with performers such as Cab Calloway, Bennie Paine and the Boswell Sisters among its popularisers. The latter can also be heard in pentecostal moments in black gospel, and a version of it is heard on recordings by Duke Ellington from the late 1920s, notably Adelaide Hall's vocal work on 'Creole Love Call', 26 October 1927. The Ellington band developed a striking 'intensional' vocabulary, particularly through its brass players like trumpeters Bubber Miley and Cootie Williams, and trombonist Sam Nanton. The orchestra's significantly designated 'Jungle Sound' is largely based on the exploration of ambiguous timbres as well as unusual voicings.

The sources of such variations from legitimate articulation are wide-ranging, but they include numerous 'folk' or 'ethnic' musics, such as Hebraic cantor traditions, as well as the more obvious African influences on American popular music.[230] For Australians, the sources were overwhelmingly American. In Australia, African-American influence permeated early public displays of expanded vocal techniques in non-indigenous society. Whiteoak cautiously suggests that nineteenth-century blackface minstrelsy might have been a conduit for such vocal practices, but is more confident that this is the case with Australian vocal 'ragging' that emerged in the last decade of the century. African-American artists provided models for such practices in Australia, incorporating husky timbres and scat effects.[231]

In alliance with the microphone, jazz extended the intensional dimensions of vocalising, eclipsing their earlier pre-technological manifestations in minstrelsy and ragging. The microphone both provided the means of mass dissemination of jazz intensionality, and enabled its possibilities to be expanded even in the huge performance spaces of urban modernity. Jazz-based vocalising explored areas that included low-volume conversational timbres and constricted glottal effects that could not have filled such spaces without the microphone taking the burden of projection.

The fact that this technological innovation appears to have been first introduced in Romanos, a relatively small venue using a relatively small band, reflects the fashion for that unforced singing style often known as 'crooning', of which Abe Romain was regarded as a skilled exponent.[232] Large dance halls had been operating well before the 1930s, and the size of dance bands had also been increasing for some time. Adelaide's Palais Royal, which opened in 1920, accommodated 2,000. Sydney's Palais Royal opened in the same year with a floor for 3,000 dancers, the same number as Melbourne's Green Mill on its opening night in 1926.[233] Among developments that brought the problem of acoustics to its flashpoint were the new fashions in popular singing styles which I have been describing. These were derived from models on recordings and in films produced with the benefit of the latest sound technology. Australians, however, then attempted to replicate them in performance conditions which had not been designed for such practices.

The advertisement for the Amplivox proclaimed that the individual voice now had the technological means to project itself into the public sphere wholly on its own terms. The importance of this was quickly recognised within the industry. In June 1934 Colin H. Keon Cohen, the Melbourne correspondent for *AMM&DBN* reported on p.26 that one of the 'most interesting features of the month' was the spread of the microphone in dance halls, and he listed five that had recently installed such equipment. His comments confirm that the new technology was now enabling local musicians to 'produce' in performance as well as 'consume' the effects being heard on recordings.

> This development, which has come so comparatively suddenly, is most interesting to thoughtful leaders and arrangers. It opens up tremendous possibilities. The gramophone has always had the advantage that it could bring out any particular instrument and tone in the others to match without necessitating any musician playing either above or below his normal tonal volume thus allowing of each giving his best. With the new conditions it should be possible, and in fact is possible for the dance hall band to do something similar ... One other aspect seems possible if we are to take a very long view of the situation. Fans are familiar now with the fact that whereas three or four feet away one is unable to hear a crooner at all, one can hear him or her perfectly, fifty or sixty feet away at the end of a large dance hall.

One of the venues listed by Cohen was Melbourne's New Embassy, opened in February 1934. There was considerable advance notice of the preparations for this new cabaret, which would compete with the well-established Rex. In keeping with the growing fashion for band singers, it was noted that the vocals 'will be a very strong point. The Embassy is comparatively small which will enable the band to play at all times within itself'. On 30 January, Reg Lewis and Barbara James left Sydney for Melbourne to begin rehearsals for the opening (*AMM&DBN* 1 February 1934, p.7), and Colin Keon Cohen attended one of the practice sessions. He listened to Barbara James sing 'Tenderly' into the microphone: 'one of the two finest that I have ever heard' (*AMM&DBN* 1 March 1934, p.22). Reviews of the opening season focus, often exclusively, on the singing of Barbara James, with the following a representative accolade:

> Barbara James has made a tremendous success, and there is little doubt that the outstanding impression taken away by the general public is of her. Her personality has got over, and I hasten to congratulate her on her success. Helped by an excellent twin speaker microphone, her voice goes over to perfection. Melbourne is indeed fortunate to possess two such outstanding vocalists as Barbara and Marjorie Shedeford [sic], both whom have received many overtures to go abroad. (*AMM&DBN* 1 April 1934, p.28)

This review has an interest going beyond the immediate event covered. Singers like these, positioned to explore the possibilities of the microphone without fear of compromising their cultural authority, were most likely to produce the boldest effects, and bring Australian song into the technological realities of the twentieth century. Both James and Stedeford, female singers associated with the latest styles and techniques and with experience in radio, were also particularly singled out for their command of the microphone. From this point on, notices of vocal performances not assisted by electrical amplification become increasingly rare.

FOURTH BREAK
TRADITION: AUSTRALIA—
BARBARA JAMES

9 December 1997, Sydney

Today I went and interviewed Barbara James again. I have been writing about her in the book I am trying to finish, becoming more interested in her work in relation to the advent of United States-sourced popular music in Australia, and the role of the microphone in this process. Apart from the questions this particular area of interest has raised, I am becoming more and more fascinated by this woman whose career began at the same moment that jazz arrived in Australia, and who is still alive, vivid, and 'full of twang', as Philip Tagg would say. I have found myself wanting to talk to her again, to absorb something of this historical aura, as well as just trying to find out things which in due course will be irretrievable. It is something like the fascination I had with Abe Romain, but complicated and textured by gender, by the physical presence, the look and sound, of this woman whose version of 'It Don't Mean A Thing', recorded exactly sixty years ago, has such erotic jouissance. Knowing that the person who sang that is still available to be talked to is a curious feeling, all mixed up with the larger matter of her life 'fitting' the history of jazz in Australia and the role which she played in that history.

I arranged the interview by phone. I asked a few questions by phone as she didn't seem very enthusiastic over yet another interview. I have found this with a lot of people who have led long and full lives—without losing their enthusiasm for living, yet they get somewhat weary of telling their stories over again: Audrey and Jack Blake, Graeme Bell, Abe Romain. I told her that it would be brief and very focussed. I knew exactly what areas I wanted to cover.

She agreed to see me at work. I had spoken to her last time at her flat, which is near and similar to Abe Romain's. Hushed, solid, dark. She works at the Kings Cross community centre, which is in the Rex Hotel building in MacLeay Street adjacent to the Alamein Fountain, quite close to where I lived for a period. I arrived on time. She was pleased with the red carnations I had bought for her. I did this just as a gift and a courtesy and out of some inarticulate feeling that I would like to be one of the many people who over the many years had given her flowers. It is likely that not so many people bring her flowers now, and it just seemed appropriate. I think that, although not intended that way, it might also have turned out to be a good thing in terms of the interview.

She seemed a little reluctant. We exchanged greetings and she reported that her health had been less than completely satisfactory but hoped it would soon improve. She was a little reserved, avoiding eye contact as she expressed the wish that she had made the appointment for next week. She was very busy. It later emerged that the centre had only just been relocated to that section of the building, and this seemed to add to the sense of spatial and psychological congestion and distraction.

I offered to come back another time, but she said no, since I had come all the way into the city to see her. It was also raining heavily. Whenever I have spoken to her I have had the sense of a very well-defined personality with a clear sense of being responsible for one's actions. One makes an arrangement, one honours it. It took a little while for her reserve to dissipate, but it did. She agreed to let me tape the interview, which she had been unwilling to do on the previous occasion. I don't know where I got that recollection; I later checked and found that I had recorded her. As I plugged the tape recorder lead into the power socket I said something to her, looking away from her as I did so. She said that I would have to speak more loudly, and as she did so she attached a hearing aid. Later in the interview she said that her hearing had been irreparably damaged during the Trocadero years from sitting next to the band night after night. So, too, she believed that her father's hearing had deteriorated because he had played banjo with his head inclined close to the body.

As we began, she said several times that she was very busy. We were frequently interrupted by the telephone or people wishing to ask or inform her of something. We talked at her desk, which was in an open workspace, virtually a wide corridor giving access to the main office so there was regular traffic as well as conversation in the background. I told her I would be as brief as possible. She said that she would try to respond to my questions, but if she didn't want to answer any she would simply decline to do so.

As we proceeded she became more engaged and in fact became quite warm to it as time passed. Gradually the emphasis shifted from her responding to questions, to opening up other lines of thought. By the time we finished she had lost what seemed to be her original lassitude. She became energised and vivacious. Perhaps because of some ill-health she had seemed a little tired and distracted at the outset. She had talked about memory and recollection. Although she had had a full and happy life, she said that sometimes people forget that memories can also cause sadness or distress. Several times she also repeated that all these things were so long ago that she could not remember some of them. Remember, remember. Her career began about eighty years ago.

By the time we finished talking she had regained some sparkle. She introduced me to her colleague, who, it turned out, had my book on Australian jazz at home, and also was a friend of pianist Peter Piercy. I hadn't seen Peter for some time, though knew he was in poor health, so she filled me in with what she knew. Barbara said with evident pleasure that I had already written about her and was doing more work on her career. She signed the booklet that goes with a CD of her recordings, and to my surprise she also happily allowed herself to be photographed and even assumed a pose for the second one. When I asked if I could have one of both of us she agreed. After the slightly intimidating opening of our talk, and in view of the slight awe in which I hold her (she can present the appearance of a rather severe headmistress who will brook no nonsense or familiarity) I was especially complimented when, posing with me, she put her arm around my shoulder. Odd, to look at the woman smiling out of the photograph taken in the Trocadero around sixty years ago, smiling in a white halter-neck gown, voluptuous shoulders, body inclined as though moving slightly to the music ... odd to look at her and to have that same arm around my shoulder as we stand to be photographed in 1997. I don't know what the feeling is called. It is prickly with all kinds of feelings—of mortality, of continuity, of entering into history, of the being-in-the-body.

Shortly before I left she talked a little about other things. She invited me to call her if I wanted to know anything else. I asked her what she was doing for Christmas. She has something organised. I suggested maybe next year. She crossed her fingers and smiled. Just before I left she introduced me to a woman who had been in the main office and I felt very proud when she said to her colleague, 'We are a mutual admiration society'.

As I walked back to the station I bumped into writer and dancer Mandy Sayer, another attractive young woman at the early end of her career that intersects with jazz, but eighty years later than Barbara. Mandy said she was just finishing her new novel which is based on her life with her father busking through the United States. There is apparently some film interest in it developing. It was raining, that humid sort of rain that reminds you that Sydney is semi-tropical. We talked for a while in the shelter of an awning, then I had a sudden thought and steered her into a bookshop, where I bought her last novel, The Cross, and asked her to sign it for me. She graciously wrote 'For Bruce—in friendship and admiration'. On the same day that Barbara James signed her CD notes for me, Mandy Sayer signed her novel, a point of very specific convergence in Kings Cross of two careers that will certainly span well over a century.

CHAPTER 5
BARBARA JAMES AND MICROPHONE SINGING

'Doowop Doowop Doowop Doowop Doowop Doowop Doowop Doowop Doowop.'

Duke Ellington, "It Don't Mean A Thing If It Ain't Got That Swing" 1932

The career of Barbara James coincided with some of the most influential developments in Australian popular music, and her recordings in the 1930s are landmarks in the transition of Australian music to the twentieth century. In particular, they reflect a striking exploitation of the microphone in extending the possibilities of vocalisation.

Barbara Florence Cecilia James was born in Carrington Street, Wynyard Square, Sydney, in 1908. Both parents were professional performers: her mother, Malvena Moore, was a singer and dancer, and her father, English immigrant Will James, played banjo, guitar and mandolin. He became Barbara's music teacher, beginning with the xylophone when she was about eight years old, later followed by saxophone and banjo. She began playing school concerts and ladies' nights, then at around the age of eleven she was contracted to the Tivoli performance circuit at a reported £15 per week. Through the 1920s she worked as a double act with her father, as well as solo, on stage, radio and in cinemas. Singing and saxophone gradually displaced the xylophone. In about 1932 the father/daughter double, billed as 'Barbara James and her Boyfriend', was augmented by pianist Reg Lewis, and Barbara 'and her Boyfriends' participated in the inaugural broadcast of 2BL, with which they maintained a busy association. She made her first recordings, as a singer, in 1933, and by the mid-1930s was at the forefront of the profession, performing in the top nightclubs and dance venues in Sydney and Melbourne. 'This was into the jazz era then', she recalled, a significant way of describing the arrival of Swing.[234]

In November 1936 she and Reg were married, and by the following year both of them became associated with the famous ballroom, Sydney's Trocadero, where she sang with the bands of Frank Coughlan, Dick Freeman and Abe Romain, most of the time in the company of Reg as band pianist. Built in 1936, with a floor that accommodated 2,000 dancers, the Sydney Trocadero in George Street quickly became the most important public dance venue in Australia. Throughout the war it was one of the favoured haunts of American servicemen.[235] Barbara and Reg left the Trocadero in 1941, and throughout the war years continued to work at the top of their profession: at the Regent, the Tivoli, and the Prince Edward, nightclubs like the Roosevelt, revue work, and a tour with Wilfred Thomas's entertainment unit for the British Pacific fleet. By the mid-1940s they had consolidated their careers and released the recordings that are the focus of this study.[236]

As noted in Chapter One, the decade from 1936 saw a decisive acceleration in Australia's shift away from Anglo-European to United States points of reference.[237] The revival of interest in African-American influenced music marked by the advent of Swing, was given further impetus with the arrival of American service personnel during the Second World War. Dance and music venues responded with renewed emphasis on the latest developments in American music. Australian women responded with changes in speech, dress, recreational conduct, sexual behaviour—changes dismissed or resented by Australian patriarchy as the infatuations of impressionable sweater girls. By the logic we have observed in relation to other cultural forms, there is no reason to expect that Australian men in positions of cultural power would initiate changes so threatening to their own authority. The channel through which the United States infiltrated Australian wartime culture was demotic and, insofar as it was gendered, it tended to be female. Applied to music, this model draws our attention to that form of United States music which is most distant from the European high art tradition—but which, of course, is also audible in Australia as quintessentially American—that is, jazz-based music.

While Australian popular music was recognising these emancipatory forces, formal music education was pulling so far in the opposite direction that the two seem scarcely related. We have already seen how resistant was the music establishment to the manifestations of 'microphone' vocalising through which modernity was being articulated in popular song. It is no surprise to find that there was no place in accredited music education for such innovation. Monique Geitenbeck's study of the role of women in the Australian music examination system discloses relationships between the politics of gender and modernity similar to those observed in Australian painting.[238] Formal standards of musical competence were determined by conservatoria in alliance with the Australian Music Examinations Board (AMEB). Their interests, ideologies and memberships overlapped. As in the post-war art schools, the overwhelming majority of music students were women. Philosophies and curricula, however, were controlled by men, and women were not admitted until the mid-1940s even at the level of examiners. Furthermore this patriarchal regime was deeply conservative, maintaining a nineteenth-century artistic profile which manifested an ethnic (Anglo-Celtic) and gender orientation. Women's roles in music-making were based on a British model which primarily confined them to genteel domesticity or public spaces where music might be a background to socialising, as in salons or teashops.[239] Any attempt to achieve respect as a concert performer required vigilance against compromising artistic standards. This could be difficult when being a woman already constituted an obstacle to employment in the art-music world.

The career of Australian singer Strella Wilson exemplified these dynamics. It extended from around 1917 to the early 1950s, and was roughly contemporaneous with that of Barbara James.[240] A pupil of Melba, Strella Wilson's aspirations were towards the concert hall, but her repertoire was categorised as 'popular songs, art songs, operettas, operas and opera arias'. 'Popular songs' in her definition consisted of 'songs in a style popular early in the twentieth century and often recorded by opera singers' (Dunbar-Hall 1997, p.121). The several hundred items include a negligible proportion from the twentieth century United States popular canon, and nothing at all from ragtime or jazz. There is virtually no evidence of the American popular music that transformed this century (Dunbar-Hall 1997, pp.149–155). She was not oblivious to it: she reportedly worked with Paul Whiteman in the United States around late 1925, and with jazz bands in England during 1930–34 (Dunbar-Hall 1997, pp.31, 67). Ultimately Wilson became an honoured Australian singer and citizen, and as she moved further into the establishment, her earlier excursions into demotic performance gradually faded from her public recollections. Although she had worked with vaudeville comic Roy Rene during the 1930s, in later years 'she conveniently avoided mentioning these shows as part of her career—perhaps they were too much a part of low culture'. (Dunbar-Hall 1997, p.71).

In all this there seems little likelihood that institutionalised vocal training in Australia would show curiosity about the innovative possibilities of contemporary popular music and technology. The singer Kate Dunbar found herself straddling an uncomfortable divide when she took singing lessons from Cecily Atkins at the NSW State Conservatorium around 1940–41. Some time into the course she also began singing informally with a suburban dance band, through which she developed microphone technique. The effects of this experience were evidently being internalised, as she realised when, while performing her exercises for Cecily Atkins, the teacher sternly ordered, 'Don't croon, Kathleen!'[241]

In 1937 J. Sutton Crow, secretary of the AMEB and of the Melbourne Conservatorium, declared that by an 'unwritten law' women were not to be used as examiners (Geitenbeck 1995, p. 197). His determination would surely have been reinforced by the recording of 'It Don't Mean A Thing If It Ain't Got That Swing' which Barbara James made that same year. What he would have heard was a comprehensive violation of the institutionalised aesthetics and ideology of singing. And he would also have heard a voice of the future.

Barbara James' first recording, on 13 June 1933, was of Noel Coward's 'Twentieth Century Blues' from *Cavalcade,* and on which she reports being a little nervous (Markham)[242]. This is not surprising since, apart from being her debut with a relatively new technology, the song incorporates the kind of unexpectedly wide intervals that were often misconceived as signalling blues or jazz.[243] In spite of its title, James's voice on this track has a rather correct English sound, in timbre, intonation and accent, producing an incongruity between delivery and lyric content. She is a little tentative in committing herself to that indeterminate third which is often (although inaccurately) regarded as distinctive to jazz and blues. It is of course important to take into account the material she is working with here. The other song later released from that session, 'Black Eyed Susan Brown', shows her much fleeter of foot and confident, probably because it is in any case a more convincing example of hot music than the somewhat creaky pastiche of 'Twentieth Century Blues'.

What is extraordinary is how rapidly her voice enlarged its expressive range over the next few years. This can be examined in terms of two parallel developments in her work. One is the movement towards the intonations of everyday speech, and the other towards the expansion of vocalising beyond normal conversational timbres. What they share is a relaxing of academically established notions of correct singing at that time. The first of these developments follows a steady trajectory. On

'The Devil and the Deep Blue Sea' (1937) and 'The Answer is Love' (1940) there is a striking increase in unforced conversational rhythms and inflections. 'I Don't Know Enough About You' (1946) is a useful foil to her first recording, as, once again, she is accompanied only by a pianist (her husband, Reg Lewis). The appeal of the performance lies in the intimate and erotic sense of someone talking softly into the ear of the 'you', the projection of what Roland Barthes referred to as the 'grain' of the voice, 'the body in the voice as it sings'.[244] Some of her latest work is from the radio program *Between You and Us*, from the late 1950s. The format is of song medleys, duetting with Reg on vocal as well as piano, linked with banter. Conversation modulates into song, with Reg singing harmonies and casually improvised counterpoint, humming intermittently over his piano solos. The impression is of overhearing an evening's companionable music-making in a living room, ranging from everyday wisdoms to a degree of good-humoured and unembarrassed sexual innuendo (as on 'You'll Find Out'). It creates the sense of a loving but often affectionately sparring contemporary domesticity, of ordinary life refracted through song.

Thus within a few years of her recording debut and overlapping with her period at the Trocadero, Barbara developed a vocal style increasingly comfortable with the projection of everyday feelings and experiences. From the point of view of voice production, the reasons included the increased assurance that comes with experience, and changing social mores that diminished constricting self-censorship and diffidence. But such changes don't occur in a vacuum: the particular kind of performance experience and its social ambience give definition to a performer's development. I hope to show that technology was also essential to this development, and the groundwork for this is an incontrovertible change in Barbara's performance practice: a lowering of her vocal register. If we consider a sample of the tracks she recorded between her debut and the heyday of her work at the Trocadero, the pattern is steady and virtually unbroken. I have identified the keys aurally, based on reissues of the original recordings. The Pitch Diagram provides an analysis of nine of her recordings dating from the beginning to the close of her recorded career, from 1933 to the late 1950s: see p. 134. These indicate a lowering of her working register from brief excursions into the lower soprano range, to the lower end of contralto.[245] Between 1933 and 1940 we hear the gradual extension of the lower register by a full fourth, with some small attenuation of the upper register. She is still hitting an easy C above middle C on 'I Don't Know Enough About You' in 1946, only a tone below the upper limit of her first recording made in 1933, 'Twentieth Century Blues', and with what sounds like greater ease. The extension of a singer's working register is of course one of the standard signs of vocal development. What can be noted, however, is that this extension is downwards in pitch, drawing her further away from the conventional registers of femininity. As the upper limit of her range indicates, this is not simply the lowering of register that comes with maturity; it is apparent within a very short time of her first recording. It coincides, in fact, with her adoption of the microphone in performance.

The drop in register achieved a number of results. They can be heard as we pass from 'Twentieth Century Blues' to 'Black-eyed Susan Brown', recorded at the same session. The fussy articulation across wide intervals of the first melody contextualises her pitching uncertainties as problems rather than solutions. On the second song, even allowing for the more bouncy tempo, her voice is very assured, as she works for the most part in what is clearly the more comfortable interval of middle C up to F. She reshapes the melody (including by 'ghosting') according to her natural compass; and is able to do this more easily because it is a jazz vehicle. Instead of finishing on a tonic, a repeated 6th puts her at the most comfortable, midpoint of her singing range.[246] This foreshadows later developments. As she expanded the intensional dimensions of her singing, these extensional dimensions were required to carry less of an expressive burden. She could if she wished contract these, manifested particularly in the preference to work in a lower and narrower pitch intervals, but she had available other devices through which to expand the overall expressive range. This recalls Al Bowlly's comment about microphone singing that 'Forcing is wholly unnecessary, and every effort can be concentrated on the quality of the voice rather than the quantity. An entirely different voice quality is the result'. (*AMM&DBN* 1 April 1935, p.27).

The reference to 'intensional' devices, as defined above, takes us to the second, parallel development in her singing. This is most strikingly explored in her 1937 recording of Ellington's It Don't Mean a Thing If It Ain't Got That Swing'. The lyric is close to musical abstraction, but grounded in sensuousness. Its outrageousness, in 1937 Australia, can be sensed if we compare it to more conventional vocalising of the period.

One of the promotional items for the opening of the Trocadero in 1936 was the song 'My music is heard around the world', probably performed by male Trocadero singer, Cardru Llewellyn.[247] Here are roughly contemporaneous performances, associated with the same site and level of popular music. Yet they represent opposite ends of a continuum along which virtually all singers of the late 1930s to mid-1940s could be situated. Broadly speaking, they correspond to the Old World/New World binary that has dominated Australia's sense of the civilised world for most of this century. Llewellyn embodies European high art conceptions of vocal production, precision of pitch and articulation, emphasis on massive projection rooted in pre-electric acoustics. This tradition had been a privileged presence in Australia since the colonial period; and popular music in its least culturally negligible forms was still basically a re-inflection of this approach heard, for example, in light opera and parlour singing.

At the other end of the continuum we have Barbara James working in a jazz style using a 'purpose-built' jazz composition.

Its written lyric is custom-made for the abandonment of the conventional vocal constraints of verbal narrative. The words of any song are but a fraction of the meaning, and often the smallest part of it. In this case, sense as something verbally denoted, or even conveyed through pitch-differentiation, is the subordinate vehicle of the song's meanings. Words are used to prepare us, but the song's 'sense' is embedded in verbal nonsense. To paraphrase:

Bars 1–4 'The meaning of this song is that it doesn't mean anything except swinging. Thus:'

Bars 5–8 'Doowop Doowop Doowop Doowop Doowop Doowop Doowop Doowop Doowop.'

Not words or pitch (which is unchanging in bars 5–8), but rhythm and sound are the subject and the vehicle. Barbara James takes even this threadbare semantic fabric and shreds it further. Instead of the symmetrical, if syncopated, 'Doowops', she scribbles across the rhythmic and acoustic space with a timbre so clotted that only the texture and rhythm count. The voice ranges from a whisper in which the flow of air more than voice is the vehicle, to a nasal projection, and extended guttural growling. She treats the lyric on the eight-bar bridge more straightforwardly, though at all times she is taking liberties with rhythm and pitch. This performance is inaccessible to notation. It is sound having no reference point other than itself. Its subject is pleasure, and in particular of a self-referential character: the pleasure of singing in this way about the pleasure of singing in this way. The indeterminate 3rds and 5ths are very confident, played with for their ambiguity. This is not someone feeling uncertain, but working indeterminacy with great confidence, and the 'affect' is of a pleasurable teasing, a flirtatious game of promise and evasion. Its commitment to pleasure and play is strikingly erotic, even now. Sixty years later this is still as authoritative a version of the song as any that would be heard live. On the basis of extant recorded evidence, it was in 1937 a radical extension of the textures of music vocalising in Australia—extension into the areas which were later expanded so energetically as by now to have become the standard. But this has not yet frozen into *cliché.* There is no precedent on Australian record for such an assured assimilation of the singing style that foreshadowed the dominant sound of the twentieth century pop voice. With this version of 'It Don't Mean a Thing', Australia arrived at the 'grain of the voice' that distinguishes the mass-mediated music of modernity.

If we can hear the future foretold in the work of Barbara James, the source of its musical form is less clear. There are a few vocalists who seem to be moving away from the rigidly-conceived distinction between song and speech, into more 'conversational' registers, intonations, phrasing. I asked Barbara James to talk about possible models she might have heard in Australia.[248] 'There weren't many Australian singers around before I was coming up. Des Tooley was around, I think.'

Born Amy Ruwald, Tooley was most active in the 1920s, but also worked in radio intermittently in the 1930s and 1940s. Her recorded work demonstrates a poised assimilation of contemporary popular singing styles as they were developing in the United States through the 1920s. Like James, her early performances were on the popular stage and in collaboration with some of Australia's most accomplished early jazz musicians including Frank Coughlan, Abe Romain and Beryl Newell. These artists also accompanied her at various times on a series of nearly forty extraordinary recordings made between 1929–33. Like James, her material was contemporary popular song dealing with contemporary lifestyles ('The Breakaway': 'Let's do the Breakaway, it's got the snappiest syncopation'), and social and private conduct, particularly relating to the pleasures and anxieties of sexual identity ('I'm Sailing on a Sunbeam', 'Swinging in a Hammock', 'Nobody Cares If I'm Blue'). She worked most comfortably in a low register, so much so that she was billed as a 'lady baritone' and 'The girl with the unusual voice'. Blindfold tests invariably elicit the opinion that the voice is male. Some of her songs had been written for a conventional male voice ('Walking with Susie'), and this contributes to a sexual ambiguity that at other times is overt. 'He's So Unusual' is based on a very explicit statement of female sexual appetite ('I've gotta have some loving ... I'm burning up for kisses'). It is a song of puzzlement but also arousal at her boyfriend's indifference or resistance to the sexual opportunities with which she provides him. 'I Wonder What Is Really On His Mind' contains a strikingly explicit double entendre that helps to explain the moral panic Edwardian-born parents experienced in the face of contemporary popular song.

When he vows to me that he
can never see enough of me,
I wonder what is really on his mind.
When he tells me I'm so sweet,
I'm really sweet enough to eat,
I wonder what is really on his mind.

This lyric is given more space in which to approximate conversational rhythms by going out of tempo in the vocal, but back into tempo for the instrumental interlude. In all this (including the category of 'lady baritone'), there is an echo of music-hall traditions, but the use of the microphone enables Tooley to discard the declamatory projection of pre-electric performance. Like Barbara James, Des Tooley frequently worked in the 'natural' timbres, rhythms and pitches of conversation. She often abandons the melody to assume the cadences of speech especially at moments of sexual ardour, a reminder of the way in which contemporary popular song brought such hitherto private and personal areas into the familiar expressive compass of everyday life. Tooley's now obscure work deserves a focussed study of its own.[249]

Had Barbara been aware of Tooley's work? She thought she had heard her on one occasion. 'She had a very deep voice'. But

James did not know the earlier recording artists work well, and had not made any particular note of it. Her comment on Tooley, 'She was fairly straight compared to me', is fully confirmed by the recorded evidence.

There is also the question of possible local antecedents for the more flamboyant developments summarised in 'It Don't Mean a Thing'. To find anything remotely resembling these explorations of unconventional vocal timbre in Australia, we have to go back beyond the advent of 'jazz' to 'vocal ragging'. The following summary of the practice is derived from John Whiteoak's account, with page references where appropriate. Ragtime vocalising flourished in Australia from the very late nineteenth century into the teens of the twentieth, and exhibited many of the characteristics of subsequent twentieth-century popular song, with 'considerable ambiguity in pitch, timbre, and the rhythmic placement of sounds' (Whiteoak 1999, p. 119). Its vocal devices included scat and a form of yodelling, and the husky voice of one of its exponents, Ben Harney, attracted the description 'crooning' (Whiteoak 1999, p.117). Ragging used growl effects, an example of which can be heard on the American Gene Greene's 1917 recording of 'King of the Bungaloos', though to my ear it is a different, relatively unaspirated technique compared to later jazz growling. The ragtime singer had great freedom:

> ... to phrase, articulate, and experiment with timbral variation in a fluidly independent way ... ragtime singers not only improvised but also provided a model of creative freedom for ragtime instrumentalists. (Whiteoak 1999, p.120)

Prominent exponents who worked in Australia were Ben Harney and Gene Greene, who visited Australia in 1911 and 1913–14 respectively. Recordings by Australian vaudevillian George Sorlie exhibit many of the effects summarised, including yodelling, 'melisma ... the interpolation of syllables, ... nonsense syllables in unison with the piano, ambiguous pitches' (Whiteoak 1999, p.158). It seems likely that the very earliest singers billed as jazz performers like Belle Sylvia also used some of these techniques (Whiteoak 1999, p.176). Subsequently jazz singing differentiated itself much more clearly from other forms of popular vocalising. As late as 1928, however, there is still at the very least a suggestion of unsurprising juxtaposing in an account in *Table Talk* of the visiting black American revue, *The Coloured Idea.* The writer describes the group's vocal quartet, the Four Coloured Emperors of Harmony:

> They faithfully express the negro sense of harmony and rhythm, even in the yodelling in which they disclose the enthusiasm of a child. The rest of the idea consists of a sambo jazz band which speaks its frequent piece from a combination of drums, saxophones, banjos, piano and asthmatic trombones; the four Covans, who dance to their legs' content: Dick Saunders, another prancer with a smile like a gash in a watermelon: and Ivy Anderson, the coloured soubrette. (Quoted by [Sutcliffe], October 1997 p.10)

The disdain that would greet any attempt today to package yodelling with jazz is not consistent with earlier and more generous traditions of what was acceptable. In contrast with later jazz enthusiasts, it seemed to cause Louis Armstrong no discomfort to record 'Blue Yodel No. 9' with yodeller Jimmie Rodgers as late as 1930.

How far might Barbara James' work in the late 1930s have derived from these multi-faceted traditions? Vocal ragging had fallen out of fashion by the end of World War I, and the early vogue for so-called jazz, through which its practices might have been translated into the early 1920s, was abruptly extinguished with the onset of the Depression in 1929. Barbara James' professional career, however had begun around 1919, and her childhood had been spent in a show-business environment. It is possible that she had assimilated the work of vocal ragtime either directly or through her parents. There is, however, no evidence that she was conscious of this being so. She was insistent about this with an emphasis that is notable for an informant who was always very clear about what she could not recall. 'Ragtime didn't come into jazz of course ... I've heard the expression ragtime, but where it came from or in what context, I don't know'. She had no involvement in ragtime: 'No, no, it was always jazz'. What Barbara and her contemporaries might have understood by these terms is, of course, very different from later constructions. Nevertheless, she had no recollection of ever hearing of Gene Greene, Belle Sylvia or Maybelle Morgan. George Sorlie was recalled 'as a name [who used to] ... take out shows'—that is, in his later capacity as an agent/promoter. She believed that her mother had worked for him, but had never heard him as a performer.

Sorlie made some recordings in 1929 that incorporated vocal ragging but these evidently represent a style that was already old-fashioned a decade earlier (Whiteoak 1999, p. 158). The singing on the Australian hot dance recordings of the 1920s, made virtually exclusively by men, shows no evidence of vocal ragging. Instead they present conventional articulation with pre-microphonic projection—the intensional explorations of ragtime singing had virtually disappeared. When in the 1930s they began to reappear in the form of crooning, conversational styles and the more extravagant vocal ambiguities of Barbara James' 'It Don't Mean a Thing', they seem to have become more of a female phenomenon, with Des Tooley the most striking exponent. This is not entirely so; witness the 1933 recordings of the Rhythm Boys, (Ray Tarrant, Jim Gussey, Dud Cantrell) who were primarily instrumentalists with Frank Davidson; of Jack Davey (beginning in 1935); and of Frank Coughlan (beginning in 1937). In each of these, and in different forms, there is some evidence of American influences ranging from hot dance to Swing. There are also press reports in the 1930s of multi-instrumentalist Benny Featherstone singing in the style of Louis Armstrong, but no recordings appear to have survived.[250] There are references in contemporary reviews that suggest other male singers presented Armstrong imitations, and to scat singing.[251]

In the absence of adequate recorded evidence it is impossible to comment on these in detail. There is, however, a great difference between a specialty Armstrong imitation, and a pervasive and personal vocal style. The object of the former is to temporarily conceal one's own vocal identity in order to draw attention to the original. In the case of Barbara James' vocal style, we are listening to a generalised assimilation of a new approach to singing. Among Australian male singers at this time, there is virtually no trace of having internalised the more extravagant intensional models like Louis Armstrong, Fats Waller, Cab Calloway, and certainly not of any of the female singers like Adelaide Hall. Nor is there any noticeable residue of earlier vocal ragging. I suggest that a major factor in its disappearance was a convergence of technology and gender. Vocal ragging was nurtured in music halls and theatres that had been built to the limits of unamplified voice and instrumentation. Their audiences were static, relatively silent, and focussed on the performer. Even under these circumstances, the physical strain of vocal ragging could evidently not be sustained for more than half an hour, even by an experienced specialist. Whiteoak (1999, p.156) cites a review of a concert by Gene Greene in Melbourne which reports that the audience kept him singing 'as long as his throat ... would stand it, and he had difficulty in escaping ... after "ragging" for half an hour'. This audience/performer dynamic is reversed in the shift from theatre-style venues to larger purpose-built dance halls in the teens of the century. In Australia, as we have seen, jazz performance quickly migrated from one to the other. In bigger spaces with unregulated acoustics it would have been physically impossible to project the vocal techniques of ragging in dance venues before the advent of electrical amplification. Since this did not occur until the early 1930s, we have nearly two decades during which the techniques fall into disuse.

This technological narrative was intersected by gender. During that same period, roughly from the end of the Great War until the early 1930s, other changes in Australian culture would also intervene. The resurgent and conservative masculine ethos that followed the war was occluded at the level of popular culture and fashion by the glitter of the 'jazz age'. It then found a more hospitable environment in the Great Depression. The conservative, patriarchal brass band movement, as well as the 'legitimate' popular music profession, reinstalled discipline and uniformity as markers of professional musicianship, with a level of success manifested in the reversion of *Australasian Band and Orchestra News* 'almost exclusively to brass band news' (Whiteoak 1999, p.220). The official consignment of ecstatic expressive modes to the realm of the feminine, and of American popular culture to the realm of corruption, almost certainly intensified the high/low binary which accompanied the cultural debates in Australia throughout the 1930s.[252] In any case it assuredly led to a hiatus in the African-American influence on Australian music and to a resumption of more traditional genre roles in the mainstream public domain. The men who had dominated recorded popular music in the 1920s were trained in pre-microphone vocal techniques, and with the coming of the Depression, jazz ceased to interest them.

With the revival of Swing in the mid—1930s this African-American stream resurfaced, but by this time a particular local tradition of popular singing had receded. That tradition, incorporating vocal ragging, was shaped by pre-electric acoustic conditions and sustained until that time primarily in vaudeville and music-hall venues. With the strain it imposed on the voice, vocal ragging was the first element of pre-amplified singing to fall victim to new performance environments. The more legitimate hot dance vocal style lingered longer because, with its bigger projection, it could still manage the new venues, but it receded along with the whole jazz *milieu* in 1929. It awaited the microphone to bring popular music into the twentieth century, and it required the attentive curiosity of those whose sense of professional competence was not threatened by it. In musical terms, that meant popular rather than art music. In terms of gender, it was women who took up the challenge more imaginatively than men.

This takes us back to the question of where they found their models. Barbara James repeatedly asserted that there were no singers in Australia on whom she consciously modelled herself, and that she was aware of no Australian predecessor who sounded like her. It is useful to link this with another comment about reasons for the interest in United States-led groups: 'Oh well, we all thought any band was good that came out from America ... Because it was American it had to be good'. As James herself suggests (Markham), the choice of models was related less to her own local antecedents and peers than to what was available on record. Over several interviews, when asked about influences, Barbara James always returned to the same group of singers: Mildred Bailey, Bing Crosby, Sarah Vaughan and especially Frank Sinatra. She also admired Ella Fitzgerald and Billie Holiday, but explicitly denied that she was inspired to model herself on them. What these people had in common apart from being American jazz or jazz-influenced performers, is that they were microphone singers. Of her acknowledged models, only Bailey and Crosby had been available on record in Australia for long enough to have been relevant to the period under discussion here—1933–1937. Mildred Bailey made her first recording in 1929 and is regarded as the 'first white singer to absorb and master the jazz-flavoured phrasing, enunciation and embellishments, improvisatory and swinging rhythm of her black contemporaries'.[253] From as far afield as Australia, James at that time could hardly have come closer to a vocal model at the fountainhead of the white jazz tradition. Bing

Crosby had worked in jazz groups as a child before forming the vocal trio the Rhythm Boys (which included Bailey's brother Al Rinker) who, like Bailey, worked with Paul Whiteman. Crosby's performance style also became internationally recognisable through a film career that began in 1930. Henry Pleasants describes Crosby as

> ... one of the first singers to master the use of the microphone and was important in introducing into the mainstream of popular singing an Afro-American concept of song as a lyrical extension of speech. As one of the first crooners, he used the microphone not so much for singing as for apparently talking (or even whispering) to a melody.[254]

In retrospect, Barbara James did not think of herself as a crooner, largely because it was a term normally applied to men. This was generally, but not invariably so, and indeed Barbara herself appeared to accept the designation during the 1930s.[255] What is both more important and less equivocal is her alertness to the possibilities of the microphone style pioneered so influentially by Crosby.

While this suggests sources for the conversational dimension of her style, these models exhibit little of the more flamboyant intensionality of 'It Don't Mean a Thing'. For that, we need to go more directly to African-American performers. Barbara had no recollection of having heard the singing of Louis Armstrong before the beginning of her Trocadero phase. Of Fats Waller's singing she said: 'I might have ... heard it in passing, but not really studied [it]'. She also used to listen to Cab Calloway. But the obvious models were Adelaide Hall's 1927 recording of 'Creole Love Call', and Ivy Anderson's 1932 recording of 'It Don't Mean a Thing'. Both of these performances, with Duke Ellington's orchestra, manifest similar wordless, glottal vocalising. She recalls that she used to listen 'a lot' to the Ellington orchestra and his singers, though regarding Hall she was definite that she 'didn't listen to her very much'. Her response to Ivy Anderson (who had visited Australia with *The Coloured Idea* in 1928) is much the same. Furthermore, the vocal arrangements of the version by Anderson and James are different in central respects. Anderson, for example, never sings the 'Doowop' sections (bars 5–8, 13–16, 29–32); she drops out and the band plays the passages. Yet these passages are precisely where James' vocalising is most adventurous. It is impossible to see the Australian version as a slavish 'cover' version of Ellington's. The most likely analogues for this extraordinary Australian recording, far from glowing like beacons in James' memory, are not specifically recalled.

This inconclusive and slightly untidy datum is an important reminder that individuals are much more than passive conduits of historical theorems. There are also the minutiae of temperament and the ambiguities of personal relationships. Barbara James' most powerful and immediate influence was that of her family and in particular her father, vaudevillian and self-proclaimed jazz musician. Questions about the beginnings of her interest in jazz go back to Will James.

> Oh yes, because he was playing jazz himself ... He was playing for dancing and jazz ... It was obvious that that's where I was going to go ... I had no alternative ... he was in jazz at that time. And I had Mother ... who had rhythm and the dancing. I had Dadda who had rhythm and the beat. Where could I get away from it?

Will James led one of the earliest groups to present themselves as a 'jazz band', first at the Wentworth Hotel circa 1920–24, and later at the Bondi Esplanade where his band included Frank Coughlan. Barbara James also recalled having heard the bands led by American musicians Frank Ellis, Ray Tellier (both at Sydney's Palais Royal), and Bert Ralton at the Ambassadors in Strand Arcade ('Dadda took me there one day'). She worked in her father's Wentworth band on xylophone; and when she later began singing she had no inclination to work outside the professional and social *milieu* of popular music.

This was a subculture in which the imperatives of high cultural performance practices were at the very least destabilised. To this must be added the fact of temperament. Barbara James saw herself as 'always a loner' (Markham), not in the sentimentally romanticised sense—which doesn't fit the evident facts of her life—but in having a clear view of her preferred options. Her choice of what was called jazz was an independent gesture. In the wave of conservatism that followed the Wall Street crash, jazz was no longer a popular or fashionable music, and the Musicians' Union itself declared it a perversion of taste, 'detestable to musicians' when used by newspapers to describe 'modern music'.[256] Nor was James simply forced into popular music by exclusion from the legitimate sphere:

> People have asked me why jazz instead of legitimate singing. I was at one time taken by a friend of my fathers who was a tenor—I was taken down to the conservatorium to an old Italian teacher down there ... who heard me sing and who ... wanted me to study for legitimate singing—or for opera I suppose—and I said no, at that time I didn't want to give up what I was doing, because I was singing and playing, loving jazz of course. And he said well I will teach you for three years for nothing. You have a ... good open throat. I said I didn't want to. (cited, Johnson & Sutcliffe 1992, p.131)

For a host of reasons, including her family background, she felt no particular pull towards the music of 'high culture'. She performed the music she chose because it gave her pleasure.[257]

This is not a romanticisation of a popular music version of the autonomous genius. It is a reminder of the plasticity of the individual's relationship with historical patterning. We might be able to see why it was likely that someone travelled along the path she did, but that is not to say it was inevitable. Barbara James is not a cultural abstraction. Nevertheless, there are aspects of her life and career which help us to understand certain incontrovertible but puzzling aspects of Australian music in the twentieth century. One of these is simply that the most adventurous Australian singers in the 1930s were women working in popular music, drawing on techniques that can be traced back to African-American music. Barbara James is the most striking example. The traditional way of seeking explanations would be to look for sources and influences that bear formal resemblances to her work. But it doesn't throw a great deal of light here: the sources she did use were available to men also, and the formal models closest to home were ignored. By the hypotheses evolving here, however, the explanations lie less in aesthetics than in socio-cultural logic in which the politics of gender, genre and technology are complicit.

The fact that, unlike instrumentalists, singers present lyrics, makes for special circumstances which seem interestingly implicated with gender, as well as with what we shall learn of 1930s performance practices. It has been suggested that Australian women singers of the 1920s and 1930s assimilated the American style more quickly and convincingly than men.[258] Recordings and contemporary media reports tend to confirm the suggestion, as does Barbara James' memory. Asked whom she regarded as jazz or Swing singers among her contemporaries, she finally named over a dozen women, but could remember no men.[259] She asserted unambiguously that women were quicker to assimilate American influences, and sang with what she called 'more natural' voices. In the early stage of her career, her male colleagues were, by her recollection, either formally trained, or modelled themselves on those who were. The conversational microphone style went against the grain of their training, in which they all took great pride (Johnson 25/6/93). I prompted her with some possible male candidates, including the brothers Frank and Jack Coughlan, but her answers were either simple negatives or hedged with qualifications. Among professional notices of the period, one of the most praised 'crooners' was Jack Davey, characteristically described by a reviewer as 'the best crooner yet heard in Sydney. For some years he has studied microphone technic [sic] and knows how to put his voice over the air' (*AMM&DBN* 1 November 1933). But for Barbara James he 'was more of a personality than a singer'. Obviously some of these replies are themselves puzzling in their implications, but puzzles for another line of inquiry. The point here is that, although two of the most influential models, Crosby and Sinatra, were men, all the evidence suggests that in Australia women outnumbered men as popular singers in the American style in the 1930s and 1940s. Most of the women had extensive radio as well as stage experience, but it is relevant here that Barbara was one of the most active in live performance, and her family background gave her a strong sense of 'stage presence' (Johnson 10/12/97).

Whatever else might remain labyrinthine, one thread seems to remain unbroken. Barbara James' testimony confirms the importance of the microphone, and its position in the genre and gender politics of Australian music. Fundamentally, it became necessary as a practical measure. The band that opened the ballroom on 3 April 1936 consisted of fourteen musicians, half of whom were horn players. She attributed her severe hearing impairment to a form of industrial deafness caused by sitting next to the Trocadero band every night for four years. The effects of amplification, however, went well beyond raising to a competitive level the volume of her existing vocal style. This now takes us back to the drop in register as observed earlier on her recordings. A comment by Pleasants resonates here with the early crooners including Crosby, he observed, the use of the microphone was accompanied by a tendency to lower pitch for the sake of enunciation and more comfortable tonalities (Pleasants 1974, p.44). The extent to which this was a conscious process on the part of Barbara James was confirmed by the unhesitating and vigorous response she made as soon as I referred to the register of 'Twentieth Century Blues'. 'I was singing in soprano range ... as time went on I went down into the chest range and extended the voice'. Asked why, she replied that it was 'stronger and better for jazz'; the change 'helped me no end'. She referred to her recording of 'I'm Gonna Live Till I Die' to illustrate the increased strength she enjoyed in the more comfortable register. This was recorded probably in the late 1950s. On aural evidence it is in G minor, with her compass between G above middle C, down to F, her lowest note on record, a range of 14 semitones. The bridge is almost wholly on the lowest two-semitone interval. In the conclusion she rises to B flat, and down a minor third to finish on the tonic. The strategic lowering of her range was facilitated by the use of the microphone, enabling her 'to project in the lower register in live performance'.

It was the microphone which also enabled her to experiment with the more closed-throat intensionality which is heard on 'It Don't Mean a Thing'. Without the mike, 'It would have been an impossible strain on the vocal chords ... I couldn't have filled the hall without the microphone' (Johnson 10/12/97). Sixty-three years earlier, she had made a similar observation when the microphone was becoming standard for vocalists:

> By careful manipulation of the 'mike', it is possible to sing thirty choruses in an evening without tiring the voice, and therefore the last number of the evening possesses the freshness of the first instead of developing weariness.[260]

Her usual technique was open-throated, but she constricted her throat for such effects. 'I wouldn't have strained my throat doing it, I wouldn't have tried to do it at the Trocadero with no microphone'.

> I could do things with the microphone that I, you know, I couldn't do personally. You know, such as, er, without a microphone light and shade doesn't come into it so much, for a start ... Sound—big sound, small sound: *to* the microphone, *away* from the microphone ... I learned that as I went. I taught myself. I watched other people a lot ... anybody that was using a microphone.

It was not only that, as a woman, she could use this technology without feeling that it demeaned her power. It was also that popular music as a genre was relatively free of the dictates of the score. And this was most especially the case with the vocalist. In the 1930s, unscored work for Swing instrumentalists was still relatively rare, the improvising soloist a special case. A further note on performance practice is necessary here.[261] Even in the 'state-of-the-art' Trocadero orchestra most of the musicians learned and played their material from orchestrations published locally. Barbara's performance was more controlled by ear, learning her repertoire from recordings because she was interested in timbral characteristics which were not evident in notation. The nights program was not planned in detail (which is why she had to be on stage continuously). Following his reading of audience mood, Coughlan would call the next song by a number that referred to the scored arrangement in the musicians' folios. The number meant nothing to Barbara, whose repertoire was in her memory. Not until the band started would she know if she would even be singing the next number, and she would take her cue from the arrangement.

Thus, while her performances were constrained by the arrangement, within that framework she had a freedom of manoeuvre denied to score singers, and was not even under the compulsion of score-prepared audience expectations. The popular music setting also allowed her to take liberties uninhibited by academic principles of vocal rectitude. In actual working conditions she could explore the possibilities opened up by the microphone and receive immediate audience feedback on their effectiveness. I asked her what made her think of producing the sounds heard on tracks like 'It Don't Mean a Thing':

> I possibly have heard somebody doing it. I don't remember who used to do that sound at that time. But I heard it somewhere. And that particular song was difficult to fill in. The extension of the bars, you know. So something had to be done to fill it in ... that's how it came about. But it was my own. I've got to do something here, so I'll do that. You know, that's the sort of thing it was. But most of my work was like that. It was my own interpretation ... You're singing it the way you feel yourself.

The comments about needing to 'fill in space', incidentally, tend to confirm that she had heard the Ivy Anderson version, and that she was determined not to copy its format slavishly.

Of course a series of interviews with someone recalling events from over half a century ago cannot by themselves sustain the arguments made in this chapter. But that material has been carefully contextualised by research. Barbara James provides what is by now virtually a unique first person testimony in the history of jazz-based music in Australia. The beginning of her career coincides with the earliest Australian 'jazz' performances. But this testimony is also the flesh and blood on the arguments, not the skeleton. Her personal history is a metaphor and dramatisation of the forces that converged to produce the song of Australian modernity, including individual temperament and background, genre, gender and technology. It is almost unimaginable that this pervasive sound of the twentieth century could have emerged from an institutionalised art music ethos. It is possible that an Australian male singer might have developed such a style at that time. But there is little evidence that one did except as a novelty impression. It is hard to imagine that anyone could have done so in the urban performance conditions of the twentieth century without the possibilities presented by the microphone.

The newness and relative spontaneity of American popular music, and its indifference to the leverage of terms like 'vulgarity' and 'sentimentality' provided a means of publicly expressing forms of experience about which we are often made to feel self-conscious; and a new way of articulating subjectivity. At the same time, the microphone made possible minimalist and intimate inflections; and enabled the singer who knew how to use it to project in large performance venues without being confined to open throat projection. It became physically possible to approximate more directly certain emotional states. As in the case of Barbara James, and I suspect Des Tooley, the microphone also permitted singers to project directionally in lower keys that were more comfortable for them. This had two important consequences. It brought singing closer to the conversational register, so that it became a way of articulating the everyday in a more recognisable way. But I also suggest that it made available to women a larger compass through which femininity could be expressed in song. The so-called *bel canto* tradition forces femininity into the upper reaches of voice production, a process which is analogous to putting them into high heels and tight dresses. That is, it restricts the acceptable range of female vocal conduct and therefore narrows the acceptable range of articulated experience. In that tradition the contralto range was most frequently associated with such roles as 'villainess, sorceress or older woman'—not the sort of place to find a decent young lady.[262]

This is not necessarily to say that in lowering the register a singer comes closer to what is trans-culturally a more 'natural' register. That is for another debate. The assertion here is that it allowed them (on Barbara James' own testimony), to settle back into a register that was more 'natural' in the sense of more closely approximating the register and projection of their ordinary conversation. There is a significant study to be made of changes in the timbre and range of women's voices as heard in song and later on film in the post-Victorian period. It is difficult to imagine the vocal balance between vaudeville-trained George Burns and Gracie Allen working for the power relations played out by Bacall/Bogart, Tracey/Hepburn.[263] Marilyn Monroe's vocal register caricatures the point. An examination of changes in the vocal register in various female *personae* on stage, film, radio and recording, may well disclose a cumulative contribution of microphone vocalising to a general shift in the acceptable public register of femininity.

It is also worth pondering a gender shift in jazz instrumentalism that appears to relate to the introduction of the vocalist's microphone. Women had enjoyed some prominence as popular musicians in the 1920s. By the late 1930s, women instrumentalists were a notable novelty in jazz-based orchestras. At the same time, while male singers dominated 1920s hot dance music, the situation is reversed from the late 1930s. It seems likely that the advent of the microphone is implicated more than coincidentally, giving women a competitive voice of their own.

Less speculative is the proposition that Barbara James is a case study in the role of female jazz/Swing singers in bringing Australian music into the twentieth century; of opening Australian culture to the vocal innovations that originated in the alliance between technology and African-American music. In so doing she helped to find a voice that could articulate the anxieties, ironies and ambiguities of heterosexual modernity. The evidence suggests that women in general were more responsive than men to these new ways of articulating and projecting these changes in white Australian subjectivity. There was a greater flexibility and receptivity on the part of women popular singers in relation to United States models, with their more developed intensional characteristics of that music including timbral ambiguities, melismatic violations of diatonic intervals. Because of their gendered position in the cultural politics of Australia in the 1930s and 1940s, women were primary channels for the infiltration of an Anglo-centric musical culture by American influences. In all this, the microphone was decisive.

Barbara did not seek to be a 'bodgie yank'. Her work continued to draw on non-American influences, particularly apparent in some of her wartime recordings which do much to evoke the same spirit as Vera Lynn's recordings of that time. She was not simply trying to be an American, but looking for a style of singing that suited her as an Australian woman working in Australia during the first half of the century. But to find that style she was drawn towards contemporary popular music styles; and it was the microphone that delivered those models to her, via recordings, radio and films. It was the microphone that had shaped those models of vocalisation. It was the microphone in her own hands that provided her with the means to experiment in performance and develop a musical language for twentieth-century Australia.

PITCH DIAGRAM

An Analysis of Nine Recordings by Barbara James Indicating a Lowering of her Working Register

Voice Sample	1933/1	1933/2	1933/3	1937/4	1940/5	1940/6	1941/7	1946/8	1950s/9
Top	74	65	67	67	67	67	67	72	67
Bottom	59	55	56	55	53	55	55	56	53

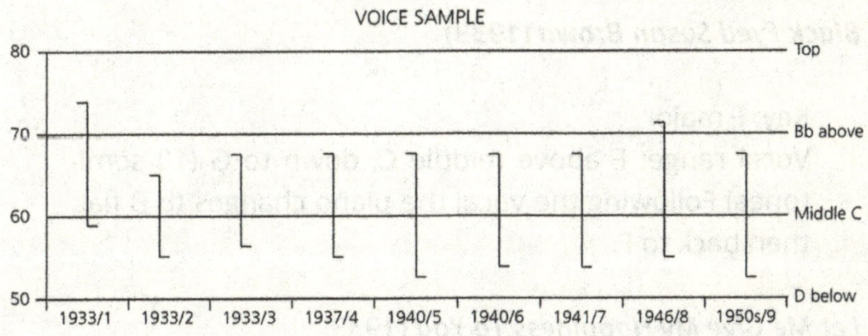

The vertical co-ordinate is based on the MIDI standards for notes, wherein middle C (the C in between treble and bass clefs) is designated 60, and the semitones above are number 61,62, etc in ascending order, with those below as 59, 58 etc in descending order.

On the chart 80 represents G#, a thirteenth above middle C; 70 is Bb above middle C; 60 is middle C; 50 is the D below middle C.

Diagram prepared by John Colborne-Veel.

Barbara James' Recordings

1. *Twentieth Century Blues* (1933)

The key is F major throughout (starting on D7 to embark on a cycle similar to Lazy River, with a bridge)
Vocal range: D, a 9th above middle C down to B (ie, 15 semitones)
This range produces a sometimes stilted effect, with an awkward crossing of the 'break' to head voice and back.

2. *Black Eyed Susan Brown* (1933)

Key: F major
Vocal range: F above middle C, down to G (10 semitones) Following the vocal the piano changes to B flat, then back to F.

3. *Let Me Give My Happiness To You* (1933)

Key: B Flat, changing to E Flat for the vocal
Vocal Range: G above middle C down to A Flat (with a passing low G); ie, 1 1 semitones.
Following the vocal there is a change to C, with Barbara singing a tag that takes her from G below middle C down to low F (ie 14 semitones) finishing on the 5th.

4. *It Don't Mean a Thing* (1937)

Key: G minor, changing to B Flat minor, then back to G minor for the vocal
Vocal range: G above middle C down to G, ie 1 octave.

5. *The Answer is Love* (1940)

She sings in E Flat then F, but occupies the same compass in both, from G above middle C down to F (ie, octave plus 2 semitones).

6. *Good for Nothing but Love* (1940)

Key: E Flat throughout, with the vocal occupying the octave below G above middle C.

7. *I Can't Give You Anything But Love* (1941)

Key: Orchestra starts in F, changes to B Flat for the vocal, with her occupying the same compass as in 6.

8. *I Don't Know Enough About You* (1946)

Key: D Flat. The vocal compass is from C above middle C down to A Flat (ie, octave plus 4 semitones). Most of the work is at the lower end, with the middle C used once as a form of emphasis. She finishes in head voice.

9. *I'm Gonna Live Till I Die* (late fifties).

Key: G minor. Vocal compass between G above middle C, down to F (14 semitones). The bridge is almost wholly on the lowest two-semitone interval. In the conclusion she rises to B flat, and down a minor third to finish on the tonic.

Items 1, 4, 8 and 9 are issued on the CD, *The Inaudible Music* (Larrikin's Yesterday's Australia Series). The others were also reissued on Barbara James: Twentieth Century Blues, Larrikin, LRH 427 1996.

FIFTH BREAK
TRADITION: EUROPE

6 January 1997, Prague

Lubomír Dorůžka, a man of stately dignity, takes Gaye and I on a walk through Prague, past the Jewish cemetery with its schizophrenic clock tower, across the river to the palace. It is cold, below freezing, 'and the snow lay all about'. We stop in a small restaurant and he buys us a coffee and a small tumbler of Becherovka, a bitter sweet local brew with a strong aroma of cloves. I have corresponded with him over several years about the Graeme Bell visit of 1947, and I go over some of the points he has raised. Marxist music historian Dave Harker had been surprised when, at a conference in Liverpool a couple of years earlier I had reported Lubomír's recollection that the Zdhanov cultural doctrines had been promulgated in Czechoslovakia in 1948. I ask him again. He is very definite that this was correct.

Lubomír talks about the pre-Nazi period in Prague. As a child at that time he recalls the era in terms of a domestic metonym. His father would arrive home from work as a civil servant around 1.30 to 2 p.m. and have the rest of the day free with his family. In the committee-bound bureaucracy of the Fascist and Soviet regimes, this remained his image of the freedoms of the First Empire. So, from 1939–45, then 1948–89—around half a century—he lived in totalitarian, highly regimented bureaucracies. In that context, the three years between the end of World War Two and the Communist coup retain a wonderful aura of freedom and possibility. For him, the soundtrack of that old footage is the dixieland which was introduced by the Australian band led by Graeme Bell.

In the restaurant U Prinz I meet and play with the band led by Luboš 'Bob' Zajíček. U Prinz is in the old town on the square, prime territory for a jazz venue, slap bang in the middle of the tourist route. But it is mid-winter and there are few tourists, though one night after I had been announced an Australian couple introduced themselves. The place is still full and the audience, from their 20s to 60s, is unrestrained in its enthusiasm for the music. As everywhere, they send up requests on the back of beer coasters. The usual mix of the well known and the recondite, some inappropriate for a small dixieland band ('String of Pearls'), others a kind of wink of shared knowledge ('Drop Me Off At Harlem'). And of course 'Sweet Georgia Brown'.

Bob is a trumpet player, born in 1937. I am astonished to learn this. He still looks in his late 40s to early 50s. He was ten years old when he first heard Bell. Bob had been playing violin for seven years, but when he heard this 'dixieland'—his first experience of the music—he was instantly a devotee. Before that the closest he had come to what would be called African-American music of the 1920s was local Swing bands, but these made little if any impression on him The Bell band changed his life. To 'us' (he said), this represented 'freedom'. He and his contemporaries began to seek out recordings. He was especially struck by Roger Bell's trumpet playing, and switched immediately to that instrument. His whole working life has been as a traditional jazz musician. He has had no other profession nor played in any other style. This remained so during the entire Communist regime which ended in 1989.

Bob speaks English haltingly, but with great care, often pausing at some length to find the right word. He runs several bands, in which he plays cornet. He solos with great accuracy and agility across wide intervals, a sharp Bix-like definition. But the tone is thicker, with a broad terminal vibrato. It reminded me of Muggsy Spanier, and when the band played 'Dinah' it was the Spanier arrangement of 1939. I hear also the echo of Ruby Braff, which he confirms, and the influence of Wild Bill Davidson. I mention this, he is pleased, and on the next evening he gives me a recording of his band with Wild Bill Davidson, of which he is justly proud. I ask him to autograph it for me, and he writes on it 'To Bruce with ...' and draws a heart, and signs it. It is difficult to carry vinyl on long trips, but when I return to Sydney four months later it has safely accompanied me through the Czech Republic, Finland, Estonia, Denmark.

He played with Graeme Bell during the latter's recent state-funded visit. He never imagined that this would happen, and regards it as one of the great and thrilling moments of his life. The analogy is with an Australian playing with, say Sidney Bechet. We played and drank and talked. He asked me back every night I was in town.

7 January 1997

Last night I went back to U Prinz and played again, but also to ask some more questions that had occurred to me. He apologised for his English, and said that trying to communicate verbally with me the night before had been very tiring. I had not really appreciated that, though realised that I should have, as I imagined myself in the same situation. To be running a band and then occupying your breaks trying to keep a foreign language visitor entertained would not be a very relaxing way of spending an evening that I would have looked forward to as stressless pleasure.

Towards the end of the evening he commented on my more mainstream jazz accent. The conversation naturally turned again to jazz in Australia and from there to the Bell visit. I asked him how he had first heard the band, his first experience of this kind of music. He had listened to the Supraphon records, which his parents had bought. And when he talked about the sense of 'freedom' that they represented, what did he mean? He repeated this point with passionate vehemence, but at first it wasn't clear whether he meant political, musical, psychological, or some permutation. But the rest of the conversation cast light. He talked about his seven years of violin study, and the insuperable difficulty he had in trying to explain his new jazz interests to his academic teachers. He found in jazz a freedom to express himself in an individual but meaningful way.

I had been thinking about the fact that he managed to earn a living as a jazz musician throughout the Communist regime, and asked him how it affected his everyday experience as a musician. Miryk (Miroslav Klimeš), one of the band's two banjo players, was sitting and drinking with us. He spoke more fluent English, but is younger than Bob, so he couldn't speak for the 1940s and 1950s. From his own experience however, he confirmed and refined Bob's account. There was little sense of general support for jazz under the Communists, and a strong feeling that it was not officially approved of—and indeed barely 'tolerated'. It seemed, however, that in spite of the suspicion with which it was regarded, its popularity made it something of a cultural link to the rest of Europe, and as such, it served some kind of purpose to the state. All band touring was booked through a state-run department and when musicians returned from tours they were required to give a proportion (I think he said 30%) of their incomes to the state. Miryk made the point that 'We made a lot of money for the state', so it seems that whatever position was taken officially, the economic imperative by which it brought in western currencies through touring bands, was overriding. The musicians confirmed that, as in the case of the Soviet Union though not so stridently, the state vacillated between two positions: jazz was either valorised as music of an oppressed proletariat, or anathematised as music of the capitalist United States. At worst, during the 1950s, there was an aura of serious disfavour, but contested by economic expediency. At best, in the 1960s, the level of encouragement increased.

This was enough talk. Through the window which looked out on to the square we could see it snowing again, but it was so hot inside with the crowd that we were down to shirtsleeves. We played the final set together and finished at midnight. As I walked back up Wenceslaus Square three hefty women emerged from a side alley and tried a co-ordinated mugging. One approached from the front, trying to distract me by pretending to ask for a cigarette and touching me, while I was aware of the other two who had circled around behind me. I tried to push her away, but she kept touching me and saying 'You have problemo?' Instead of backing away, I put my face within an inch of hers, then yelled 'Polish' at the top of my voice. They vanished. I was surprised, I didn't think I looked like a tourist mark, plodding through the snow with an instrument case. Someone said later that it was because of my leather jacket. The Czechs don't wear them in winter because they don't keep out the cold.

CHAPTER 6
AUSTRALIAN JAZZ ABROAD

> Australia ... [is] ... the most in all countries of the world for jazz
>
> *MY 47, Prague, 1947*

> It is from 'downunder' that the English jazz revival movement received its greatest single stimulus
>
> *Rex Harris, 1952*

We have been looking at ways in which Australian jazz brought Australian music into the realm of modernity through the influences of technology and gender. This has disclosed the importance of expressive sites that encourage the exploration of hitherto marginalised areas of the modern subjectivity. Jazz musicians and participants found opportunities for articulating identity in ways blocked by established traditions, but which became democratically available partly by developments in the mass reproduction of images, and through an encouragement to push at the limits of received expressive forms and practices. Two such areas were dance and singing, largely because of their unmediated physicality. The emancipative forces of the early twentieth century also operated through jazz recordings and instrumental jazz performance. Nonetheless, instruments, radios, record players still cost money, while dancing and singing bypass even these obstacles. Anyone with a voice may sing. Anyone with a body may dance. We are conditioned to accept constraint as a fact of an expressive regime that requires training, status, money. One requires the privileges associated with class, ethnicity and gender; there are rules relating to aesthetic decorum. The more bureaucratised our society, the more tightly woven are these constraints. There are limits to how far liberating possibilities can be explored within the formal controls of dominant art music traditions, or later, the market-dominated media monopolies of popular musics also. As we move farther outside these zones of control into the unregulated musical badlands, possibilities open up. Yet even here, a musical instrument evolved under hegemonic scrutiny will limit the exploration of subjectivity in the 'now'. Trumpets, pianos, clarinets, are still tempered, resistant to radical violations of approved order, and instruments such as the trombone and violin which are, so to speak 'unfretted', must still normally operate within that regime. Voice and dance are potentially the most unconstrained forms of musical expressiveness. And the suggestion is reinforced in the next stage of the discussion, to which dance is central. Other patterns recur as we consider the contribution made by jazz to the projection of Australia into the international consciousness of twentieth-century music. This discloses a level of influence in other parts of the world, which is equalled by probably no other expressive form, and certainly by no other form of music.

Since the mid-1970s, increased institutional support has expedited overseas tours for Australian musicians. Dale Barlow's work with, *inter alia,* Cedar Walton and Art Blakey; James Morrison's frequent international collaborations; Bob Barnard's recent sojourns in New York and his United States movie work (he shared trumpet responsibilities with Warren Vaché on the soundtrack for *The Gig*); the overseas successes of such groups as Clarion Fracture Zone, Wanderlust, the catholics, Ten Part Invention and its rhythm section the Engine Room; the Wizards of Oz; the New Wolverines; the Golden City Jazz Band and the Graeme Bell All Stars. These are just examples of many encounters that have recently confirmed internationally the authority of Australian jazz musicians.

Major Australian honours or awards appear to be granted to jazz musicians with more alacrity once their merit has been confirmed overseas. Don Burrows began touring abroad in the 1950s. By the time he received his MBE in 1976 and, more recently, the AO and in 1994 an Australian Artist's Creative Fellowship, he had established himself as one of the world's two best-known Australian jazz musicians. The other is Graeme Bell, whose 1978 MBE came thirty years after the international acclaim that greeted the first of his overseas tours. Sandy Evans had established herself on the international jazz circuit before receiving her Creative Fellowship in 1995. Although the subject of a devoted cult following, Bernie McGann worked in obscurity from the 1950s. As a consequence of touring opportunities opening up in the 1990s, he has been hailed internationally as one of the worlds major jazz voices on the alto.[264] This has been followed by the recent presentation of Australia's Don Banks Award.

Other Australian musicians have worked overseas for extended periods, and established themselves at the highest professional levels in Europe, Asia and the United States. As I write, the list includes trombonists Campbell Burnap and Max Collie; bassists Barry Dillon, Lyn Christie, Nicki Parrot; drummers Colin Bailey, Tony Buck; guitarists Peter O'Mara, Steve Brien, Steve McKenna, Carl Orr; reed players Lisa Parrot, Andrew Speight, Barry Wrattan; trombonist Adrian Mears; singer Chris McNulty. Judith Durham achieved fame with the Seekers, but remained overseas working in her original role as a jazz singer before returning to Australia. In the traditional sphere, drummer Viv Carter worked with Acker Bilk, Ken Colyer and Dick Charlesworth in the 1950s; he is currently active as a performer in Sydney. Trombonist/pianist Ian Pearce spent the early 1950s in Britain where he joined Mick Mulligan.[265] He is still active in Hobart. Mike Sutcliffe has recently documented the work of Melbourne-born trombonist Orme (aka Orm) Stewart in the UK in the 1950s, playing with Roy Fox, touring and recording with Joe Daniels and Freddy Randall, with whom he toured the United States in an exchange arrangement with Louis Armstrong's group. Stewart currently works in Melbourne in brass band, big band and light classical settings. From the late 1960s into the 1970s reed player Graham Spedding worked with leading traditional groups in the United Kingdom, and his earlier career included touring in China and the Soviet Union, discussed in more detail below. At the contemporary experimental end of the spectrum: following success in Sydney in the early 1960s, New Zealand-born Mike Nock settled in the United States where he led the seminal fusion group the Fourth Way as well as working with major figures like Coleman Hawkins and John Handy. In 1985 he returned to Sydney, where he teaches and performs. New Zealand-born pianist Julian Lee went to the United States from Sydney at the invitation of George Shearing to work as his arranger, and worked in the same capacity for Gerry Mulligan, Chet Baker, Frank Sinatra, Peggy Lee—some of this in his role as producer for Capitol Records.

There is also a large category of Australians who spend lengthy periods overseas in other professional capacities, but whose commitment to playing brings them into close touch with local jazz communities. In the course of his career in the diplomatic service, reed player Greg Gibson became prominent as a performer in Kuala Lumpur, Bangkok, Brussels and London. Subsequent to his training at the Royal Military College, Duntroon, fellow reed player Lachie Thomson was posted to Bangkok. There he became a mainstay of the local jazz movement, forming the Bangkok Jazz Club in 1962, and playing with the (saxophonist) King of Thailand's Orchestra. Cornettist Tony Newstead's career in communications technology and with the World Bank brought him into contact with an international jazz community, producing nearly fifty tracks recorded in the United States with luminaries like Willie 'The Lion' Smith, Wild Bill Davidson, Art Hodes, Danny Barker, Max Kaminsky.[266] Because such 'day gig' musicians don't focus solely on their music performance activities, this is a difficult category to map. On the basis of my research and contacts (and as an active member of this category myself), it seems that virtually all such jazz musicians who travel extensively, and maintain their chops, find themselves working overseas at a professional level.

Australian jazz musicians have also impressed the international community with the versatility that arises from the difficulty of making a living solely out of jazz in Australia. Ron Loughhead became staff arranger for Decca Records and for the BBC during seven years in London from 1955. While based in the United Kingdom with Max Merritt and the Meteors, saxophonist Bob Bertles also worked with Cliff Richard and Cilla Black, as well as with Ian Carr's contemporary jazz group Nucleus. Bassist Bruce Cale played in the United States with a range of jazz legends including Zoot Sims, Bobby Hackett, John Handy, but also composed for the Los Angeles Philharmonic Orchestra. Bassist John Ryan recorded with Cat Stevens, Mike Nock with Dionne Warwick; drummer Barry Woods played session work for Tom Jones and Engelbert Humperdinck.

The distinguished history of Australian jazz musicians abroad would have to include a full account of the Australian Jazz Quartet/Quintet (AJQ) which worked in the United States through the mid-1950s. They out-billed musicians like Miles Davis and Art Blakey, winning local polls, breaking ground in the cool style, with reed player Errol Buddle pioneering the use of double reed instruments in jazz settings. Buddle and recruit American bassist Ed Gaston returned to Australia, but two other members have settled in the United States. Vibist/drummer Jack Brokensha runs a highly successful business in the competitive area of music production. Pianist Bryce Rohde spent a few years back in Australia where he initiated some of the most decisive projects in jazz experimentalism, before returning to the United States, where he established himself as a musician in California.[267]

One of the least-known tours by Australian bands abroad, though in many ways most ground-breaking, was that of the

Southern Cross Jazz Band in 1957. In February of that year banjoist Mick Fowler (later prominent in Sydney's Victoria Road development Green Bans), and trumpeter Terry McCardell were approached by the Eureka Youth League to assemble a band for the sixth World Youth Festival to be held that year in Moscow. Recruiting trombonist Ken Longman, reed player Graham Spedding and pianist/accordionist Alan Lynch, they called the group the Southern Cross Jazz Band and departed on 24 June for what was to be a spectacularly successful three-month tour. It appears that this scored a number of 'firsts': the first formal appearance of Australian musicians in the Communist bloc, in the Soviet Union, and in the People's Republic of China. In the Cold War climate of 1957, this is most worthy of remark. Yet on their return to Australia, little general notice seems to have been accorded this tour, and today it is scarcely known even in the jazz community. Alan Lynch died in 1971 and Mick Fowler in 1979. Both Ken Longman and Graham Spedding are in musical semi-retirement.[268]

Australian jazz musicians were establishing international credentials from the beginning. Ross's Jazz Band was formed in Melbourne in 1924 and went on to tour England and the United States as the Three Australian Boys. They made fourteen tracks for English Parlophone and also played the prestigious Palace Theatre in New York before returning to Australia by 1933.[269] By later definitions the match between the 'jazz' name and actual performance practices was probably uneven, but their inspiration appears to have included America's 'King of Jazz' Paul Whiteman, who had recorded 'From Monday On' on 28 February 1928, some eight months before their version.

In the 1920s the Whiteman band employed some of the most influential white jazz pioneer musicians and arrangers, and was generally regarded by white America and internationally as the pinnacle of jazz. When Australian trombonist Clarrie Collins was chosen by Whiteman from among several hundred applicants to replace Boyce Cullen during the filming of the high budget 1930 colour movie, *King of Jazz*, it was the highest of jazz accolades. It headlined the account of his overseas experience in *Australian Music Maker and Dance Band News* when he returned to Australia.[270] He did not appear in the film but performed on the soundtrack. His subsequent career showed no decline from that exalted position. In the 1930s he worked in England with Jack Hylton and Ambrose, leading the band at the Lido in Paris, and played equivalent stints in Hamburg, Budapest, touring Germany with a Berlin-based show band. In 1933 he briefly led the band in Switzerland for a Boswell Sisters tour, and was back in the United States in 1934, where he worked with Leopold Stokowski for the soundtrack of *The Big Broadcast of 1935*, and with Fred Waring. During the war, by now working under the name Larry Collins, he played tours, concerts and broadcasts in the United States, including a billing with Duke Ellington and Louis Armstrong. He also taught trombone: it was reported in Australia's *Music Maker* (21 October 1946) that he had given lessons to the brass players in the bands of Duke Ellington and Count Basie. Collins remained active internationally throughout a career that continued into the 1970s.[271]

For Australians, Frank Coughlan became the musician who most comprehensively represented Swing, from the moment he led his band for the opening of Sydney's Trocadero in 1936, to its closure at the end of the 1960s when Coughlan again was the bandleader. Like Clarrie Collins', Coughlan's early career found him working in the top ranks of overseas hot dance bands including those of Jack Hylton, Fred Elizalde (with Adrian Rollini) and Al Starita. Like Coughlan, New Zealand-born Abe Romain is now best remembered as a successful bandleader at the Sydney Trocadero. Like Coughlan, however, he had already achieved the highest level of professional success overseas. Between 1930 and 1940, Romain spent two extended periods in England and Europe, working with a number of bands including as first saxophone with Jack Hylton. He toured the United Kingdom and the Continent for eighteen months, and recorded several hundred titles with the band. Back in England in 1936 he worked with Harry Roy, recorded and toured extensively, this time as far as South America.[272]

Both Hylton and Harry Roy must have come to expect the best from expatriate Australians. Perth-born trombonist/pianist Abe Walters also tried his chances in England in the late 1930s and joined Harry Roy's No. 2 band at Southend before going on to work with Freddy Gardiner and Lew Stone. He also became closely involved in the after-hours 'bottle party' activity at clubs where visiting American jazz musicians played engagements, in the course of which he worked with Benny Carter and Coleman Hawkin. In 1941 he played with Carroll Gibbons, Sid Phillips and Ambrose, before being invited by Ciro's nightclub to form and lead his own band, the beginning of a long period as a prominent London bandleader until he retired in 1963.[273] Similarly, bandleader Cec Morrison was feted when he travelled extensively overseas in the early 1930s. In the United States he met counterparts in the industry and presented a radio broadcast of what was called 'Kangaroo Jazz', which evidently consisted of his own symphonic arrangements of what was perceived as jazz. Among the flood of letters in response, a professional musician in Chicago described his intense dislike of jazz until converted by Morrison's work: 'I hope Mr. Morrison will remain here long enough to educate our own jazz leaders into what jazz might be'.[274]

The list could continue. Benny Featherstone reputedly met Duke Ellington and Louis Armstrong in England in 1933, played as a multi-instrumentalist at London's Silver Slipper, and in 1945 sat in with Jimmie Lunceford in the United States. Barbara James and her husband Reg Lewis took their Swing-based experience overseas in 1949 and opened with Harry Roy at the Café Anglais in December. They also enjoyed success on BBC radio (where another expatriate Australian Swing musician, Jim Davidson, had been appointed assistant head of Variety in 1948), and later on television. By the time they had returned to Australia they had established themselves beyond England through tours that covered Europe, the Middle East and Asia.[275] Clearly, some of the foregoing are only marginally associated with jazz, though they all developed their careers in popular music during an era in which African-American innovations increasingly had to be incorporated into the competencies of the professional popular musician. And some of those mentioned were also dedicated jazz proselytisers and performers, from Coughlan to the Southern Cross Jazz Band.[276]

The Graeme Bell Tour, 1947–8

The Southern Cross' tour through China and the Soviet Union was not the first the Eureka Youth League had initiated.[277] Among those prominent as League organisers in the 1940s was an amateur drummer and jazz enthusiast Harry Stein. In 1947 a major event in the youth project of the international Communist movement was the staging of the World Youth Festival in Prague. Stein was invited to send a delegation from Australia. He approached Graeme Bell and offered to organise fundraising events to support the tour. Bell accepted with enthusiasm and the band members gradually wound down their own affairs, leaving jobs, selling businesses and possessions to help pay for the venture. They and their spouses (one of whom was pregnant) embarked on a journey to a destination which was virtually unimaginable to an Anglo-Saxon Australian at that time. They undertook all this in the chaotic conditions prevailing in that immediate post-war period, and with virtually none of the support systems now available to travellers. When they departed from Melbourne by ship on 17 July 1947, their joint funds had raised only enough for one-way tickets.

They arrived in Prague on 24 August. There were some fifty nationalities represented at the Festival, but by all local accounts the Bell band dominated the event. Their performances included open-air concerts to audiences of over 5,000; their recorded music was piped through loudspeakers in Wenceslaus Square. That concert was filmed by a United Nations film crew.[278] The two weeks they had planned to stay in Czechoslovakia turned into four months of residency work, recording, lecturing, and a 44-town tour.[279]

The band departed for England on 9 December 1947, playing a concert in Paris en route. They arrived in London on 15 December and based themselves in England for the next eight months, with forays into Holland and Belgium. In France they played at an international jazz festival where their performance elicited a review in *Melody Maker* which included the following summary:

> The band has a firm, relaxed style that is more rhythmic than most of the current jazz groups. Individually the men are much better than most, and as a group they have done a much better job than any seven or eight musicians playing in the same idiom. That includes Spanier, Lu Walters [sic], Condon, Hodes, Parenti, and Wilber.[280]

In the same issue, English saxophonist and critic Derek Neville wrote, 'Theirs is the best dixieland music I have heard, and I think they can show Claude Luter's band the way home'.

In the United Kingdom, however, the band encountered initial hardship. The unfamiliarity of the environment—its weather, its manners and infrastructures—was exacerbated by the failure of agents' undertakings to materialise. In time, however, the band's resilience and the creative opportunism of manager Mel Langdon secured a toehold on the English jazz scene. A 'sight unseen' booking at the Birmingham Town Hall at which a crowd of some 2,300 shouted for encores, led to pub gigs and concerts. They opened their own jazz club in London, toured extensively, played BBC broadcasts and around two dozen recording sessions, both as a unit and in the company of local musicians, most notably Humphrey Lyttelton. At an average of two per month these yielded over 100 tracks.[281] Graeme's meticulous journal lists over 100 gigs during their stay—an average of one every two days, in a period that included a very slow start and several intervals of rest and recreation. They embarked on the Orion in August 1948, a year after leaving home.

In assessing the band's impact it is important to bear in mind that Czechoslovakia in 1947 was still devastated physically and economically by the effects of the war.

> One of the places we played in this former German territory was Chomutov. It had a tramway system and a population of about 100,000. Any former beauty had been destroyed by British bombs. The streets were dirty and littered with rubble, over which evil-looking weeds had sprawled. Starved for entertainment, the audience here was one of the most uninhibited on the tour. (Bell 1988. p.92)

The association drawn with 'evil' through the relatively innocuous image of plants spontaneously springing up through the streets draws on a significant tradition in Australia of constructing modern Europe as a site of cultural disease.[282] This in turn helps to account for the Bell band's energy and confidence in the European environment, and the position they secured in Czech memory. With the Communists taking power only weeks after the band departed, their visit coincided with a brief interval of freedom between two totalitarian regimes. Prior to the arrival of the Australians, jazz in Czechoslovakia was primarily an idea, with particular appeal to youth.[283] Wartime Swing orchestras were scarcely regarded as jazz, so that in terms of local perceptions little live jazz had been heard in Czechoslovakia before the arrival of the Bell band. Likewise, there appear to have been few American recordings of the music available, and radio exposure had been primarily via proscribed transmissions.[284] These circumstances had invested the music with an aura of subversive anti-totalitarianism, implicated in complex ways with the idea of local sovereignty. After the defeat of the Germans 'jazz became something of a synonym for freedom'.[285]

The Bell band performances thus acquired resonances the members could never have anticipated. Emmanuel Uggé, president of a local record club, Gramoclub, became an energetic advocate for the band:

> The musicians who are the part of the Australian delegation had to travel 25,000 km so that Prague could finally listen—for the first time in her history—to jazz. Pure, uncorrupted by commercialism and fashion. Jazz created from spontaneity, improvised music of people as played by its creators in New Orleans.*[286]

All accounts speak of the band's musical conviction and the enormous excitement generated by its performances. The following are representative:

> The performance of all members of the band is characterised by its perfection ... we can see here the mutual spiritual background and the commonly inspired act of creation the analogy of which could not be found probably anywhere, America, the country of jazz not excluded.*[287]

> ... probably the best combination of its type in Europe at the present time.*[288]

> Australia ... [is] ... the most in all countries of the world for jazz.*[289]

> For the first time we heard really pure jazz.*[290]

> ... the best band playing improvised jazz today.*[291]

The Bell band virtually started the jazz movement as such in Czechoslovakia, providing a working model for a music already deeply inscribed with socio-political meanings.[292] Bands and clubs were formed in the immediate wake of their visit, and jazz secured space in local broadcasting; a session recorded by Bell for Prague Radio was broadcast four times within a matter of weeks. The decision of Supraphon to record the band for commercial release opened up similar opportunities for subsequent groups.

In addition the band had a significant influence on the overt politics of Czechoslovakia during the Communist regime which began shortly after they departed. Lubomír Dorůžka used the image of the Trojan horse when discussing the jazz component of the International Youth Festival.

> But the results of the festivals often backfired. If Moscow tried to pose as a friend and host to young people, it also had to make certain allowances in its cultural policy, and by letting in some kinds of popular young culture it sometimes brought a dangerous Trojan horse inside its walls. Ten years later, 1957, the same festival was held in Moscow. The young modern jazz ensembles—especially the one led by Michel Legrand—started a new wave in modern jazz trends in USSR which later caused quite a headache to party officials—exactly the same as Graeme Bell did in Prague. In 1947. the Zhdanov ideological doctrines were not yet publicly announced and Trad Jazz might not have been so condemnable from their point of view. But nevertheless, the Graeme Bell visit influenced further development in Czechoslovakia not only musically but also ideologically.[293]

The evidence suggests that the spectacular success of the Bell band produced a faltering of centralised cultural control which in turn initiated a sequence of tactical adjustments of policy. In the words of Petr Sedlak, all the propaganda of commoes became counter-productive'.[294] Škvorecký elaborates on the dilemma. Although Stalinism condemned the music, the proliferation of traditional jazz in the wake of the Bell tour made it difficult to proscribe:

> ... it was really the only form of jazz suffered at the depressing congregations called youth entertainments, where urban girls in pseudo-national costumes got up and sang bombastic odes to Stalin in the style of rural yodelling. (Škvorecký 1980 p.17)

And because of the fact that it was young people particularly in whom and by whom the meanings of jazz were generated, the effects continued to be felt for decades, especially as this imprinted generation emerged into positions of cultural influence. Jiří Šlitr, for example, became a pianist in a band whose formation was inspired by Bell's tour, and this momentum helped carry him to an influential position in Czech culture. As a composer, he incorporated traditional jazz elements into early rock, and several generations of young people grew up to the sound of his music. With Jiří Suchý he founded Prague's Semafor Theatre which marked the beginning of the New Wave in performing arts and was a significant force in the developments which led to the 'Prague Spring' of 1968. Currently, he and Suchý are regarded as

> ... indisputable seminal figures, recognised by every critic and historian, and living in the hearts of all those who listened to and hummed their songs. One—and certainly not the least important—of its roots had also something to do with Graeme Bell's visit. High trees cast long shadows. In this case the shadows were very agreeable and fruitful.[295]

Long shadows indeed: in the 1970s, digitally remastered recordings of the Bell bands Supraphon recordings sold out as soon as they appeared. When Bell returned to Prague as the guest of the government in 1993, he was rapturously received by audiences, including by young jazz followers, as the father of the Czech jazz movement. He was remembered also as embodying a brief interval of buoyancy and optimism between two long episodes of repression in the history of twentieth-century Czechoslovakia. Otaker Novotny, who now lives in Tasmania, recorded his recollections of the visit in a letter to me:

> They engendered so much exuberance and good will and gave out such a spirit of joyous optimism to all present that you felt that finally after all the ugliness and deprivation experienced, in my country, that there was hope for the future and something to work towards. Little did we realise that shortly, the Swastika would only be replaced with the dreaded 'Hammer and Sickle'. (6 November 1994)

All these impressions are confirmed by press reports, by the documentary film of the Bell's 1993 visit which was made by a Prague TV production company, and by every Czech with whom I have communicated.[296]

The Bell band was the first jazz band to visit the United Kingdom for about two decades. The musicians' union had embargoed American bands but, as British subjects, the Australians were provided with work permits.[297] This embargo was almost certainly one of the reasons that English jazz culture was centred on recordings, even more so than in Australia. In Britain a jazz club meeting was a relatively cerebral affair, usually incorporating a record recital, some discussion, a lecture and some live music.[298] Among performers, George Webb is regarded as the pioneer of the British traditional jazz movement. He formed his Dixielanders in 1944 (some years after

Graeme Bell had formed his first bands in Australia). Webb was a moving force in the establishment of the Hot Club of London in 1946, but both the Club and the Dixielanders were dissolved at a final meeting on 31 January 1948, at which the newly arrived Bell band also performed. Ralph Venables, reporting the night in the U.S. journal *Down Beat* on 25 February 1948, described the night's music as tired and ragged until 'sparked' by the Australians, whom he described as 'unquestionably the greatest jazz band outside America'.

Two days after the closure of the Hot Club of London, the Bell band opened its own venue, the Leicester Square Jazz Club, which became the base from which they established an influence that led English jazz historian Rex Harris to declare:

> It is from 'downunder' that the English jazz revival movement received its greatest single stimulus—in the shape of GRAEME BELL (*born 1914*) and his 'Australian Jazz Band'[299]

This was to have a powerful bearing on the way in which popular music in England was produced and consumed, and by whom, for some decades after the war. It discloses continuities in youth music scarcely noticed by writers focussed on rock'n'roll, which did not appear until the mid-1950s. Peter Lewis sees the pre-rock era in England as totally bereft of any music for the exuberant and improvisational dancing of young people. Dick Bradley's surprise as he peers back to the pre-rock history of Britain and finds only a Dark Age of youth dance music, is another representative example of this point.[300] Although he acknowledges the earlier British jazz scene, there is a tacit inclination to equate popular and youth music exclusively with rock, so that, inevitably, he finds ruptures where there are also continuities.

Bell's performances extended the social functions of jazz by enlarging it as a musical and recreational space, giving greater room for audiences to express themselves. To some extent this was achieved through changes in the musical form and format. He extended instrumental combinations beyond the sanctions of the British traditional jazz canon to that time. His colleague Ade Monsbourgh was central to this; his multi-instrumental authority made it possible to double up any of the horns, producing unexpected textural combinations. More important was his very personalised use of the alto saxophone, horrifying the purists, but introducing a new voice into English traditional jazz.[301]

Unlike local bands, the visitors replenished their repertoire with their own compositions. The Bell brothers and Monsbourgh were prolific jazz composers, and their material formed a very substantial part of the band library, to the extent that some of it has passed into the English repertoire and is still performed.[302] Their repertoire was broader than English practice, going beyond jazz standards to include Noel Coward compositions and English music hall songs. Also notable was the character of the band's ensemble work. All reviewers, including those on the Continent, were struck by the cogency of its collective improvisation and its complete lack of any form of 'score'. Apart from print notation, which was equally absent from equivalent English practice, the Bell band was also uninterested in the studied reproduction of the canonical recordings. Any specific performance was thus more immediately a response to that moment and its collective meaning.

Above all, that moment incorporated the active participation of the audiences. Local press announcements for English jazz events of the period spoke of 'meetings'. In recognising the importance of reuniting jazz with dance, Graeme Bell changed the social function and meaning of traditional jazz. He abolished ritualised record recitals, lectures and discographical discussions from club functions. In a letter dated 20 January 1948, barely a month after arriving, he wrote to a friend in Holland:

> There are some good jazz musicians in England but they have made the great mistake of divorcing jazz from dancing so therefore do not reach a very wide audience. This concert hall stuff will kill jazz unless they bring it to the dancing patrons as well.

Bell provocatively announced his jazz functions as 'dances', deliberately invoking completely different forms of social conduct. It was his 'jazz for dancing' policy which above all encapsulates his impact on popular music in Britain. It is worth quoting his own account of this project:

> The jazz clubs of Britain (mostly called rhythm clubs in those days) would meet in an upstairs or back room of a boozer. Record recitals would be given, devoted to various jazz greats, and papers would be delivered delving into the origins and development of the different styles of playing. Chewing seriously on their pipes and sipping their beers with thoughtful expressions, the members would nod quietly to the beat of their 'pure' jazz. Questions of any interesting key changes or incorrect harmonies or matters of intonation and chord structures or stability of tempo were rarely discussed, but matrix numbers, the label and date and place of recording were of paramount importance.
>
> We found this approach so stuffy. It contradicted the very reasons that attracted us to jazz in the first place; the breaking free of the restrictions, rigidity and seriousness of European music ... The whole function of this 'classic' jazz was being ignored, and the celebratory joining together of listener and musician was missing. Audience response in the form of handclapping is the fuel from which the musician receives his lift ...

> So we decided to open up our own club with the slogan 'jazz for dancing'... With posters and flyers proclaiming 'Jazz for Dancing' and 'You *Can* Dance to Jazz' we opened on Monday, 2 February 1948, on a regular, once-a-week basis. After paying their admission at the door, the people started coming in ... the women in particular had come to jive and jitterbug. (Bell 1988, p.105)

The final observation reactivates the issues raised in an earlier chapter regarding jazz, dance and emancipative gendered practices, now also resonating into generation and class. Although the jazz establishment was outraged, Bell's policy was enormously successful in attracting a new audience by providing a public space for high energy recreational dancing of a kind that seems hitherto non-existent in post-war Britain. The novelty produced a particularly interesting result, as Humphrey Lyttelton has described:

> It seems difficult now to imagine the stir which this revolutionary and sacrilegious notion caused in purist circles. 'Dancing to jazz?' they cried. 'Whatever next! How can anyone possibly *listen* to jazz or appreciate it when they are leaping about on the dance floor?' And I must say that it did not take a jazz purist to be alarmed by the first exhibitions of jazz dancing which took place at the Leicester Square Dance Club above the Café de L'Europe. The premises were hired from the N.S.P.C.C. for every Monday night, and the younger generation of jazz fans turned up there to let off steam. Many of them were students from the Art Schools and from the various branches of London University, and they had unlimited reserves of steam. Young people came too from shops and offices, seizing the opportunity to assert themselves by dressing

> up in bright, highly original fashions and letting their hair down (sometimes literally) ... At this time there was no established pattern for jazz dancing. The sort of jiving which was done in the ballrooms smacked too much of Swing music and 'jitterbugging' to be countenanced at all ... and of course no one knew anything about the dances which were originally danced in New Orleans at the beginning of the century. So the dancers at the Leicester Square Jazz Club just invented steps of their own. Led by the art school contingent—the least inhibited of those present—they flung themselves on to the floor and just did the first thing that came into their heads.[303]

The social demand for this recreational outlet was reflected in the Club's popularity. The band's Australian experience of playing every kind of venue and dance, and a flair for showmanship, implicated rather than excluded audiences. Band manager Mel Langdon's astute exploitation of existing publicity networks also drew jazz closer to popular discourse than was felt to be altogether proper by local purists, who also doubtless felt anxious about the general level of energetic fun which the Bell band introduced into their music-making. A regular club newsletter, called *Puffo*, took a distinctly irreverent approach to the discographical solemnity of the more conventional British jazz clubs. Within a few weeks the LSJC numbered over a thousand members, and found it necessary to open on other nights of the week. Band manager Langdon secured a booking at the Hammersmith Odeon, the first jazz concert there since the Original Dixieland Jazz Band in 1919. This booking spread their influence even more widely.

The swaggering energy which helped to make the Australian band so popular, was also enhanced by two fortuitous circumstances: the sporting victories of the visiting Australian cricketers under the leadership of Donald Bradman; and the doubles victory at Wimbledon by the Australians Frank Sedgman and John Bromwich. Both of these events coincided with the Bell band's tour. The connection was publicly noted. Newspapers in Brighton declared an 'Australian invasion' when all the tours converged on the town. Bell watched Sedgman's victory, and when the latter attended a Bell concert the same night, Roger improvised blues lyrics in the tennis player's honour. The public intersection of the visiting contingents magnified their overall visibility. It also reinforced the sense of a freewheeling energy that contributed to the local construction of contemporary Australian identity, and helped to rework the image of the music they played.

The Bell success also materially benefitted English jazz musicians. The final Hot Club concert at which the Bell band made its London debut was described by Jim Godbolt (1984, p.213) as 'the start of a new era in British jazz'. The wider profile the Australians established for their music began to make it possible to earn a living as a jazz player (Godbolt 1984, p.214). In particular, Humphrey Lyttelton, later to become one of the elder statesmen of British jazz, received his 'first lucky break' when his band deputised for the Australians at the LSJC during one of the latter's tours.[304] Lyttelton became the most influential force in the next phase of English traditional jazz, and there is evidence that his expansion of the traditional format was inspired by his earlier collaborations with Bell.[305] More generally, it is possible to trace a continuity from the transformation of the social function of jazz and the consequent enlargement of its audiences, through to the 'trad boom' of the early 1960s. Even today the influence of the band is audible in current repertoire, certain stylistic and instrumentation conventions, and in English record collections.

The Bell band returned to Australia with their reputation enhanced; so much so that they were immediately offered a national tour by the ABC. On a second visit to Britain, lasting from 1950 to 1952, they were feted, treated like (and indeed played for) royalty. This was the most immediate legacy of their earlier groundbreaking work. But it was the earlier tour that was most influential on the subsequent course of popular music; an influence that manifested itself musically, socially and politically.

The Australian Style: 'A Puzzling Reputation'

Max Harris was one of the few commentators to have recognised the significance of these events. Calling for a more serious documentation of the history of traditional jazz in Australia, he asked:

> ... how many people recall that perhaps the first effective impact of Australia on the overseas cultural scene occurred long before the expatriate trek of Nolan, Boyd, Perceval and Pucker The tour of the Bell group to Poland [sic], Czechoslovakia and Britain in the 1940s caused an excitement and stimulation of the jazz idiom in Europe that no national group outside the Americans had effected before. In one area of the performing arts Australia acquired a mystic and puzzling overseas reputation.[306]

There are two 'puzzles': why was Australian jazz able to establish such authority? Why is this almost totally unremarked in Australia? I shall conclude this chapter by considering the first of these, which in turn will throw light on the second. How could an Australian expressive form so low in local cultural capital, exercise such unparalleled influence elsewhere?

Harris' reference to the self-exiled Australian painters suggests the beginning of an answer. Albert Tuckers reported explanation of his departure was that he was a 'refugee from Australian culture'.[307] Apocryphal or not, this reflects a pervasive attitude of 'serious' Australian artists in all media who have made the European or another overseas pilgrimage: Australia was a philistine wasteland. True or not, this is a subservient and pliant state of mind in which to approach one's destination. One goes to Paris, London or more recently New York in order to learn what cannot be learned in Australia. The musicians in the Bell band did not travel in order to subsume themselves to the models they found in Europe and the United Kingdom. In jazz terms these were virtually non-existent in the Australian imagination. Nor was the occasion of their departure in the nature of an escape from intolerably unsympathetic conditions. It was a response to an invitation.

There are other reasons, however, arising from the Australian jazz scene at that time. The band members were well-developed individual musicians, in a mature, cohesive band that had been working in a robust jazz movement that was not Eurocentric. Reviews and other responses constantly refer to the members as fully and even aggressively articulated personalities both on and off the stand, with Monsbourgh, the Bell brothers and 'Pixie' Roberts presenting particularly forceful profiles. The general impression of Antipodean cockiness' recorded by Jim Godbolt, English agent and jazz chronicler, is representative (and rather more measured than some reports).[308]

The Bell band had also been developing as a unit for a considerable time before it undertook the journey to Prague. The cohesiveness of an experienced improvisational performance group is unlike that of any other performance, either collective or individual. It knows that its dynamic is unique to the group, and this in turn generates extraordinary confidence in performance. This band was also very much its own creature. The international jazz revival is often dated from the foundation of the Yerba Buena Jazz Band formed by Lu Watters in San Francisco, which became a major inspiration in other countries with its first recordings in 1941.[309] It has sometimes been dismissively asserted that the Bell band was an imitation or 'extension of the bands put together by Watters or the even later work of his alumni such as Turk Murphy.[310] The Bell members, however, had been forming their tastes and playing for up to nearly a decade before the Watters recordings became available, and had been 'workshopping' their way into existence as a band for some time. Their sources, repertoire, instrumentation and musical ideas were in very significant ways distinct from, and less doctrinaire, than the Watters ventures.[311]

The band that went to Europe was also embedded firmly within a local culture. The annual Australian Jazz Convention, founded in 1946, disclosed a national traditional jazz movement. Throughout the 1940s its centre was Melbourne, where there were dedicated jazz venues, functions and residencies, sustained by a number of bands apart from those led by Bell.[312] Of special importance was the journal *Jazz Notes*, founded by the Melbourne solicitor and jazz spokesman Bill Miller, which provided a forum for the energetic discussion of jazz and the local scene.[313] The Bell band was not an imitation of something heard on recordings, but a collection of individuals engaging through their music with a very specific place and time. One significant manifestation of this was the large number of original compositions in the band repertoire, a characteristic which was absent from the British scene, and which virtually disappeared from traditional jazz in Australia during the later New Orleans purism. Melbourne was also distinctive in the links it created between its jazz scene and the broader community of radical arts and politics. In the words of Max Harris (1973, p.15), the jazz musicians were integral to that whole homogeneous movement over the full spectrum of the arts that mysteriously convulsed the ultra-conservative Melbourne of the 1940s'. His radical literary journal, *Angry Penguins*, supplemented *Jazz Notes* as an occasional forum for jazz debate.[314]

The intense communality that informed the jazz culture produced a music that came to be seen as regionally distinctive. To a level apparent nowhere else outside the United States, the original compositions emerging from Australian traditional jazz in the post-war decade explicitly projected an interest in the evocation of local landscape, flora, fauna, history, and particular personalities.[315] Simply giving a song a title like 'Mulga Rag', of course, produces no more than a nominal linkage with a sense of place. But in conjunction with other characteristics of the evolving style of traditional jazz, however, a distinctive style was able to develop. Clunies-Ross' 1979 article remains the most focussed study of this phenomenon. He notes that the so-called revivalist movements in England and the United States were conservative in seeking to preserve an earlier moment in the history of jazz. In Australia, uniquely, traditional jazz underwent a process of further development, through which it achieved a characteristic Australian style'.[316] This view is shared by the Australia Music Centre: its monograph on Dave Dallwitz links him with other Australian traditionalists of the 1940s in the development of a 'unique idiom' in Australian jazz.[317] From Max Harris, a public intellectual who was central to some of the most crucial episodes in Australian culture and modernity, comes the same conviction. Jazz was our 'national' art form with, he was inclined to believe, a sound of its own. 'I don't think any other country in Europe would lay claim to a sustained jazz tradition as Australia can do'.[318]

Given some resistance to these ideas among Australians themselves, it is important to note how far the arguments advanced by Clunies-Ross correspond with overseas opinions.[319] Clunies-Ross (1983, p.7) cites an American critic who wrote in *Down Beat* (12 July 1979) that 'the trad revival in Australia, near-stagnant throughout the rest of the world throughout the last quarter century, has developed valuable insights into the jazz of an earlier day'; he identifies Roger Bell, Ade Monsbourgh, Dave Dallwitz, and singer Penny Eames (of a much later generation) as original artists of international stature; they and a few others simply have no equivalents on the imitative, joyless American and European trad scene'. In a recent reference work with a global scope, the authors refer to the almost disturbingly original contributions of such Bell sidemen as Ade Monsbourgh';

and assert that 'in Australia itself a jazz scene flourishes which (it could be argued) produces the most stimulating music of any outside America'.[320]

This assessment germinated with the Bell tour of 1947–8. The esteem in which the band was held led to the general belief that Australia had produced perhaps the only distinctive re-articulation of the style since the United States classic period. Rex Harris' assessment of the band's impact on the British scene, as noted above, was echoed in Jim Godbolt's reference to the 'fresh approach' it introduced.[321] This was reinforced by a decision reported in a letter from Mel Langdon, dated 30 March 1948:

> The name of the band has been changed from Graeme Bell and his Dixieland Jazz Band to Graeme Bell and his Australian Jazz Band—so many sins have been committed in the name of Dixieland.

Godbolt recalled that in his discussions with Langdon regarding the promotion of the band, the band's agent would solemnly insist, 'There's something I've got to make quite clear to you son. The billing is Graeme Bell and his *Australian* band' [italics in the original].[322]

It is clear that the Bell band took with them something perceived to be an Australian jazz style robust enough to prevail in its international negotiations. Its source lies in conditions specific to the post-war Australian traditional jazz movement, and ironically in the country's 'isolation', so often regarded as a cultural handicap. As outlined in Chapter One, the end of World War II left Australian popular music in a state of high stimulation, yet bereft of the systematic exposure to overseas models which would saturate the country from the mid-1950s, with rock'n'roll in tandem with American cultural marketing strategies. In 1946 the Australian scene was well developed with bands already seasoned in local 'field conditions'. They had thus evolved a high degree of regional specificity before being overtaken by what Clunies-Ross called the 'spectatorial' phase of the revival. This was characterised by attempts to systematise the music through written commentary, very largely the project of American and European writers, and which allowed for little deviation from a standardised version of authenticity. Clunies-Ross (1979, p.67) summarises the argument thus:

> Because musicians in Australia began playing jazz before the spread of this static conception, they developed a freer style and adopted a creative rather than a preservative approach to the music. Thus it acquired a characteristic accent of its own, as compared to the international style of traditional jazz which was to flourish later.

To this account we can also add the fact that as a musical form disdained by both the art music and the professional popular music sector, traditional jazz was relatively free to develop spontaneously in a large and uncrowded cultural space.

Of course, exactly what the 'Australian' style consists of takes us into more ambiguous areas. An overseas fan introduced to Australian jazz by the Bell band could mistake a group of highly distinctive individuals for a representative regional or national sound. The special quality of Ade Monsbourgh could be seen as integral to the Australian style. To a greater or lesser extent these difficulties attend any attempt to define the connections between the qualities of music and place. Is one hearing 'Russian-ness' when one hears Prokofiev, or the unique Prokofiev, whom we know is Russian? The analysis of what makes this 'Australian' sound is complicated further by the undeveloped state of the symbolic discourse for a music like jazz, making its distinctive coloration resistant to notation. What is clearly documented, however, is the widely-held belief that Australia did develop a distinctive contribution to jazz history, and we can investigate some of the ways in which that was linked to a supposed national character.

The amateur status of most participants in this phase of Australia's traditional jazz movement was crucial to this. Graeme Bell's status as a professional musician was highly unusual among his contemporaries, for whom traditional jazz did not generally function as an essential source of income. They remained relatively free of the constraints of commercial and 'legitimate' artistic imperatives, and untroubled by constraints of professional competence. Amateurism could also be better accommodated to a larger cultural perspective. The separateness-from-society that is part of the ideology of the professional 'artist' is not such a determining force in the psychological profile of musicians who also hold down a day job. Their musicianship was formed in a vivid relationship with a local culture, in front of audiences who were also friends and, in increasing numbers of cases, even family.[323]

The music's rootedness in a social rather than a professional community relates to Max Harris' suggestion that the character of this music reflects something of the Australian mythology of 'mateship', a personal dynamic which is conspicuous for overriding other intersecting loyalties in determining conduct. Recalling the phenomenon several decades later, Harris (1973, p.15) speculated that:

> ... the Australian jazz underground provides the last surviving embodiment of Lawson's mateship imperatives ... the old musicians ... have enjoyed a sustained and reassuring empathy with their now paunchy and raddled audiences. There has been an unchanging human environment in which the tradition has been able to survive and develop. Jazz has built an ethos of mateship around itself.

This suggests an affinity between the Australian jazz style and something seen as the 'Australian character', to a much greater extent than musical forms accorded greater significance in our national life. Max Harris's evocation of the mateship ethos has a clear parallel in the collaborative attitude imperative in the improvised collectivity of the traditional style. Amateurism also has obvious affinities with a range of other *supposed* Australian characteristics, from the suspicion of virtuoso professionalism (the 'tall poppy' syndrome), to the 'she'll be right' spirit that improvises workable solutions from whatever is lying around. The Australian style grew out of a pragmatic musical eclecticism largely necessitated by the intermittent access those musicians had to the source material. Our remoteness from the primary and secondary source material (Clunies-Ross' 'spectatorial' phase) for the early jazz tradition helped to produce an *ad hoc* approach to the music that gave larger meaning to the word 'improvisatory'. In the absence of the blueprints of later eras and styles, Australian traditional jazz in this period improvised its way into existence in a fluid response to local conditions.[324]

All these characteristics can be seen in the originality and eclecticism of the Bell band's repertoire, its use of instruments and combinations not explicitly sanctioned by the canonical 'texts', and by a breezy and swaggering indifference to English conceptions of musical and social decorum. Jim Godbolt (1984, pp.213, 214) noted that the Australians were not as 'hidebound' as the English groups, and were eager to take the doctrinaire seriousness out of the music and turn it into irreverent fun. If these sound like familiar English stereotypes of Australians, it is partly because the Bell band was in substantial ways helping to create them. In England traditional jazz was largely appropriated by intellectuals; in Australia, however, within the limits imposed by the white, Anglo-Celtic and masculinist post-war ethos, it was a relatively classless music whose participants presented a comprehensive socio-economic profile. Indeed, it was one of a limited number of recreational forms in which such barriers were regularly abolished.[325] A notion so evasive as 'national character' is constructed as much from outside the group identified by nation as from inside.[326] British descriptions of the Bell band often disclose much about their own expectations of 'colonials'. The aggressive egalitarianism of the Australians was frequently interpreted as ockerism and ratbaggery, and their style as brashness in social conduct and music. From published reports and in correspondence I have conducted with English witnesses to the tour, it is clear that the band's confidence often affronted expectations of what was appropriate demeanour:

> When the band returned to Australia Graeme Bell's parting shot, quoted in Melody Maker, was that, 'If British bands stuck at it and rehearsed they should improve.' The Australians brought a breezy humour, fresh approach and a wide repertoire to jazz presentation, but modesty was not one of their shining attributes, and their leader was patently unaware of the word.[327]

Strengthened by the virile success of Australian sportsmen, such characterisations were generalised to become part of the 'national character'. The Bell band's first European tour decisively altered the subsequent history of popular music and its relationship with the larger cultural field in Europe and the United Kingdom. This achievement on its own confers on them a unique status among our cultural exports. But they also established Australia as a distinctive presence on the international jazz scene, and were also among the first to fortify an overseas perception of the Australian national character in the post-war era.[328]

SIXTH BREAK
WHEN IT WORKS—A GOOD START

12 October 1991, Edinburgh

Because the pubs don't go in for any air-conditioning, the heat and fug are often unbearable. However cold the weather, I am always stripped back to a T-shirt within minutes of entering a pub. And a couple of times I've been on the point of leaving because of the smoke. The clothing always has to be aired or washed next day. Lots of jazz here. And everyone invites you for a sit-in. The first pub I tried was Preservation Hall in Victoria Street on a Saturday afternoon. I didn't take my trumpet, because of the conspicuousness of it, which can be a bit embarrassing all round. Also if I decide that I don't want to play it's a bit hard to explain things away politely if you're carrying an instrument that proclaims you're on the prowl for a blow.

It's a great ratty looking place, basically a big square room with a hollow square bar—like the British formations at Waterloo—in the middle. A stage occupies one side, and tables and chairs in the serviced areas. Fireplace. Amusing epigrams painted on the walls. Scottish nationalist pictures—a huge reproduction of the famous one of the Scots Guards at Waterloo, and an appalling painting of a kilted highlander on whose knees someone has stuck a couple of bandaids. I later learned that it was Toto the drummer. I sat at the bar. I was feeling good from a temperate lifestyle, swimming, a lot of walking, weight good. I timed my arrival for what I thought on the basis of the advertisements would be the last hour, so I could make myself known without necessarily getting tied up in a long drinking session. I drank orange juice.

The stage is large, and the musos appeared not actually to

have started (which turned out to be right—the advertised time was wrong). I thought I was looking at a gig in mid-flight, the band about to play its next number in the last set. But I was watching a band about to play its first number, and what was interesting is how ragged it looked, spread out over the stage, looking tentative and unfocussed. I hadn't realised until then how the appearance of the musicians on stage reflects the progress of the gig, and what registered to me was, what a ratbag looking band. I would not have thought that if I had been as a spectator part of that process of mobilisation—if I had known it was the last few minutes before the first number of the day. Attentive to this now, I watched how the band over the afternoon played itself into existence as a physical spectacle, now bunching, now opening up. When I looked for it, it was a bit like watching a flock of birds wheeling, massing, opening, closing, in response to something that defined it as a flock.

Now that I have been to so many jazz gigs here, I realise that that first day in the 'Prezzy' put me in touch with the most paradigmatic jazz venue in Edinburgh. The kind of place where, for me, live jazz works best. The gig is the site of a continuing community which really only comes into existence at that time. The people generally know each other, but don't all systematically and regularly have any other space or time where they become this identity. They probably don't share much professionally. The audience/band included a house painter, an architect (who had designed the city morgue), a guy who runs a sandwich shop, Orwell's biographer Bernard Crick, a number of Edinburgh's unemployed, a retired accountant. I doubt that all these people would exchange opinions on social issues and life-styles, and indeed would probably have a vigorous falling out if they did. So this 'community' exists only at this time and through this activity. The 'unemployed' are not unemployed while they are here. Academics are not demarcated as such in this place. Nor are racists, masons, taxi-drivers, housewives, bus conductors. I don't know whether this is a 'bad' thing or a 'good' thing, but it's certainly an interesting thing that slips by demographers.

The barriers between musician and audience are also down. The stage is merely a slight elevation enabling better acoustic projection, not a line of demarcation between audience and 'artist'. The PA is not suavely hidden in niches behind stylish facades. The speaker boxes and bass cube are just sitting there on stage. Leads straggle across the stage to a visible powerpoint surrounded by finger smudges. The musos don't disappear into the wings or some mysterious sanctum backstage during the breaks. Gigs I've done at the Opera House or places like the Supper Club at the Regent are always a sort of morbid memory, remembered as being in a darkness. Not literally, of course.

You've got spotlights in your eyes, but beyond their glare it's as though you're in a cave, there's no-one there, just an occasional faceless and featureless susurrating wash of applause. Backstage sitting in dressing rooms that have the same convergence of too much light and too little: the unmasked globes around the make-up mirrors, the shadowy space elsewhere. Picking at your supper, looking at your watch. The only jazz performers I've seen thrive on the Green Room are the ones who feel that saying you're in there means you've arrived. I reckon you've left. Excluded others, excluded yourself. I like the money you get for these gigs, but you earn it in alienation. The Regent gigs always made me think, 'I know why I'm here, it's for the money. But why are those people out there? And who are they?' They are gigs that seem to be endless. You just want to get home and watch a late movie and have a drink. It's because the performance spaces are so strategically divisive and alienating for everyone.

That's one of the great things about this kind of jazz venue. It pays bugger all, but you enjoy yourself. Like here in the 'Prezzy', the musos wander over to the bar, and drink with everyone else. It's smoky, rough, drunken, relaxed, with the usual complement of regulars with strange edgy mannerisms that would be difficult to accommodate anywhere else. There's one guy, there every week, who looks a bit like Robert Shaw with twitches. Talks endlessly, stands in front of the band raving, gets barred from time to time (but it's never enforced—he's always back and people are glad to see him). There's no other place I can imagine him having a role, or at least that particular role. His role is to be a bit off the wall and to be thrown out occasionally. And it seems to be a necessary role in the overall scenario and I quite like that. One week I watched him stare lugubriously out of the window at the bucketing torrents of rain lashing against the glass (I really don't want to let go of these things). For a very long time I watched him standing uncharacteristically silent and motionless, pondering what he saw. (What was happening in his mind? Remembered rain? Funes the memorious?). Finally he broke out of this brown study and walked away from the window. As he passed me he said with gloomy assurance, 'Ut's pussin' dain'.

CHAPTER 7
CONCLUSION: JAZZ AND AUSTRALIAN CULTURAL POLITICS

> Question: In your definition, what is good music?
>
> Pierre Boulez:... [At] the professional level. If a score is not really well put together, well written, then I am already suspicious of something.
>
> *(1988)*

The foregoing chapters have attempted to exemplify some of the contributions made by jazz to the formation of Australian culture in the twentieth century. They have been considerable and in some instances decisive among the range of musics practised in this country. Jazz has been the primary musical signpost of the advent of Australian modernity. In the first half of the century it musically channelled progressive developments in matters of gender, the arts, technological innovation, and was prominent in projecting a distinctive Australian presence internationally. When we turn to discussions of Australia's transition into the modern era, however, we find that jazz is virtually inaudible. A review of this anomaly will provide concluding points of departure for further analysis of the way in which that transition has been mapped, in relation to the place of music and other popular forms in Australian cultural debate.

In assessing how jazz is situated in accounts and valuations of Australian culture, we gain a preliminary glimpse from the bibliography at the end of this book. This is able to list only four works seeking to give a general overview of Australian jazz, one of which is confined to the post-war years. There is a two-part discography covering the period up to 1996. There is one bibliography of Australian jazz compositions, to 1978.[329] There are several personal memoirs and biographies, though in some cases only occasionally intersecting the jazz world. Interestingly there are also at least three Australian novels with a jazz setting.[330] Nevertheless scholarly interest in Australian jazz and other popular musics is increasing: Warren Bebbington's recent *Oxford Companion to Australian Music* includes substantial coverage; similarly John Whiteoak's *Playing Ad Lib*; the forthcoming Currency *Companion to Australian Music and Dance* which Whiteoak is co-editing with Aline Scott-Maxwell; and Kay Dreyfus' *Sweethearts of Rhythm.*[331] My own data-base of research on Australian jazz grows annually, if slowly. Nonetheless, in relation to the overall level of research into Australian culture and music, and in the public policies that accord cultural validation, we find that jazz is scarcely represented.

In the larger context of Australian cultural history, this neglect extends to music as a whole. This is a subject for its own inquiry, especially given that of all the arts, music is arguably the most pervasive. The most recent published survey conducted by the Australian Bureau of Statistics (ABS) on attendance by Australians at cultural venues is for the year ending March 1995. In that period there were 5,403,100 individual attendances at libraries, 3,134,100 at art galleries, 2,336,300 at non-musical theatre. When we turn to music, a total of 9,001,100 attended concerts categorised as of popular, classical, dance, and opera or musical.[332] These formal recreations are only a small fraction of our daily experience of music, which we encounter in restaurants, shopping malls, workplaces and transport, as background to other entertainments such as TV and film. Yet publishers' catalogues and bibliographies confirm that studies of our culture and identity are overwhelmingly dominated by the examination of verbal and visual narratives.

In studies of a form that is already neglected, the voice of jazz is scarcely audible. In the standard narrative history of Australia's music', jazz is not accorded an entry in the index. The *Australian Directory of Music Research*, covering work up to February 1977, lists around 150 musicology projects, of which only a handful involve jazz. The most recent full-length bibliographical survey lists only 29 entries under jazz, out of a total of 2,218.[333] In light of earlier parallels between the history of jazz and film it is notable that a recent Australian film bibliography which covers books, articles and reviews, includes nearly 15,000 items, of which some thousand are book-length studies.[334]

One of the most persuasive forms of recognition our society accords any cultural activity is financial support, and particularly government funding, which supposedly encourages artistic worth. The main support mechanism for the Commonwealth Government is the Australia Council (AC). In an earlier published study I analysed figures available up to the time of the *Australia Council Annual Report 1993–4*.[335] Although the AC Annual Report for 1996–7 has been published, I shall refer back to the *Report* for 1995–96 (designated *AC 1995–96*) to bring the analysis more into coincidence with the latest figures available from the ABS, above. That picture is complicated by changes in the AC operating structure introduced in April 1996; but the asymmetries to which I call attention are so persistent and massive that it is impossible to believe they have been significantly affected by the reforms in AC structure. Given the thrust of what follows, it is important to stress that since the establishment of the Council in 1973 jazz has benefited significantly from commonwealth patronage. This has been particularly so through the establishment of the various Jazz Co-ordination programs. Jazz musicians have also been recognised through Creative Fellowships. We have noted before the awards to Don Burrows and Sandy Evans. In 1994 the former received a three-year Commonwealth Government Creative Arts Fellowship to the value of $330,000, one of eleven presented in that year. In 1995, Sandy Evans received one of ten Young Australian Creative

Fellowships, to the value of $33,000 over a year. Financially, Australian jazz is unquestionably better off with the Australia Council than without it.

Let us look at some relativities, however. How much recognition does jazz enjoy in relation to other forms of music funded by the Council? In *AC 1995–96* the figure given for 'Total Arts Support Payments' is $63,684,000. While this pie is considerably larger than the $49,218,000 million at the time of my last analysis covering 1993–94, it has several more parties sitting at the table: 'Audience Development and Advocacy' and 'Major Organisations' were not included in the equivalent earlier figure *(AC 1993–94* p.78; *AC 1995–96*, p.76). The largest single share in 1995–96, 30% or $18,960,000 again went to Performing Arts. Of that amount music received 21% ($4,059,000), of which $610,134 went to what could be described as jazz projects, for 34 projects out of 250 successful music applications.[336]

Thus, jazz received 15% of the money disbursed to music, for 13.6% of the number of music grants made. While this is a jump of just over 5% since 1993–94, it remains a low figure as a measure of the official recognition of a music employing numbers of musicians equal to classical music in general, for around 2.4 times the audiences. Participation figures are considerably higher than for opera, which receives millions each year in funding from government and private sources.[337] In December 1995, for example, the Australian Opera consolidated accounts (in which is included figures for the Australian Opera and Ballet Orchestra) recorded grants of $4 million from private and corporate donors (11% of the opera company's revenue), and $9 million from government grants (24% of revenue).[338] If these figures dwarf the level of jazz support, it dwindles even more embarrassingly when it is remembered that the Music Fund's grants for dance projects are not included. These also subsidise music—though rarely, if ever, jazz. Nor have the grants made to music and dance under the 'Major Organisations' category been included (where jazz is a negligible presence). These in 1995–96 amounted to in excess of a further $66 million (*AC 95–96*, p.97). To appreciate the significance of these figures, it is necessary also to know that the Music Fund does not in general support vernacular or popular musics such as rock, pop, country music. An infinitesimal share of the pie is enjoyed by some folkloric and ethnic music projects, but in terms of the mainstream categories, the music subsidised by the Music Fund of the Australia Council can be described as jazz, art or concert music including the contemporary, and that designated as avant-garde. All this means, in bold outline, that when we take such factors into consideration, the jazz share of the music funding pie shrinks to a single-digit figure.

The silence of jazz in the musical accounts of Australia persists as we browse through other areas of cultural legitimation. In October 1994 the first statement of cultural policy ever to be articulated by an Australian Commonwealth government was presented in the form of the document called *Creative Nation.*[339] In its one hundred pages, it mentions jazz only once. When Eric Myers reviewed jazz for the country's only national newspaper, the *Australian*, he reported that his arts editor would accept his recommendations 'only if there was absolutely nothing else from such areas as classical music, opera, dance or the theatre. Jazz was the lowest priority and the last resort'.[340] While there have been episodic increases in coverage, the level is still not commensurate with the level and recognised quality of jazz activity. In its *Preliminary Announcement* brochure of 1995 the Australian National Academy of Music's 'Mission and Program' impassively perpetuates the complete exclusion of jazz (and all vernacular forms of music such as popular, folk, multi-cultural) from the category of Australian music.

Now at the turn of the century the debates on republicanism, on the rights of indigenous peoples, on Australia's relationship with the Asia-Pacific region, have been conducted with increasing urgency, brought to a focus by the millennial Olympics in Sydney. This climate has produced an expanding literature on the country's social history, particularly as articulated through popular culture. In the media, in scholarly studies, and in educational programs, there has been an intense interest in the articulation of collective identity through literature, painting, film. Scholars have recognised that of all expressive forms music is perhaps the most powerful, immediate and democratic:

> The musical event, from collective dances to the act of putting cassette or CD into a machine, evokes and organises collective memories and present experiences of place with an intensity, power and simplicity unmatched by any other social activity.[341]

Yet in the context of Australian arts discourse, the level of attention paid to music as a way of mapping our culture is slight. And within that sparsely-inhabited category, jazz has a negligible presence.

Why this might be so is a significant statement about Australian cultural politics, and I have pursued this inquiry in some detail in this and other publications. What emerges is an overview of significant patterns in the politics of Australian culture and music. These can be approached with reference to two broad areas. First are the ideologies that have shaped the concept of Australian culture in the twentieth century, in particular the relationship between modernism and modernity. The overview presented in Chapter Two discloses attitudes to the 'popular' and to mass-mediated culture, and to the play of gender within that field. A second group of factors involves assumptions about cultural capital, about what kinds of musical models matter. This centres upon the idea of the musical 'product' and how it is embodied.

What these two points of reference—culture in general and music in particular—share is that they are framed by politics. That is, in determining what is valued, relations of power take precedence over, and indeed shape, standards of artistic value.

The inaudibility of jazz is not fundamentally to do with formal aesthetics nor with public morality, though these have been vigorously emphasised in the marginalisation of the music. Aesthetic values are socially contingent: Picasso's cubist images remained unchanged while he was being recuperated by the art establishment. Nor is there any evidence that jazz has produced any generalised pattern of moral depravity. Indeed, it was suppressed by two of the most cruel and immoral regimes of the twentieth century: Hitlers and Stalin's.[342]

But before proceeding to an examination of the way jazz is located in recent discourses of the Australian musical landscape, it is necessary to make a few observations about the way that landscape itself is mapped. The whole of my discussion thus far has implied that 'jazz' is a genre having some objective existence in a field also occupied by other genres from which it is distinguishable: classical, rock, folk, country and western, liturgical, world music, pop and its proliferating and fusing sub-categories like rap, hiphop, techno, metal, trance and so on. Such taxonomies are essential to music discourses, for promotion, distribution, review and analysis. As I have suggested at a number of points, the genre known as 'jazz' is also largely a discursive construct, determined by history and place. To a large extent, the history of Australian jazz is the history of a struggle for control of the word's meaning. Nonetheless, there is still considerable room for a common understanding of what is meant by 'jazz' even while the edges of the definition are under continuous review.

At a deeper level, there is a further problem with the word 'jazz' as the pivot on which these discussions swing. This is to do not with the particular genre, but with the whole notion of genre itself as a principle of musical categorisation. Many of the generic terms by which we distinguish one musical form or practice from another, presuppose a cultural field which has not yet been intersected by mass mediations. The revolutionary change brought about by sound recording and mass distribution of music was this: the technology made it possible for the first time to experience music at places and times other than those of its performance. It is no longer necessary to go to the 'country' to hear country music; to church to hear religious music; to Arnhem Land to hear particular forms of Australian indigenous music; or to Bulgaria or Lebanon to hear their 'ethnic' or 'world music' manifestations. Without rearranging our lives, we can hear these musics at any time, in any place. They can be heard adjacent to each other or even superimposed. Mass mediations have abolished the geographic and historical constraints on the basis of which such genres were evolved.

Those mediations have also abolished traditional class constraints. Before the invention of sound recording, the musically illiterate could only gain access by attending a performance. But access to performance was regulated along class lines by economics—the cost of concert admission and the inaccessibility of salon performance. The sound recording changed this political dynamic utterly. In the twentieth century the genre, or aggregation of genres, called art music can no longer adequately differentiate itself on grounds of exclusivity. The anxieties thus generated among people who see their cultural capital being devalued are a further reminder that cultural value is at least as much (and I would say more), a function of politics as aesthetics. This leads me forward to the main lines of inquiry in this concluding chapter.

The unreflective use of genres as a basis for the discussion of music can be a minefield. One of the dangers it presents has been the subject of this whole book. Traditional discourse of music is commonly based on notions of genre and the formal properties that constitute its 'authenticity'. These are deployed as measures of aesthetic value, but at a historical moment that is deeply inappropriate.[343] The consequence is that such discourse is profoundly out of touch with contemporary music practices and the enfolding social dynamics. Nevertheless, it provides the authoritative models for education, public policy, support and promotion, with exclusionary consequences that are socially divisive, intimidating and futile as a definitive standard for musical practice in Australia.

The Aesthetics of Exclusion

Chapter Two sought explanations for the inaudibility of jazz in the early histories of Australian modernism, largely through the social and cultural conditions prevailing at the time. Today, many of those conditions no longer obtain. All musical forms, for example, had access to, and have by now increasingly become absorbed into, the apparatus of mass distribution. There must therefore be additional factors at work in the process of determining cultural value. I suggest that we find the answers to this in practices and competencies that distinguish jazz (and other similarly marginalised musics) from art music as it evolved through the nineteenth century. Central to this is the extent to which jazz is an improvised music that comes into being spontaneously and emerges from social praxis. I have taken up the problems of the term 'improvisation' elsewhere, but here I intend it to refer to variations—harmonic, timbral, rhythmic—which originate at the moment of performance in response to the total performance ambience.[344] Paul Berliner's massive study of jazz thinking and practices is a sustained testimony to the continuing centrality of improvisation among the distinctive elements of jazz.[345] This is not to deny mutual influences between jazz and conventional notation-based music; nor that some dimension of unscored variation is wholly absent from the latter; nor again that the improvisational thrust of jazz is at every moment convincingly audible in performance. My point is that in practice and in print, jazz musicians universally hold improvisation to be a constitutive presence in the music.

It thus violates models based on score-based discipline of musicians and audiences; and the doctrines of artistic autonomy evolved in the nineteenth century.[346] Rowse and Hawkins, *inter alia,* have demonstrated the extent to which the official discourse of art in Australia is still dominated by neo-Romantic aesthetics of transcendence, in spite of episodic interruptions which seek recognition of alternative ways of conceiving the relationship between art and culture.[347] Art music remains a bastion of the mythology of autonomy that underpinned the modernist rejection of mass culture. This involves privileging the canonical text as a model of transcendence and universality, in which the design of the composer/genius is preserved and sanctified. In this model the role of the musician is to bring to the highest pitch the academic virtuosity required to 'read' the text accurately.[348]

When a vernacular music like jazz attempts to find a place in this discourse, however, it finds itself in a Procrustean bed. The hierarchical structures around which operatic and orchestral performance and composition cluster are not central features of jazz activity. The aesthetic forcefield that arranges itself around the 'serious' music composer, for example, is an inappropriate model for the relationship between composer, performer, audience, music-text and venue, in jazz. When it seeks to situate itself within the domain of autonomous art, jazz finds it more difficult to conceal its social origins; and this is especially true of styles and performance practices in which the improvisational textures are most densely matted, and entwined with the performance environment. That is, the more overt the level of collective improvisation, and the greater the inter-activity with audiences and extrinsic conditions, the less leverage jazz has in a musicology that privileges the autonomous text. The centrality of improvisation in jazz (and to varying extents in other musics designated through terms such as 'ethnic', 'folk', 'pub rock') requires the deployment of criteria of analysis, evaluation and support which are scarcely to be found or understood through high art music discourse. There is abundant literature on this; significantly it is to be found mainly in cultural studies and ethnomusicology.[349]

To begin with, the theoretical competencies are very different for the jazz musician. It is frequently reported that basic classical training is an impediment to effective jazz performance (and of course vice versa). The exercises designed for orchestral playing develop skills essential in score-based performance; but they do not develop the competence to improvise over sequences that change key, sometimes as often as every beat in a bar—or even to recognise what is happening. Furthermore, the instrumental competencies in each case require very different skills. As we have noted, the dimensions of expressive complexity for jazz are not simply 'extensional', but 'intensional'.[350] These include spontaneously-generated rhythmic and timbral ambiguities, the latter comprising rasps, smears and growls, often sentimentalised as 'making the instrument talk'. From Percy Grainger's 'kaleidoscopic density' to Charles Keil's 'engendered meaning'—as opposed to syntactic embodied meaning'—attempts have been made to articulate these dimensions of expressiveness. Because they are transgressive in terms of art-music discourse, however, it is hard to describe them without at the same time demeaning them.[351]

Similarly, while art music demands rigorous adherence to a text, jazz belongs to a category of music in which degrees of formal unruliness are endemic. Charles Keil has developed the theory of participatory discrepancies as central to the expressive power of vernacular music. By this he means the discrepancies in the generation of patterns of tension and release in improvisatory practices: groups of musicians who are not hitting the beat at exactly the same moment, who are not articulating exactly in tune, who drop in and out of the performance, as people drop in and out of a conversation.[352] Many writers think of this as the essence of 'swing', and indeed computer research is now generating a 'wave-guide' technology: having spent decades trying to produce 'perfect' and uncontaminated sounds, Yamaha are now experimenting with asymmetries and indeterminacies in their synthesiser programs to increase their expressivity.[353] Thus it is recognised that central to the power of some of our expressive music forms, is a set of practices defined in art music discourse as musical incompetence. Doctrines of formal perfection, central to institutionalised policy, education, administration, are diametrically opposed to the modes of expressivity of vernacular music.

Jazz is also distinguished from art music models in the absolute priority of the ear in performance. Brian Brown, jazz musician and former jazz studies director at the Victorian College of the Arts, summarises the evidence also accumulated by Berliner: 'The ear is the truest guide in the end'.[354] The jazz ear is attuned not only to the formal music activity, but also to the enfolding soundscape. Because the performance moment is everything, that soundscape is actually part of the 'text', part of what is being read and generated. Related to this is a fundamental question of attitude'. The formal teaching and evaluation of music for the most part focuses on the development of instrumental virtuosity and theoretical command. But absolutely crucial to effective collective improvisation is a readiness to yield control, to suspend cognitive design: to hear what conventional music training would call an irrelevance, and embrace it. In ignoring performance conditions, traditional formalist analysis leaves improvisational music significantly unintelligible. The myth of the artistic genius in full cognitive control of the act of creation has relatively little to do with public (and even solitary) improvisational practice. The collective improviser must be open to the other instruments—a drum punctuation, a chord substitution, competition for the same note, but equally so to a noise from the crowd or street traffic. These require the constant revision of planned manoeuvres. Jazz musicians habitually play with, as well as against, the sounds of conversation, bar noises, poker machines, a passing siren. Any attempt to understand a musical statement made without reference to the enfolding soundscape is bound to fail. Precisely those things a score-based musician must ignore in order to produce an effective performance, is what an improviser must take into account.[355]

The role played by cognitive design in jazz is also contested by what is known as kinaesthetics. Among the ways in which the orchestral score enacts the ideology of the Enlightenment is its subordination of body to mind, to the design of the genius/composer. Transcribed as a score it is then performed by musicians whose training is devoted to the disciplines necessary to the realisation of that design. In the case of the improviser that relationship is much more ambiguous. Jeff Pressing, jazz musician and academic, has analysed the formal structure of improvisations conducted for the experimental situation.[356] He hypothesises that some of its patterning is 'stored to a significant degree in the kinaesthetic representation, rather than aural'. That is, in a musical improvisation certain patterns are attributable not so much to audialisation (the projection of a particular sound pattern originating in the mind), as to physical organisation of space (a habitual sequence of movements of the hand on the keyboard). Thus, one of the bases of improvisation is kinaesthetic—that is, the outcome of a physical mannerism rather than the projection of a cognitive design. It may be associated, for example, with fingering patterns that have become habitual in particular keys. Improvisational music often reflects the very opposite of cognitive control: the sounds issuing proclaim a loss of orientation, a confused immersion in the irreversible process growing out of the complex convergence of space, time, memory and instrumental competence; kinaesthetics, internalised vocabulary, and the performance conditions. Far from being the articulation of an artistic design, such moments (familiar to every improvising performer) are points of crisis which are more likely to produce unexpected, unplanned 'improvisation that will transcend sustained control. It is the alternation between different levels of control and moments when it is lost or surrendered, that generates the tensions that distinguish muzak from music.

The relationship between cognitive and physical control is

thus extremely complex. For all improvising musicians there are times when they let their fingers do the talking. And it remains to be argued why the intervention of kinaesthetics, of the habits of the body, is in principle likely to produce anything less aesthetically valid than the habits of the mind—even assuming that distinction can in practice be made.[357]

In this connection, a further line of demarcation within the jazz field itself emerges to emphasise which particular elements of jazz practice are in most contention with the paradigms of musical modernism. The statistical review that opened this chapter did not by any means reveal a total exclusion of jazz from official recognition. A glance at which styles enjoy most favour gives further emphasis to the arguments I have been articulating. One area in which that emphasis is most apparent is that of jazz education.[358] The seminal tertiary diploma course in jazz studies was inaugurated at the New South Wales State Conservatorium of Music in 1973. Others followed, and today there are eighteen similar tertiary programs in Australia.[359]

The encounter between jazz and the Australian academies, however, has produced ambiguous effects. With important exceptions, and to varying degrees, the traditional/modern bifurcation sketched in Chapter One has been manifested in the biases of academic jazz programs, to the benefit of the modern styles. In consequence this dichotomy has been rearticulated in terms that imply the distinction between art music and folk music or 'high' and 'low'. Where traditional jazz receives attention, it is generally not on its own terms, but as a stage on the path to aesthetic completion, rather like the neanderthal represented at some intermediary point in the evolution of man. I stress again that this is a tendency, to which there are notable exceptions: my concern is with bias in the overall profile.[360] Once jazz is situated within the orbit of musical academia, no matter how strenuously individual teachers might seek to follow the trajectory of jazz aesthetics, it cannot help but behave like a satellite of the dominant centre. This is formally inscribed in the course handbooks and anecdotally proclaimed in the overall musical orientation of the instructors and graduates.[361]

The traditional jazz style marginalised by academic modernism is, as this book has attempted to show, a crucial vehicle of modernity in and beyond Australia. Ade Monsbourgh is particularly important in this movement. He is frequently identified as the leading architect of an Australian jazz style; as a composer, performer, mentor, he is certainly one of the most significant jazz musicians Australia has produced.[362] Yet he is barely known, let alone given appropriate recognition, within the national academic community. The effect on jazz education is a radical distortion of our musical history, which would be lamentable enough at any time but which is staggeringly anachronistic in the current regionalist consciousness of centrifugal postmodernism. It also undermines the value which traditionalists impute to their own work. Ade Monsbourgh himself has confessed that in the current climate of opinion, he often felt he ought to be playing in a style other than that which has made him so profoundly influential:

> I've been trying to ... make excuses for myself for still being interested in 'Potato Head Blues'... when I should be thinking about playing as many notes as I can in three seconds'[363]

Apart from producing a deformation of history, this bias also neglects a highly significant formal skill: sustained polyphony between three or four horns, supported by a rhythm section. This is virtually the distinguishing practice of all forms of so-called traditional jazz from New Orleans to dixieland. This disappeared from developments subsequent to Swing, and did not regain any prominence until the 'free' jazz movement of the 1960s, with the difference that conventional concepts of tonality were now abandoned. Even so, its exponents frequently invoked the New Orleans tradition of collective improvisation as a model in terms of both form and social purpose.[364] It is noteworthy that among the post-bop styles generally privileged over the pre-bop in the conservatoria, 'free jazz' is represented most sparsely. Continuous collective improvisation is both a formal musical skill involving the cultivation of a distinctive vertical (synchronic) and horizontal (diachronic) aural alertness, and a vehicle for socialisation. This emphasis on communality is peripheral to, even antipathetic to, the hierarchical tradition of the solo artist.

Collective improvisation is singularly difficult to accommodate in a text-centred ethos, simply because it is so resistant to notation. As improvisation (and this of course is true of a bop solo as well as traditionalist collectivity), it cannot be written down beforehand; but as collective it is virtually impossible to transcribe later from a recording. This was recognised from the beginning, in the work of the ODJB from the earliest days of jazz recording:

> At the time of these recording sessions, the complex scores of these musical productions existed only in the minds of the musicians. Attempts at copying five-piece band arrangements note for note from the records were, in fact, totally unsuccessful, owing to the dozens of odd musical effects and subtle refinements of rhythm for which there were no known symbols. The publishers were finally content to settle for standard orchestral arrangements derived solely from the melody.[365]

The intractability of collective improvisation to the form of a scored 'opus' constitutes a radical disadvantage to legitimacy as high art. Key notions in the dominant cultural discourse have served to privilege particular artistic myths—the sacrosanct work of art (the composition), the shaping genius (the composer), the performers and audiences regimented to his/

her will. One outcome of this ideology is the sacralisation of the Composition—the Opus—as the centre of music production/consumption, against which all alternatives are to be seen as deviations, as for example in the form of radical experimentation. The authority of the notion of composition and its embodiment, the score, is abundantly signalled in music scholarship and criticism. Eminent Sorbonne musicologist André Pirro expressed the point with schematic clarity when he informed his pupil and successor Jacques Chailley, 'I never go to concerts any more. Why listen to music? To read it is enough'.[366]

Jazz cuts across this in two ways: it evades the authority of the 'score' in both production and consumption. Because it is virtually an oral/aural music, jazz can be practised without a text. The score-centredness of art music means that it can only be performed by musicians who have subscribed to an approved symbolic order, access to which is restricted according to such criteria as class, race, economics, gender. Anyone with ears, however, can learn jazz, and in fact without an 'ear' it is generally held to be impossible. It was also the first major musical genre to be disseminated predominantly on sound recordings. That is, it could be heard and reproduced out of earshot of the original without access to the score or to the performance. The recording, however, obviously becomes the jazz equivalent of the score—sometimes even more dictatorial—and its function in the political economy of music is therefore extremely ambiguous. On the one hand, the recording industry has a considerable measure of control over access to its products. On the other, the recording provides direct access to the sound of music for consumers, and advances in domestic sound technology can further democratise music (re)production.[367]

Where a particular musician sits on the continuum from collective to solo improviser shifts, of course, from moment to moment. However, the combination of an aesthetic of the individual *agon*, and an academic ethos which emphasises training to the highest level of internationalist professionalism, will find the soloist jazz model more congenial than one in which the individual yields to the collective dynamic of the local moment. Yet, when centralised at the expense of other musical insights activated in collectivity, this has a severely limiting effect on the way in which music functions as a mediator for the individual and society. Internationalist virtuosity becomes a fetish, advertising the separation of the musician from the rest of the community, erasing all traces of individual and regional identity.

To address the connection between improvisation and social identities is not flippant in the context of urban modernity, in which the spontaneous harmonising of difference is crucial. In our high density centres of population we have to improvise our way into collective harmony every day. This is not a fanciful conceit. In the transition to the mass centres of urban modernity, the traditional frameworks within which social conduct is regulated have been largely disrupted. The cultural script or 'score' is full of blanks and erasures. Urban life is a constant negotiation with the unexpected. When we enter a space full of strangers we enter into a complex process of unscripted collective improvisation. Such an improvisation can only be harmonised by the most attentive alertness to signals and by the most rapidly deployed and rearticulated repertoire of responses. This is as close to a description of the dynamic of jazz as I can imagine. Every time we move through a crowded street we enact a combination of 'compositional design'—a planned timetable and destination—and improvisational realisation of that design. That light is red, that group stands in the way, that stranger asks for the time, that roadworker tells me the way is closed, these drivers are attempting to travel at right angles to me as I cross the road, there a cyclist darts out from an unexpected quarter. And if we have no particular destination, if we are that quintessential urban modernist, the *flâneur*, then interactive improvisation is the key to our negotiations with our environment. Improvisation is central to social conduct in modern society. We need constantly to read and respond positively to the unpredicted signals of strangers according to a shared vocabulary, if we are to transcend the terror of 'the man of the crowd'.[368]

It has been a basic contention of this book that among musical forms, jazz played a pivotal role in the transition to modernity of Australian society—both as the latter reflected upon itself and as it projected itself internationally. This is not only the case within the sphere of music, but in the wider terrain of public and domestic life. That this role has made barely any imprint upon cultural commentary is largely attributable to the dominance of a cultural policy that continues to be shaped by aesthetics constructed on a deep bedrock of nineteenth century social conditions and ideologies. Already in the inter-war period, the gap was widening between a conservative hegemony locked into an earlier Anglo-European *milieu,* and the more erratic orientations of everyday life in mass-mediated modernity. It is now wider than ever.

I conclude by reaffirming the point made in the preface: that different musics require different skills; and no one form is intrinsically superior to another. I make it because traditional musicology so often interprets the claim that art music discourse cannot be all things to all musics, as an attempt to displace that discourse altogether. John Sangster's *Lord of the Rings* cannot be played by a symphony orchestra, and a jazz quartet as such will not produce the most approved reading of a Beethoven string quartet. Such exercises will most often exhibit the equivalent of an 'accent', which, it should be remembered can also have a charm of its own. Diversity and hybridity are the norms of music in social practice—and social practice in music—not the exception. This is nowhere more apparent than in the extraordinarily rich diversification of Australian jazz over the last decades. What gives jazz its particular character cannot be disclosed through a language written for some other kind of music; and the nature and sources of its decisive contribution to Australian society cannot be properly evaluated while relying on cultural models built for other purposes.

TURNAROUND
WHEN IT DOESN'T WORK—
NOT THE END

5 October 1991, Edinburgh

This afternoon I strolled into one of the local jazz pubs after having had a really pleasant lunch with Peter Marks at Bernard Crick's place. I walked into a different universe. One of those shambles that can overtake unscripted performance spaces. Most unscripted gigs work wonderfully, and rarely less than well. But some days a spirit is abroad. I don't know what it is—the moon, the ghost in the machine. But I've experienced this in so many bands, that unpredictable collective dementia, that I know it has nothing to do with any one individual, but some kind of succubus that takes over everybody.

There was a big football match on yesterday, between Scotland and Japan. Coincidentally, today most of the usual band members were afflicted with illness or sick relatives who required TLC. The usual singer wasn't there, and her dep, Liz, was also a good singer, but my heart went out to her because she had to front chaos. So, a different band, almost wholly made up of deps. One of those situations where everybody knew everybody, had all played with each other, but not in this particular permutation. There was a dep guitarist, saxophonist, trumpeter, bassist, and the epicentre, a Glaswegian trombonist who started pissed and finished the day flat on his back.

I caught the scent of mice playing while the cat was away, because the few regular members seemed to me to be starting a few sheets to the wind. They started ragged and late, as bands are apt to do when it's a loose, pickup day that feels a bit like a lost cause even before you start. You could have driven a semi between the pitching of the trumpet and the trombone, but the pervasive problem (which meant that the pitch problem never got attended to) was that nobody was listening to anyone else. Individually and at their best they were all very good musicians, but each played as though he was the only horn player on stage. It was like the Dodgems except that they didn't seem aware that they were constantly crashing into and skidding off each other. Peter's ears told him that something wasn't working and mine told me what wasn't. It's axiomatic, for example, that unless the horns are listening very sharply and with reflexes in good shape, it's best if only one at a time backs a singer, maybe in relays of eight or sixteen bars if everyone wants a go. Not these boyos—they all blazed away together at any note that drifted into view from the singer. Talk about the OK Corral. A lot of innocent bystanders among the chord changes bit the dust.

I (still abstemious) made a mental note which read: 'Do Not Sit In!'. And was thinking that I would leave, but wait until the end of the first bracket just to be polite. But while announcing the last number, the drummer announced that I would be coming up in the next bracket, and does this extravagant wrap up on me that it would have been really rude to cold-shoulder. In due course, following a band break which most of them treated as the last chance for drinks before prohibition, I get up to play. I am surprised to see that the dep trumpeter comes on stage too. This is a little unusual, creating the likelihood of congestion in the lead, but it wouldn't normally worry me except for the heavy traffic I've been listening to. A singer calls Route 66 (one of the dullest songs I know) and takes the mike in his hand. We kick off. It's like the starting bell at a stockcar demolition derby. No room no room, so I don't even try to contribute to the mayhem, figuring to wait for a bit of solo space. The trombonist who, closeup, has the features of an open-cut coalmine, begins to talk into my ear in a loud but incomprehensibly haphazard way, trying to talk me into participating in the massacre. Suddenly the singer stops and yells, 'Take it Bruce!', and thrusts the mike into the trumpet bell. Now I'm not feeling real relaxed at this point, so my intonation lacks definition, my lip is cold, my breathing jagged, and the resultant less-than-polished sound is boring out through the loudspeakers, fit to make the roof flap. Meantime, while I am playing Jack the Lad is still trying to tell me some incomprehensible piece of Glaswegian jazz folklore and trying to make some arrangement that would involve us meeting in a pub and swallowing its contents. His voice comes and goes somewhat, as the mouth from which it issues is in turn connected to a body that is swaying alarmingly. But it is never less than a dull roar of glottal vowels and spraying sibilants washing over my shell-like. Are you getting all this down Officer?

After about eighteen bars of this (ie in the middle of a chorus) I just stop—every attempt to point the trumpet away from the mike having been treated by the sit-in singer as an unsuccessful challenge to his persistence and agility. There is mischief here now. Others take solos. The singer raunches a few final choruses, and I think I will just play a note to contribute to the final chord. Who do I think I'm kidding? They don't do anything as bland as hold a resolving chord. It becomes a contest to see who can play the most fascinating cadenza. Next, a pleasant Sinatra-ist gets up to sing 'Lady is a Tramp'. Another signal for all-in, hell-for-leather backup. By this time the trombonist is baying in my ear to the effect that, 'It's OK. I'm from Glasgow and we drink a lot there.' A sort of palsied helplessness drives me off the stage, trumpet back in locked case; return to join Peter at the bar and call for a pint of Old Peculier which I pay for with a trembling hand. By now the trombonist has spotted the cowbell on the drum kit, and is kneeling looking into it as though it's a periscope, making various maritime noises not unconnected with foghorns. Interesting counterpoint to the singer, this:

> 'She gets too hungry for dinner at eight'
> (Steady as she goes lads!)
> 'Hates California, it's cold and it's damp'
> (Hoooot. Stand by to board!)
> 'That's why the Lady is a tramp'
> (Target closing to starboard. Ding Ding)

The drummer is caught between the pull of drunken mateship, the spirit of the moment, and a residual professional embarrassment. Now the trombonist has thought of a new lark. He has removed the slide from his trombone and is bawling out in simulated distress, 'Oh, I've broken the wee thing. It's broken'. Liz has to return to the stage and looks at me enviously, sitting at the bar. I figure: 'I'm not being paid for this, so why the fuck should I suffer?' Then with a twinkle of retributive malice in her eyes she takes the mike, eyeballs me and announces, 'And we'd like to have Bruce Johnson rejoin the bandstand', knowing how rude it would be to decline. Also I do like Liz's singing, and sucker that I am I feel for the situation she is in. Back on the stand. They're all pissed except the trumpeter, though it is suggested that one of the other guys is sniffing something. They play something, and I stay out of it, refusing solos and trying to get out of earshot of the trombonist who's beginning to suspect that I'm not having a ball. So he starts articulating at length his philosophy of jazz gigs and how they are supposed to be like this. And of course he's almost right: when they're good it's partly to do with the same thing that makes them this kind of bad. If you put in place watertight safeguards against this kind of anarchy, you also ensure that its potential amplitude is narrowed in every direction. But his arguments don't persuade me at this particular moment that this is how they are actually supposed to be.

He pauses in his apologia and abruptly presents his glass to me. 'Taste it!' he says. I have no idea why, just then, with all the rest of the band blaring around us. As Peter said later he probably wanted me to join him on whatever planet it was he was calling from.

'No', I say'.

'Taste it!' sez he.

I sniff it.

'Smells like whisky,' sez I perceptively.

'TASTE IT!!' he yells. I take the hint of a sip.

'It is whisky,' I tell him.

And he looks at me and shrugs morosely before turning away to aim a few more clumsy kicks at the battered body of the song lying on the stage. I think some of my irritation is seeping through.

Sax player asks me what I would like to play, and I think, fuck it, we'll do a song I'm right on top of, that's such a standard that everybody's instincts could over-ride the stampede, and we'll do it on my terms. I call 'Perdido'. So we play it in and at the end of the ensemble chorus the sax player gestures to me to take the two-bar break. Well, I'm not ready right now, but sometime around now. So I do what I should have done earlier that is more important than filling the two bar break. Put in a plungerless harmon (easier to control your breathing), walk to the mike in my own time and take charge of the discourse for a little while. At last I play well. I also impose my own will on the final choruses, setting the riffs. For the first time in the final bracket, some cohesion is produced. The song is finished. Honour is tattered but intact. I put the trumpet away with such a look of finality at Liz that she knows better than to try to blackmail me back on to the stage.

Another song finishes the day. The trombonist collapses on his back, supine on the stage. The trumpeter says to me, 'Bit of a shambles, eh?' probably hoping I would smile politely and say something nice, which normally I would. But I am feeling too mean-minded for that, locked in my own trivial irritation. I agree with him. After some time the trombonist resumes what might loosely be called a standing position. After all, there's a limit to how much attention you can call to yourself by lying motionless on the ground. He rats around in a satchel he has on stage, and produces a clown-sized tartan bow-tie which he dons. I dunno how much more of this I can write down. A clown's tartan bow-tie! And presents himself at the bar and orders a double scotch.

So what happened there? I guess it was a way in which the day, the football win, the hangovers, the specificity of everybody there just then suddenly erupted with the musical means at hand. At the time I felt petulant, embarrassed, impatient. Can't help that; when you're standing on a stage, unmistakably there, evidently aiding and abetting such mayhem, my temperament just doesn't seem to be able to carry it off. But in spite of my own prima donna flouncing and petulance, whenever that happens I know I'm alive, I register everything so sharply. I suppose if we want to drive an interesting road in an interesting way, we have to be prepared to lose control. I know that it's part of my 'design' that I don't really want that kind of thing to happen to me on stage. But I really want to play a kind of music—jazz, for example—where I know it is a possibility. I suppose I want to live in a society like that too. And if it does have to happen from time to time to remind me that it can, that's an acceptable price.

SELECT BIBLIOGRAPHY

Adams, Brian, *Sidney Nolan: Such is Life.* Milsons Point NSW: Vintage, Random House Australia, edition of 1992.

Anderson, Benedict, *Imagined communities: reflections on the origin and spread of nationalism.* London: Verso 1983.

Australia Council, *Annual Report.* Sydney: Australia Council, 1993–94, 1995–6

Australia Music Centre, *Catalogues of Australian Compositions VIII: Jazz.* Sydney: Australia Music Centre 1978.

Australia Music Centre, 'Dave Dallwitz' in the *Australian Composers* series. Sydney: Australia Music Centre 1981; see also [Myers, Eric].

Australian Bureau of Statistics, *Cultural Trends in Australia: A Statistical Overview 1997,* ABS Cat. 4172.0. Canberra 1997.

(*The*) *Australian Opera Annual Report 1995.*

Baer, Nancy Van Norman, *Theatre in Evolution: Russian avant-garde stage design 1913–1935.* Great Britain: Thames & Hudson 1991.

Balliett, Whitney, *Jelly Roll, Jabbo & Fats: 19 Portraits in Jazz.* Oxford University Press 1983.

Barthes, Roland, 'The Grain of the Voice', *Image-Music-Text,* trans Stephen Heath. Great Britain: Fontana/Collins 1977, pp. 179–189.

Bebbington, Warren (ed), *The Oxford Companion to Australian Music.* Melbourne: Oxford University Press 1997.

Bell, Graeme, Scrapbooks, State Library of NSW.

Bell, Graeme, 'Reconstruction of European Tour (not Czecho) 1947–1948' (MS).

Bell, Graeme, *Graeme Bell, Australian Jazzman: His Autobiography.* Frenchs Forest NSW: Child & Associates 1988.

Bell, Philip, and Roger Bell, *Implicated: The United States in Australia.* Melbourne: Oxford University Press 1993.

Benjamin, Walter, 'The work of art in the age of mechanical reproduction', in Hannah Arendt (ed), *Illuminations,* trans Harry Zohn. London: Jonathan Cape 1970.

Berliner, Paul E, *Thinking in Jazz: The Infinite Art of Improvisation.* Chicago and London: The University of Chicago Press 1994.

Berman, Marshall, *All That Is Solid Melts Into Air: The Experience of Modernity.* London and New York: Verso, 4th Impression 1989.

Bisset, Andrew, *Black Roots White Flowers: a history of jazz in Australia.* Second Edition, Sydney: ABC Enterprises 1987.

Bolton, Geoffrey, *Spoils and Spoilers: a history of Australians shaping their environment.* North Sydney: Allen & Unwin, Second Edition 1992.

Boulez, Pierre and Michel Foucault, 'Contemporary music and its public', *Melbourne Journal of Politics,* 17, 1985/86, pp.42–50.

Bourdieu, Pierre, *Distinction: a social critique of the Judgement of Taste,* trans Richard Nice. Cambridge Mass: Harvard University Press 1984; first published in French, 1979.

Bourdieu, Pierre, *The Field of Cultural Production: Essays on Art and Literature,* ed Randal Johnson. Cambridge: Polity Press 1993.

Bourdieu, Pierre, *Language and Symbolic Power,* trans Gino Raymond and Matthew Adamson, ed John B. Thompson. Cambridge: Polity Press 1992.

Bradley, Dick, *Understanding Rock'n'Roll: Popular Music in Britain 1955–1964.* Buckingham: Open University Press 1992.

Brantlinger, Patrick, *Bread and Circuses: Theories of Mass Culture as Social Decay.* Ithaca: Cornell University Press 1983.

Breen, Marcus, 'Popular Music', in Stuart Cunningham and Graeme Turner (eds), *The Media in Australia: Industries, Texts, Audiences.* St Leonards, NSW: Allen & Unwin, 2nd ed 1997, pp. 143–162.

Brisbane, Katharine (ed), *Entertaining Australia: an illustrated history.* Sydney: Currency Press 1991.

Brown, Marshall, 'Origins of modernism: musical structures and narrative forms', in Scher, Steven Paul, *Music and Text: Critical Enquiries.* Cambridge, Cambridge University Press 1992, pp.75–92.

Bruton, Dean, *The Contemporary Art Society of South Australia 1942–86: Recollections.* Bedford Park SA: Flinders University 1986.

Burke, Janine (ed), *Dear Sun: The Letters of Joy Hester and Sunday Reed.* Port Melbourne Victoria: William Heinemann Australia 1995.

Burt, Warren, 'If it works, it's wonderful' (interview with Pierre Boulez), *Meanjin,* 2, Winter 1988, pp.253–265.

Bushell, Garvin, *Jazz From the Beginning.* Oxford: Bayou Press 1988.

Cameron, Barbara, 'The Flappers and the Feminists', in Margaret Bevege, Margaret James, Carmel Shute (eds), *Worth Her Salt: Women at Work in Australia.* Sydney: Hale & Iremonger 1982, pp.257–269.

Carey, Hilary M., *Believing in Australia: a cultural history of religions.* St Leonards: Allen & Unwin 1996.

Carlsson, Susanne Chauvel, *Charles and Elsa Chauvel: Movie Pioneers.* St Lucia, Queensland: University of Queensland Press 1989.

Carr, Ian, Digby Fairweather and Brian Priestley, *Jazz: The Essential Companion.* London: Paladin, Grafton Books 1990.

Carr-Boyd, Ann, 'Australia', in H. Ryker (ed), *New Music in the Orient: Essays on Composition in Asia since World War IL* Buren, The Netherlands: Frits Knuf Publishers 1991, pp.49–60.

Centre for Studies in Australian Music, *Register of Theses on Australian Music.* Melbourne: Centre for Studies in Australian Music 1996.

Chailley, Jacques, *40,000 Years of Music: Man in Search of Music,* trans Rollo Myers. London: Macdonald 1964.

Chauvel, Charles, Shooting Script for *Greenhide,* held by ScreenSound Australia, formerly the National Film and Sound Archive, NFA 221.

Chester, Andrew, 'Second Thoughts on a Rock Aesthetic: The Band', *New Left Review,* 62, 1970, pp.73–82.

Chevigny, Paul, *Gigs: Jazz and the Cabaret Laws in New York City.* New York/ London: Routledge 1991.

Chilton, John, *Sidney Bechet: The Wizard of Jazz.* London, Basingstoke: Macmillan 1987.

Clare, John, aka Gail Brennan, *Bodgie, Dada and the Cult of Cool.* Kensington NSW: UNSW Press 1995.

Clark, TJ, 'Clement Greenberg's Theory of Art' in Francis Frascina (ed), *Pollock and After: The Critical Debate.* London: Harper & Row 1985, pp.47–63.

Clunies-Ross, Bruce, 'An Australian Sound: jazz in Melbourne and Adelaide 1941–51', in P. Spearritt and D. Walker. (eds), *Australian Popular Culture,* North Sydney: George Allen & Unwin 1979.

Clunies-Ross, Bruce, 'Dave Dallwitz & Australian Jazz: A Reply to Mr. Linehan,' *Jazz: The Australasian Contemporary Music Magazine,* May/June 1983, pp.6–8.

Cohen, Sara, *Rock Culture in Liverpool: popular music in the making.* Oxford: Clarendon Press 1991.

Collins, Diane, 'The Movie Octopus', in P. Spearritt & D. Walker (eds) *Australian Popular Culture,* Sydney: George Allen & Unwin 1979, pp. 102–120.

Commonwealth Government of Australia, *Creative Nation: Commonwealth Cultural Policy October 1994.* Canberra: National Capital Printing 1994.

Copeland, Peter, *Sound Recordings.* London: British Library 1991.

Cottle, Drew, 'Dancing Out The Depression: The Sydney Trocadero's earliest years, 1936–39', *New Music Articles (NMA),* 3, 1984, pp.38–40.

Covell, Roger, *Australia's Music: Themes for a New Society.* Melbourne: Sun Books 1967.

Crafts, Susan D., Daniel Cavicchi, Charles Keil, *My Music.* Hanover New Hampshire: Wesleyan University Press 1993.

Crisp, Deborah, *Bibliography of Australian Music: an index to monographs, journal articles and theses,* Australian Music Studies 1. Armidale 1982.

Croft, Julian, 'Responses to Modernism, 1915–1965' in Laurie Hergenhan (ed), *The Penguin New Literary History of Australia.* Ringwood Vic: Penguin 1988, pp.409–429.

Crow, Thomas, 'Modernism and mass culture in the visual arts' in Francis Frascina (ed), *Pollock and After: The Critical Debate.* London: Harper & Row 1985, pp.233–66.

Cunningham, Stuart, *Featuring Australia: The Cinema of Charles Chauvel.* North Sydney: Allen & Unwin 1991.

Cusack, Dymphna and Florence James, *Come In Spinner.* London: Heinemann 1951.

Dahlhaus, Carl, *Foundations of Music History,* trans. J.B. Robinson. Cambridge: Cambridge University Press 1983.

Dance, Stanley, *Duke Ellington.* Alexandria, Virginia: Time-Life Records 1978

Dark, Eleanor *The Little Company.* Sydney: Collins 1945.

Davidson, Jim, *A Showman's Story: The Memoirs of Jim Davidson.* Adelaide: Rigby 1983.

de Certeau, Michel, *The Practice of Everyday Life,* trans Steven Rendall. Berkeley: University of California Press 1984.

Dever, Maryanne (ed) *Wallflowers and Witches: Women and Culture in Australia 1910–1945.* St Lucia Qld: University of Queensland Press 1994.

Diller-Anderson, Gae M., *The First twenty-Five Years of Vaudeville at the Sydney Tivoli, 1893–1917: Sexual Difference and the Female Vaudevillian.* Unpub. Diss., MA (Hons), University of New South Wales 1991.

Dorůžka, Lubomír, 'Jazz in Czechoslovakia: 1945–1993'. Unpub. paper delivered in Darmstadt, Autumn 1993.

Dorůžka, Lubomír, Extract from Unpub. paper delivered in Lugano, March 1993.

Douglas, Louise, *Truckin' at the Troc.* Unpub. Diss., Macquarie University, NSW, 1983.

Dreyfuss, Kay, *Sweethearts of Rhythm: The story of Australia's all-girl bands and orchestras to the end of the second world war.* Sydney: Currency Press 1999.

Drummond, Philip J., *Australian Directory of Music Research.* Sydney: Australia Music Centre 1978.

Dunbar-Hall, Peter, *Strella Wilson: The Career of an Australian Singer.* Chatswood NSW: Redback Press 1997.

Eagle, Mary, 'Modernism in Sydney in the 1920s', in Ann Galbally and Margaret Plant (eds), *Studies in Australian Art,* Melbourne 1978.

Easthope, Anthony, *Literary into Cultural Studies.* London and New York: Routledge 1991, p.79.

Ehrlich, Cyril, *The Piano: A History*. London: JM Dent & Sons Ltd 1976.

Eisenberg, Evan, *The Recording Angel: Explorations in Phonography*. New York: McGraw Hill 1987 (Note: the same text is published as *The Recording Angel: Music, Records and Culture from Aristotle to Zappa*. London: Picador, 1988, with a different ISBN no).

Feather, Leonard, *The New Edition of The Encyclopedia of Jazz*. NY: Horizon Press 1960.

Ferres, Kay, 'How to be a singer though married', in Ian Craven (ed), *Australian Popular Culture*. Melbourne: Oxford University Press 1994, pp. 149–160.

Finnegan, Ruth, *The Hidden Musicians: music-making in an English town*. Cambridge: Cambridge University Press 1989.

Fiske, John, *Reading the Popular*. Boston: Unwin Hyman 1989.

Fiske, John, *Understanding Popular Culture*. Boston: Unwin Hyman 1989.

Frascina, Francis (ed), *Pollock and After: The Critical Debate*. London: Harper & Row 1985.

Ford, Joan, *Meet me at the Trocadero*. Cowra NSW: Joan Ford 1995.

Foster, Roland, *Come Listen to My Song*. London, Sydney: Collins 1949, p.34.

Frith, Simon, 'Art versus technology: the strange case of popular music', *Media, Culture and Society*, 8/3, July 1986, pp.263–79.

Frith, Simon, 'The Industrialisation of Popular Music', in James Lull (ed), *Popular Music and Communication*. Newbury Park, Beverly Hills, London, New Delhi: Sage Publications 1987, pp.53–77.

Furia, Philip, *The Poets of Tin Pan Alley: A History of America's Great Lyricists*. New York, Oxford: Oxford University Press 1990; the 1992 edition used here.

Geitenbeck, Monique, 'The Role of Women in the Australian Music Examinations Board from 1930 to 1950', in Nicholas Brown et al (eds), *One Hand on the Manuscript: Music in Australian Cultural History 1930–1960*. Canberra: Humanities Research Centre Monograph Series No. 9, Australian National University 1995, pp 189–200.

Gelatt, Roland, *The Fabulous Phonograph 1877–1977*, Second Revised Edition. New York & London: Collier Macmillan 1977.

Gerstner, Robin, 'War Literature, 1890–1980', in Laurie Hergenhan (ed), *The Penguin New Literary History of Australia*. Ringwood Vic: Penguin 1988, pp.337–352.

Godbolt, Jim, *All This and 10%*. London: Robert Hale 1976.

Godbolt, Jim, *A History of Jazz in Britain 1919–50*. London: Quartet 1984.

Goddard, Chris, *Jazz Away From Home*. New York and London: Paddington Press 1979.

Goodall, Peter, *High Culture, Popular Culture: The Long Debate.* St Leonards NSW: Allen & Unwin 1995.

Greenberg, Clement, 'Avant-Garde and Kitsch', in Francis Frascina (ed), *Pollock and After: The Critical Debate.* London: Harper & Row 1985, pp.21–33.

Greenberg, Clement, 'Towards a Newer Laocoon', in Francis Frascina (ed), *Pollock and After: The Critical Debate.* London: Harper & Row 1985, pp.35–46.

Greenwood, Kerry, *The Green Mill Murder.* Ringwood Vic: McPhee Gribble 1993. Haese, Richard, *Rebels and Precursors: The Revolutionary Years in Australian Art.* Ringwood Vic: Penguin 1981.

Hale, Patricia, 'The Dancing Years: Popular Dancing and the Trocadero', *Public History Review,* 1997, pp. 99–115.

Hall, Richard, 'White Australia's Darkest Days', *Sydney Morning Herald Good Weekend,* March 15 1997, pp.[17]-23.

Harris, Max, *The Angry Eye.* Potts Point NSW: Pergamon Press 1973.

Harris, Rex, *Jazz.* Harmondsworth, Middlesex: Penguin 1952.

Harrison, Charles and Paul Wood (eds), *Art in Theory 1900–1990: An Anthology of Changing Ideas.* Oxford UK and Cambridge USA: Blackwell 1992.

Haskins, Jim, *The Cotton Club.* New York: Random House 1977.

Hasse, John (ed), *Ragtime: its History, Composers and Music.* London: Macmillan 1985.

Hawkins, Gay, *From Nimbin to Mardi Gras: constructing community arts.* St Leonards, NSW: Allen & Unwin 1993.

Hayes, Mileham, Ray Scribner and Peter Magee, *The Encyclopedia of Australian Jazz.* No publisher, place or date listed; it appeared in 1976.

Heath, Leslie, *Sydney Literary Societies of the Nineteen Twenties: Cultural Nationalism and the Promotion of Australian Literature.* Unpub Doctoral Diss, Schools of English and History, University of NSW 1996.

Heathcote, Christopher, *A Quiet Revolution: The Rise of Australian Art 1946–1968.* Melbourne: The Text Publishing Company 1995.

Holmes, Katie, '"Diamonds of the Dustheap"? women's diary writing between the wars', in Maryanne Dever (ed) *Wallflowers and Witches: Women and Culture in Australia 1910–1945.* St Lucia Qld: University of Queensland Press 1994, pp.38–48.

Hoorn, Jeanette, 'Misogyny and Modernist Painting in Australia: How Male Critics Made Modernism Their Own', *Journal of Australian Studies,* 32, March 1992, pp.7–17.

Hoorn, Jeanette, (ed), *Strange Women: Essays in Art and Gender.* Carlton Vic: Melbourne University Press 1994.

Horkheimer, Max and Theodore Adorno, *The Dialectic of Enlightenment,* trans John Cumming: NY: Continuum Press 1972.

Hoskings, Reg, 'Collecting Jazz Records—the 78 Era', *Australian Record and Music Review* 11, October 1991, pp. 10–11.

Huyssen, Andreas, *After the Great Divide: Modernism, Mass Culture, Postmodernism.* Indianapolis: Indiana University Press 1986.

Johnson, Bruce, 'Is There an Australian Jazz?' *Jazz: The Australasian Contemporary Music Magazine* Part 1, December 1981, pp.6–8; Part II, February 1982, pp.20–23.

Johnson, Bruce, 'Dave Dallwitz and the Southern Jazz Group' *Jazz: The Australasian Contemporary Music Magazine* Part 1, March/April 1982, pp.10–13; Part 2, May/June 1982, pp.10–13; Part 3, August 1982, pp.10–13.

Johnson, Bruce, 'Traditional Jazz in Australia', *Jazz: The Australasian Contemporary Music Magazine,* December 1982, pp.4–6.

Johnson, Bruce, 'Graeme Bell At Seventy', *Jazz: The Australasian Contemporary Music Magazine,* Winter/Spring 1984, pp.8–11.

Johnson, Bruce, 'Bruce Johnson Comments', *Jazz: The Australasian Contemporary Music Magazine,* Summer/Autumn 1986, pp.26–27.

Johnson, Bruce, *The Oxford Companion to Australian Jazz.* Melbourne: Oxford University Press 1987.

Johnson, Bruce, 1992A 'Orality and jazz education', *New Music Articles.* 10, 1992, pp.39–43, 46.

Johnson, Bruce, 1992B 'The Great Divide—Australian Traditional Jazz and the Academies', *Journal of Australian Studies,* 34, September 1992, 32–42.

Johnson, Bruce, 1992C 'Jazz: A Test Case for Popular Music in the Australian Academies', *Institute of Popular Music Occasional Paper 3.* Liverpool: University of Liverpool 1992.

Johnson, Bruce and Mike Sutcliffe, 'Barbara James: a career in Australian popular music', *Australasian Drama Studies,* 21, October 1992.

Johnson, Bruce, 'Hear Me Talkin' To Ya: problems of jazz discourse', *Popular Music,* 12/1, January 1993, pp.1–12.

Johnson, Bruce, 'Art, Jazz and Uncle Tom's Cabin', *Jazzchord,* 13, May/June 1993, p.8.

Johnson, Bruce, 'Klactoveesedstene—Music, Soundscape and Me' in Helmi Järviluoma (ed) *Soundscapes: Essays on Vroom and Moo.* Finland: Dept of Folk Tradition, University of Tampere 1994, pp.39–47.

Johnson, Bruce (1995A), 'Jazz and the Cultural politics of Australian Music', *Context,* 10, Summer 1995, pp. 11–26.

Johnson, Bruce, 'The Production and Consumption of Jazz in Live Performance in Australia', *Jazzchord* 25, Jun/Jul 1995, pp.6–7.

Johnson, Bruce, 'Australian Jazz in Post-war Europe: a case study in musical displacement', *Perfect Beat—The Pacific Journal of Research into Contemporary Music and Popular Culture,* 2/3, July 1995, pp.49–64.

Johnson, Bruce, 'Towards a new cartography: rethinking Australia's music history' in Nicholas Brown et al (eds), *One Hand on the Manuscript: Music in Australian Cultural history 1930–60*. Canberra: The Humanities Research Centre 1995 pp.243–257.

Johnson, Bruce, 'The Music Industry: Selling Empty Boxes', *Realtime*, 9, October-November 1995, p.15.

Johnson, Bruce, 'Resituating Improvisation', *Journal of Improvisational Practice*, 2/1, 1996, pp.6–11.

Johnson, Bruce, 'In the Jumble, the Genre Jumble: the prison house of popular music discourse'. Unpub Paper delivered at *Rock as a Research Field* Symposium, University of Aarhus, Denmark, 4–10 April 1997. A version on-line as 'Watching the Watchers' under Archive link: www.arts.unsw.edu.au/jazz/.

Johnson, Bruce, 'Doctored Jazz—Early Australian Jazz Journals', *Perfect Beat: the Pacific journal of research into contemporary music and popular culture*, 3/4, January 1998, pp.26–37.

Jonas, Gerald, *Dancing: The Power of Dance Around the World*. London: BBC Books 1992.

Jones, Steve, *Rock Formation: Music, Technology, and Mass Communication*, Foundations of Popular Culture 3. Newbury Park, London, New Delhi: Sage Publications 1992.

Kater, Michael, *Different Drummers: Jazz in the Culture of Nazi Germany*. New York: Oxford University Press 1992.

Kay, Brad, sleeve note to *Reflections in Ellington: The 1932 band in true stereo, and on the road with the great 1940 band*. Everybodys EV-3005. 1985.

Keepnews, Orin and Bill Grauer, *A Pictorial History of Jazz*. UK: Spring Books, New Revised Edition 1966.

Keil, Charles and Steven Feld, *Music Grooves*. Chicago: University of Chicago Press 1994.

Keil, Charles, 'The Theory of Participatory Discrepancies: a Progress Report', *Ethnomusicology: Journal of the Society for Ethnomusicology*, 39/1, Winter 1995, pp.1–19.

Keil, Charles and J.A. Prögler, 'Rejoinders', *Ethnomusicology: Journal of the Society for Ethnomusicology*, 39/1, Winter 1995, pp.97–104.

Kerman, Joseph, *Musicology*, London: Collins 1985.

Kermode, Frank, 'Poet and Dancer before Diaghilev' in *Modern Essays*. Great Britain: Fontana 1971.

Kernfeld, Barry (ed), *The New Grove Dictionary of Jazz*. Vols 1 & 2. London & New York: Macmillan 1988.

Kirkpatrick, Peter, *The Sea Coast of Bohemia: Literary Life in Sydney's Roaring Twenties*. Queensland: Queensland University Press 1992.

Kramer, Lawrence, *Music as Cultural Practice.* Berkeley, Los Angeles, London: University of California Press 1990.

Leppert, Richard and Susan McClary (eds), *Music and Society: the politics of composition, performance and perception.* Cambridge: Cambridge University Press 1987.

Levine, Lawrence W, *Highbrow/Lowbrow: The Emergence of Cultural Hierarchy in America.* Cambridge Massachusetts: Harvard University Press 1988.

Lewis, Laurie, *Arthur and the Nights at the Turntable: The Life and Times of a Jazz Broadcaster* First pub. London: Excalibur Press 1996; this edition, Wingen NSW: K'Vrie Press 1997.

Lewis, Peter, *The Fifties: Portrait of a Period* [On the title page: *Portrait of an Age*]. London: Cupid Press 1989.

Lewis, T, *Empire of the Air: The men who made radio.* New York: Edward Burlingame 1991.

Linehan, Norman, 'Dave Dallwitz: The Creation of a Myth', *Jazz: The Australasian Contemporary Music Magazine,* January/February 1983, pp.20–21.

Lomax, Alan, *Mister Jelly Roll.* New York: Duell, Sloan and Pearce 1950.

Lyttelton, Humphrey, *I Play As I Please: The Memoirs of an Old Etonian Trumpeter.* London: MacGibbon & Kee 1954.

Mackay, Mary, 'Almost Dancing: Thea Proctor and the modern woman', in Maryanne Dever (ed), *Wallflowers and Witches: Women and Culture in Australia 1910–1945.* Queensland: University of Queensland Press 1994, pp.26–37.

Mangan, Kathleen, *Daisy Chains, War, then Jazz.* Hawthorn Vic: Hutchinson of Australia 1984.

Maróthy, János, *Music and the Bourgeois, Music and the Proletarian.* trans Eva Rona. Budapest: Akadémiai Kiadó 1974.

Matthews, Jill Julius, 'Dancing modernism', in Barbara Caine & Rosemary Pringle (eds), *Transitions: New Australian feminisms.* St Leonards NSW: Allen & Unwin 1995, pp. 74–87.

McCardell, Terry, *Jazz Speaks All Languages.* Sydney: Australian Jazz Convention Trust Fund 1985.

McClary, Susan, *Feminine Endings: Music, Gender and Sexuality.* Minneapolis: University of Minnesota Press 1991.

McCorquodale, Phyllis, *The Lure of the Dance: some aspects of ballroom dancing in Australia in the inter-war years.* Unpub Hons Diss, School of History, University of New South Wales 1985.

McCredie, Andrew, *Musical Compositions in Australia, including select bibliography and discography.* Canberra: Australian Government Printing Office 1969.

Megaw, M. Ruth, '"Happy Ever After"; the image of women in four Australian feature films of the Nineteen Twenties', *Journal of Australian Studies*, 7, November 1980, pp.55–71.

Melly, George, *Owning Up*. Harmondsworth Middlesex: Penguin 1970.

Melman, Billie, *Women and the Popular Imagination in the Twenties: Flappers and Nymphs*. New York: St Martin's Press 1988.

Middleton, Richard, *Studying Popular Music*. Buckingham: Open University Press 1990.

Mitchell, Jack, 'Jazz, Art and the Communist Party', *Jazz: The Australasian Contemporary Music Magazine*, Winter/Spring 1985, pp. 16–18.

Mitchell, Jack, *Australian Jazz on Record 1925–80*. Canberra: Australian Government Publishing Service 1988.

Mitchell, Jack, 'Graeme Bell in Europe 1947–1948: Recordings Known, and Radio Broadcasts Which May Have Been Recorded', *Australian Record and Music Review*, 16, January 1993, pp.14–17.

Mitchell, Jack, *More Australian Jazz on Record*. Canberra: Australian Government Publishing Service 1998.

Mitchell, Tony, *Popular Music and Local Identity: Rock, Pop and Rap in Europe and Oceania*. London and New York: Leicester University Press 1996.

Munn, H.O., *The Story of the Original Dixieland Jazz Band*. Louisiana: Louisiana State University Press 1960.

Murdoch, James, *Australia's Contemporary Composers*. South Melbourne and North Sydney: Macmillan 1972.

Murray, Scott, *Australian Cinema*. St Leonards NSW: Allen & Unwin/ Australian Film Commission 1994.

[Myers, Eric], 'Dave Dallwitz' in the *Australian Composers* series. Sydney: Australia Music Centre 1981; see also Australia Music Centre.

Myers, Eric, 'An Interview with Geoff Bull', *Jazz: The Australasian Contemporary Music Magazine*, December 1981, pp. 18–21.

Myers, Eric, 'Errol Buddle: A New Era', *Jazz: The Australasian Contemporary Music Magazine*, August 1982, pp.4–8.

Myers, Eric, 'Errol Buddle: Some earlier eras', *Jazz: The Australasian Contemporary Music Magazine*, October 1982, pp.20–23.

Myers, Eric, 'Errol Buddle and the AJQ' *Jazz: The Australasian Contemporary Music Magazine*, January/February 1983, pp.22–26.

Myers, Eric, 'Eric Myers writes', *Jazzchord* 19, May/June 1994, p.5.

Myers, Eric (ed), *Australian Jazz Directory*. Sydney: Jazz Co-ordination Association of NSW Inc, First Edition 1994, Second Edition 1998.

Nanry, Charles, 'Jazz and Modernism: Twin-born Children of the Age of Invention', *Annual Review of Jazz Studies*, I, 1982, pp.146–154.

Nehring, Neil, *Popular Music, Gender, and Postmodernism: Anger is an Energy.* Thousand Oaks California, London, New Delhi: Sage Publications 1997.

Ohmann, Richard, *Selling Culture: Magazines, Markets, and Class at the Turn of the Century.* London, Verso 1996.

Page, Geoff, *Winter Vision.* Queensland: University of Queensland Press 1989.

Pearsall, Ronald, *Popular Music of the Twenties.* Totowa NJ: Roman & Littlefield 1976.

Philp, Angela, 'From Wallflowers to Tall Poppies? The Sydney Society of Women Painters, 1910–1934', in Maryanne Dever (ed), *Wallflowers and Witches: Women and Culture in Australia 1910–1945.* Queensland: University of Queensland Press 1994, pp.1–12.

Pigot, J., '"Decadent, Savage and Primitive": Hilda Rix Nichols and Modernism', *Journal of Australian Studies*, 32, March 1992, pp.26–33.

Pike, Andrew & Ross Cooper, *Australian Film 1900–1977: A Guide to Feature Film Production.* Melbourne: Oxford University Press 1980.

Pleasants, Henry, *The Agony of Modern Music.* New York: Simon & Schuster 1955.

Pleasants, Henry, *The Great American Popular Singers.* New York: Simon & Schuster 1974.

Poole, Gaye, *The Big Day: Scoring the Wedding.* Unpub. paper presented at the 6th Annual Conference of the International Association for the Study of Popular Music, Australian/New Zealand, Adelaide, June 1998.

Potter, John, *Vocal Authority: Singing Style and Ideology.* Cambridge: Cambridge University Press 1998.

Potts, Donald and Annette Potts, *Yanks Downunder 1941–5: the American Impact on Australia.* Melbourne: Oxford University Press 1985.

Potts, John, *Radio in Australia.* Kensington NSW: University of New South Wales Press 1989.

Pressing, Jeff, 'The Micro- and Macrostructural Design of Improvised Music', *Music Perception*, 5/2, 1987, pp. 132–72.

Prögler, J.A., 'Searching for Swing: Participatory Discrepancies in the Jazz Rhythm Section', *Ethnomusicology: Journal of the Society for Ethnomusicology*, 39/1, Winter 1995, pp.21–54.

Pumphrey, Martin, 'The Flapper, the Housewife and the Making of Modernity', *Cultural Studies*, 1/2, May 1989, pp. 179–84.

Quirey, Belinda, *May I Have The Pleasure? The story of popular dancing.* London: Dance Books 1987.

Reis, Brian, *Australian Film: A Bibliography.* London & Washington: Mansell 1997.

Rickard, John, 'Music and Cultural Hierarchy', in Nicholas Brown et al (eds), *One Hand on the Manuscript: Music in Australian Cultural History 1930–1960*. Canberra: The Humanities Research Centre 1995, pp. 181–8.

Rimsky-Korsakov, Nikolay, *Principles of Orchestration, with musical examples drawn from his own works*, trans Edward Agate. New York: Dover Publications, Inc 1964.

[Rix, Peter?], *Contemporary Music Summit: Report on the Contemporary Music Summit for the Minister for Communications and the Arts, Michael Lee*. Canberra: Dept of Communications and the Arts 1995.

Rowse, Tim, *Arguing the Arts: the finding of the arts in Australia*. Ringwood Vic: Penguin 1985.

Sabine, James, *A Century of Australian Cinema*. Port Melbourne: William Heinemann Australia 1995.

Sadie, Stanley (ed), *The Norton/Grove Concise Encyclopedia of Music*. New York and London: WW. Norton & Co 1994.

Sayer, Mandy, *Mood Indigo*. Sydney: Allen & Unwin 1990.

Schafer, R. Murray, *The Tuning of the World*. Toronto: McLelland & Stewart 1977.

Scher, Steven Paul, *Music and Text: Critical Enquiries*. Cambridge: Cambridge University Press 1992.

Schuller, Gunther, *Early Jazz: Its Roots And Musical Development*. New York & Oxford: Oxford University Press 1968.

Schwartz, Elliot and Daniel Godfrey, *Music Since 1945: Issues, Materials and Literature*. New York: Schirmer/Macmillan 1993.

Seeger, Charles, *Studies in Musicology 1937–75*. Berkeley and Los Angeles: University of California Press 1977.

Shapiro, Nat and Nat Hentoff, *Hear Me Talkin' To Ya: The Story of Jazz by the Men Who Made It*. London: Peter Davies 1955.

Shepherd, John, *Music as Social Text*. Cambridge: Polity Press 1991.

Škvorecký, Joseph, *The Bass Saxophone*. Toronto: Lester & Orpen Denny 1980.

Škvorecký, Joseph, *Talkin' Moscow Blues*, ed Sam Solecki. London: Faber & Faber edition 1989.

Starr, S. Frederick, *Red and Hot: The Fate of Jazz in the Soviet Union 1917–1980*. New York/Oxford: Oxford University Press 1983.

Stedman-Jones, G., 'Working-Class Culture and Working-Class Politics in London, 1870–1900: Notes on the Remaking of a Working Class', *Journal of Social History*, VII, Summer 1974, pp.460–508.

Stein, Harry, 'If Those Walls Could Only Speak', *Jazz: The Australasian Contemporary Music Magazine*, Winter/Spring 1985, pp.22–26.

Stein, Harry, *A Glance Over an Old Left Shoulder*. Sydney: Hale & Iremonger 1994.

Stokes, Martin, (ed), *Ethnicity, Identity and Music: The Musical Construction of Place.* Oxford/Providence USA: Berg 1994.

Strinati, Dominic, *An Introduction to Theories of Popular Culture.* London & New York: Routledge 1995.

Struthers, Steven, 'Technology in the art of recording' in Avron White (ed) *Lost in Music: Culture, Style and the Musical Event,* Sociological Review Monograph 34. London & NY: Routledge & Kegan Paul 1987, pp.241–258.

[Sutcliffe, Mike], 'Australians Overseas: The Three Australian Boys', *Australian Record and Music Review,* 1, April 1989, p.2.

[Sutcliffe, Mike], 'The Australian Hot Jazz Classics', *Australian Record and Music Review,* 6, July 1990, pp.11–13.

[Sutcliffe, Mike], 'The Career of Clarrie Collins', *Australian Record and Music Review,* 7, October 1990, pp.3–10.

[Sutcliffe, Mike], 'Des Tooley', *Australian Record and Music Review,* 8, January 1991, pp.8–13.

[Sutcliffe, Mike], 'The Career of Abe Walters', *Australian Record and Music Review,* 9, April 1991, pp.3–12.

[Sutcliffe, Mike], 'Artie Shaw in Australia', *Australian Record and Music Review,* 13, April 1991, pp.3–8.

[Sutcliffe, Mike], 'The Career of Abe Romain', *Australian Record and Music Review,* 19, October 1993, pp.3–13.

[Sutcliffe Mike], 'The Red Arrows', *Australian Record and Music Review,* 20, January 1994, p.20.

[Sutcliffe, Mike], 'Jazz on Record', *Australian Record and Music Review,* 24, January 1995, pp.20–2.

[Sutcliffe, Mike], 'Tony Newstead in the USA' *Australian Record and Music Review,* 25, April 1995, pp.20–21.

[Sutcliffe, Mike], 'American Servicemen musicians in Australia 1942–1945', *Australian Record and Music Review* 28, January 1996, pp. 15–16.

[Sutcliffe, Mike], 'Australian Jazz Compositions' Part 3, *Australian Record and Music Review,* 32, January 1997, p.22.

[Sutcliffe Mike], 'Sonny Clay and the Coloured Idea', *Australian Record and Music Review,* 35, October 1997, pp.3–13.

Tagg, Philip, *Kojak: 50 Seconds of Television Music—Towards the Analysis of Affect in Popular Music.* Unpub. Diss, University of Göteborg 1979.

Tagg, Philip, 'Musicology and the Semiotics of Popular Music', *Semiotica,* 66, 1/3, 1987, pp.279–298.

Tagg, Philip, 'Music for Moving Pictures: Academia, Education and Independent Thought'. Unpub. Paper, Colloquium *Musica e Cinema,* Siena, August 1990.

Tagg, Philip, 'Towards a Sign Typology of Music', in R. Dalmonte (ed),

Secondo Convegno Europeo di Analisi Musicale. University of Trento 1992, pp.369–378.

Tagg, Philip, 'From Refrain to Rave: The Decline of Figure and the Rise of Ground', published in *Popular Music* 1994, also online at www.liv.ac.uk/ipm/tagg/taggwbtx.htm.

Théberge, Paul, *Any Sound You Can Imagine: Making Music/Consuming Technology.* Hanover, New Hampshire: Wesleyan University Press 1997.

Topliss, Helen, *Modernism and Feminism: Australian Women Artists 1900–1940.* Roseville East NSW: Craftsman House 1996.

Tulloch, John, *Legends on the Screen: The Australian Narrative Cinema 1919–1929.* Sydney: Currency Press 1981.

Turner, Bruce, *Hot Air, Cool Music.* London: Quartet 1984.

Turner, Graeme, *Making it National: Nationalism and Australian Popular Culture.* St Leonards NSW: Allen & Unwin 1994.

Van Der Merwe, Peter, *Origins of the Popular Style: The antecedents of Twentieth Century Popular Music.* Oxford University Press 1989.

Varnedoe, Kirk and Adam Gopnik, *High and Low, Modern Art and Popular Culture.* New York: The Museum of Modern Art 1991.

Varney, Jack, *Zing Went The Strings—Tales of a City Slicker.* Unpub. memoir, ca 1993.

Vine, Carl, 'Art for Whose Sake?', *ABC Radio 24 Hours,* August 1993, pp.44–50.

Walker, David, 'Introduction', P. Spearritt & D. Walker (eds), *Australian Popular Culture.* Sydney: George Allen & Unwin 1979, pp.1–16.

Walter, James, 'Controlling the Technology of Popular Culture: The Introduction of Television in Australia' in Ian Craven (ed), *Australian Popular Culture.* Cambridge, New York, Melbourne: Cambridge University Press 1994, pp.66–78.

Waterhouse, Richard, *From Minstrel Show to Vaudeville: The Australian Popular Stage 1788–1914.* Kensington: NSW University Press 1990.

Waterhouse, Richard, *Private Pleasures, Public Leisure: A History of Australian Popular Culture Since 1788.* South Melbourne: Longman 1995.

Whiteoak, John, *Early Modern Jazz in Australia: The Introduction of Bop* Unpub. Honours Diss, Dept of Music, La Trobe University, Vic 1986.

Whiteoak, John, 'Robert Rooney and the McKimm/Rooney/Clayton Music Collaboration: Melbourne, 1960s', in Jenepher Duncan and Merryn Gates (eds), *From the Homefront: Robert Rooney Works 1953–1988.*

Clayton Vic: Monash University Gallery, Monash University 1990, pp. 15–21.

Whiteoak, John, 'From Jim Crow to Jazz—Imitation African-American Improvisatory Musical Practices in Pre-Jazz Australia', *Perfect Beat—The Pacific Journal of Research into Contemporary Music and Popular Culture,* 1/3, July 1993, pp.50–74.

Whiteoak, John, *Australian Approaches to Improvisatory Musical Practice 1836–1970: A Melbourne Perspective.* Unpub. Diss, Ph.D., Dept of Music, La Trobe University September 1993.

Whiteoak, John, *Playing Ad Lib: Improvisatory Music in Australia 1836–1970.* Sydney: Currency Press 1999.

Williams, Alistair, *New Music and the Claims of Modernity.* Aldershot England: Ashgate Publishing 1997.

Williams, John F., *Quarantined Culture: Australian Reactions to Modernism 1913–1939.* Melbourne: Cambridge University Press 1995.

Willis, Anne-Marie, *Illusions of Identity: The Art of Nation.* Sydney: Hale & Iremonger 1993.

Willis, Paul, with Simon Jones, Joyce Canaan, Geoff Hurd, *Common Culture: Symbolic work at play in the everyday cultures of the young.* Milton Keynes: Open University Press, reprint of 1996.

Wilmer, Valerie, *As Serious As Your Life: The Story of the New Jazz.* Melbourne, New York, London: Quartet 1977.

Winter, Jay, *Sites of Memory, Sites of Mourning: The Great War in European Cultural History.* Cambridge: Cambridge University Press 1995.

Wolff, Janet, *Aesthetics and the Sociology of Art.* (London: Macmillan, Second Edition 1993.

Wolff, Leon, *In Flanders Fields: The 1917 Campaign.* London: Longmans, Green & Co, 1960 edition for Readers Union.

Primary Source Journals (Australian*)

* *Angry Penguins Broadsheet*

* *Australasian Band and Orchestra News*

* *Australian Dance Band News*

* *Australian Music Maker*

* *Australian Music Maker and Dance Band News*

Cadence (United States)

Coda (United States)

Down Beat (United Stares)

* *Everyones*

* *Graphic*

Jazz (Czechoslovakia)

**Jazzchord*

Jazz Forum (United States)

* *Listener In*

* *Melbourne Argus*

* *Melbourne Truth*

Melody Maker & Rhythm (UK)

Mladá Fronta (Czechoslovakia)

* *Music Trader*

MY 47 (Czechoslovakia)

* *Quarterly Rag*

Ohlas (Czechoslovakia)

Osvobozeny (Czechoslovakia)

* *Radio Call*

* *Soundblast*

Svobodné Slovo (Czechoslovakia)

* *Sydney Morning Herald*

* *Table Talk*

* *Victorian Dance News*

Correspondence (With The Author*)

Bell, Graeme, to Dick (surname not known) January 20 1948

* Davies, J.R.T. August 24 1984

* Dorůžka, L. January 22 1994

* Dorůžka, L. March 11 1994

* Dorůžka, L. August 14 1994

* Lyttelton, H. July 31 1984

* Novotny, Otaker, November 6 1994

* Sedlak, P. Undated; received in February 1994 in Tampere, Finland

* Škvorecký, J. November 12 1993

* Stewart-Baxter, D. August 22 1984

* Šváb, Ludwig, March 14 1994

Interviews

Bailey, Judy, with Bruce Johnson (notes) Sydney 20/2/98

Banks, Don, *De Berg Tapes* (National Library, 1972)

Bell, Graeme: The most substantial, generating an eleven-page transcription, was conducted in Sydney, June 22 1984. I have referred in passing also to a discussion dated at April 11 1994, and additionally to the following:

Bell, Graeme: tape-recorded responses to a set of questions submitted by Czech researcher Anna Tousikova, December 21 1993.

Brown, Brian, with Bruce Johnson (recorded) Melbourne 24/7/91

Connor, David, with Bruce Johnson (notes) Sydney March 1998

Crichton, Pat, with Bruce Johnson (notes) Perth 13/8/91

Dorůžka, Lubomír, with Bruce Johnson (notes), Prague January 1997

Dunbar, Kate, with Bruce Johnson (notes) Sydney 20/3/98

Falk, Susan, with Bruce Johnson (notes) Sydney March 1998

James, Barbara, with Lyn Markham (broadcast on 20/4/85 on ABC's *The Coming Out Show*)

James, Barbara, with Mike Sutcliffe (recorded) Sydney 22/5/92

James, Barbara, with Bruce Johnson (recorded) Sydney 25/6/93

James, Barbara, with Bruce Johnson (notes of telephone conversation) Sydney 5/12/97

James, Barbara, with Bruce Johnson (recorded) Sydney 9/12/97

James, Barbara, with Bruce Johnson (notes of telephone conversation) Sydney 10/12/97

Klimeš, Miroslav, with Bruce Johnson (notes) Prague, January 1997

Le Doeuff, Maurie, with Bruce Johnson (recorded) Adelaide 7/8/91

Monsbourgh, Adc, with Bruce Johnson (recorded) Melbourne 30/7/91

Opekar, Ales, with Bruce Johnson (notes) Liverpool March 1994, Prague

January 1997, Kanazawa July 1997

Romain, Abe: I have conducted a number of interviews in person and by telephone with Romain, the most relevant being (notes) Sydney 13/1/91

Zajíček, Luboš (notes) Prague January 1997

NOTES

Chapter 1

1 · Arguments about the origin of the word 'jazz' continue. To me the most plausible etymology is, like many terms associated with demotic music including 'rock', immersed in sexual activity. To 'jazz it up' is to make it sexy. Approached phonetically, the title of a song transcribed as 'Jazzin' Babies Blues', acquires a different resonance if it is known that 'Jism' appears to have been an African-American word for semen.

2 · Among the many accounts of Morton's early career, see Gunther Schuller's entry on him in B. Kernfeld (ed), *The New Grove Dictionary of Jazz.* London & New York: Macmillan 1988, Vol.2 pp.136–9; Whitney Balliett, *Jelly Roll, Jabbo & Fats: 19 Portraits in Jazz.* Oxford University Press 1983, pp.16–30. Morton's own reminiscences were recorded for the Library Congress by Alan Lomax, who then adapted them in the book *Mister Jelly Roll.* New York: Duell, Sloan and Pearce 1950.

3 · On the migration to Chicago, see James Lincoln Colliers entry on Jazz in *The New Grove Dictionary of Jazz,* 1988, Vol. 1 p.585; on 'territory' jazz activity, see G. Schuller, *Early Jazz: Its Roots And Musical Development.* New York & Oxford: Oxford University Press 1968, pp.65 ff. Garvin Bushell's *Jazz From the Beginning.* Oxford: Bayou Press 1988, is one of a number of memoirs recording early activity that was arguably jazz outside New Orleans (see esp.p.10). The balance of provincialism and urban sophistication in the encounter between early jazz and the Northern cities is recorded anecdotally throughout the literature of jazz, including N. Shapiro and N. Hentoff, *Hear Me Talkin' To Ya: The Story of Jazz by the Men Who Made It.* London: Peter Davies 1955, Chapt 7.

4 · On minstrelsy in nineteenth century Australia, see Richard Waterhouse, *From Minstrel Show to Vaudeville: The Australian*

Popular Stage 1788–1914. Kensington: NSW University Press 1990.

5 · Andrew Bisset, *Black Roots White Flowers: a history of jazz in Australia*. 2nd ed, Sydney: ABC Enterprises 1987, pp. 13–14.

6 · The band is represented by these two songs, recorded in 1919, on *Steppin on the Gas: Rags to Jazz 1913–1927*, New World Records NW 269

7 · See J. Mitchell & M. Sutcliffe in B. Johnson, *The Oxford Companion to Australian Jazz*. Melbourne: Oxford University Press, 1987 p.72.

8 · Roger Covell, *Australia's Music: Themes for a New Society*. Melbourne: Sun Books 1967, pp.20–1.

9 · Geoffrey Bolton, *Spoils and Spoilers: a history of Australians shaping their environment*. North Sydney: Allen & Unwin, Second Edition 1992, pp 131–2

10 · For amplification of the following see Johnson 1987 pp.1–76. In the light of subsequent scholarship, I now believe my account overstated the unfamiliarity of black American music to Australians. See in particular, Richard Waterhouse 1990. John Whiteoak, in *Playing Ad Lib: Improvisatory Music in Australia 1836–1970* (Sydney, Currency Press 1999), has proposed convincing reconstructions *of* early music improvisational practices in Australia. See also Whiteoak, 'From Jim Crow to Jazz—Imitation African-American Improvisatory Musical Practices in Pre-Jazz Australia', *Perfect Beat—The Pacific Journal of Research into Contemporary Music and Popular Culture*, 1/3 July 1993, pp.50–74.

11 · *Australian Band News*, July 26 1926; Eric Myers (ed), *Australian Jazz Directory 1994*. Sydney: Jazz Co-ordination Association of NSW Inc 1994, pp.36–97.

12 · Presented under the name The Ambassador's *Jazz* Orchestra for a radio broadcast in 1926 (Johnson 1987, p.73; my italics).

13 · *Australian Band News*, July 26 1926.

14 · Frank Coughlan, 'A Short History of Jazz in Australia', *Australian Music Maker and Dance Band News* December 1936, p.7.

15 · Whiteoak, John, *Australian Approaches to Improvisatory Musical Practice 1836–1970: A Melbourne Perspective.* Unpub Diss, Ph.D., Dept of Music, La Trobe University September 1993; p.62. This thesis was the basis of Whiteoaks *Playing Ad Lib,* (1999) which appeared just before this book went into print. I have re-referenced citations to the later work where possible. In the transition from PhD thesis to a book, however, a certain amount of documentation was inevitably edited out, requiring in some instances that I retain the thesis citation.

16 · See further [Mike Sutcliffe] 'Sonny Clay and the Coloured Idea' in *Australian Record and Music Review,* 35, October 1997 pp.3–13, and Richard Hall, 'White Australia's Darkest Days', *Sydney Morning Herald Good Weekend,* 15 March 1997, pp.[17]-23.

17 · See Mitchell and Sutcliffe in Johnson 1987, pp.71–2.

18 · When referring to the style known as 'Swing', I have used the capital 'S' in order to distinguish it from the trans-stylistic verb, 'to swing'.

19 · Jim Davidson, *A Showman's Story: The Memoirs of Jim Davidson.* Adelaide: Rigby 1983, pp.30–31.

20 · Waterhouse, Richard, *Private Pleasures, Public Leisure: A History of Australian Popular Culture Since 1788.* South Melbourne: Longman 1995, p.165.

21 · See further Chapter 6.

22 · Donald Potts and Annette Potts, *Yanks Downunder 1941–5: the American Impact on Australia.* Oxford University Press 1985, pp.29–30.

23 · Jack Varney, *Zing Went The Strings—Tales of a City Slicker* Unpub. Memoir, ca 1993, p.23.

24 · The ambience is vividly conveyed in two novels set in wartime Australia, and, interestingly, both written by women: Eleanor Dark, *The Little Company* and Dymphna Cusack and Florence James, *Come In Spinner.* The literary reflections of the influence of gender in responses to the Americans are briefly adverted to by Robin Gerstner, 'War Literature, 1890–1980', in Laurie

Hergenhan (ed), *The Penguin New Literary History of Australia.* Ringwood Vic: Penguin 1988, p.347.

25 · See further, Johnson 1987, pp.87–90.

26 · The fullest account of this movement is given in his *Graeme Bell Australian Jazzman. His Autobiography.* Frenchs Forest NSW: Child & Associates 1988. See also Harry Stein, *A Glance Over an Old Left Shoulder.* Sydney: Hale & Iremonger 1994.

27 · The Trustees and the Steering Committee of the AJC resist the term 'Festival' in order to deflect the implication of a commercial profit-making venture. I use the term here in its broadest generic sense.

28 · See further Bruce Johnson, 'Doctored Jazz—Early Australian Jazz Journals', *Perfect Beat the Pacific journal of research into contemporary music and popular culture, 3/4* January 1998, pp.26–37.

29 · See further, Johnson 1987, John Clare, aka Gail Brennan, *Bodgie, Dada and the Cult of Cool.* Kensington: UNSW Press 1995.

30 · See Reg Hoskings 'Collecting Jazz Records—the 78 Era', *Australian Record and Music Review,* 11, October 1991, pp. 10–11, and [Mike Sutcliffe], 'Jazz on Record', *Australian Record and Music Review,* 24, January 1995, pp.20–21.

31 · See [Mike Sutcliffe], 'The Australian Hot Jazz Classics', *Australian Record and Music Review,* 6, July 1990, pp. 11–13.

32 · See Marcus Breen, 'Popular Music', in Stuart Cunningham and Graeme Turner (eds), *The Media in Australia: Industries, Texts, Audiences.* St Leonards NSW: Allen & Unwin, 2nd edition 1997, pp. 143–62.

33 · Kernfeld 1988, Vol. 1, p. 580.

34 · On the basis of Statistics of the Military Effort of the British Empire of the Great War (1922), Wolff estimates half a million allied and 270,710 German casualties for the Flanders campaign and Cambrai (Leon Wolff, *In Flanders Fields: The 1917 Campaign.* London: Longmans, Green & Co. 1960 edition for Readers Union, p.210).

35 · Cited by Whiteoak 1999, p. 140.

36 · R. Murray Schafer, *The Tuning of the World.* Toronto: McLelland & Stewart 1977, p.145.

37 · The term 'sonic anaphone' is part of the typology developed by Philip Tagg for the study of 'affect' in music. It can be thought of as the quasi-programmatic 'onomatopoeic' stylisation of 'non-musical' sound, e.g. Schubert's babbling brooks, Baroque opera thunder, William Byrd's bells or Jimi Hendrix's B52'; Philip Tagg, 'Towards a Sign Typology of Music' in R. Dalmonte (ed), *Secondo Convegno Europeo di Analisi Musicale.* University of Trento 1992, pp.369–378. The theoretical and methodological background to this typology was developed notably in his unpublished doctoral dissertation *Kojak: 50 Seconds of Television Music—Towards the Analysis of Affect in Popular Music.* University of Göteborg 1979, and in published summary in 'Musicology and the Semiotics of Popular Music' *Semiotica,* 66 1/3, 1987, pp.279–298.

38 · On Jack Hylton, see Chris Goddard, *Jazz Away From Home.* New York and London: Paddington Press 1979, pp.23–4; on Parnakh, see Nancy Van Norman Baer, *Theatre in Evolution: Russian avant-garde stage design 1913–1935.* London: Thames & Hudson 1991, p.136.

39 · Peter Van Der Merwe, *Origins of the Popular Style: The antecedents of Twentieth Century Popular Music.* Oxford University Press 1989, pp.271–6.

40 · See Whiteoak 1999, p.24.

41 · Richard Middleton, *Studying Popular Music.* Buckingham: Open University Press 1990, p.41.

42 · On 'inadmissable sounds' in modernist music, see below, Chapter Two; in early Australian jazz bands, Johnson 1987, p.4.

43 · Johnson 1987, p.11.

44 · See Whiteoak 1999, pp. 120–1. The topic is developed further in chapters 4 and 5, below.

45 · Furia, Philip, *The Poets of Tin Pan Alley: A History of America's*

Great Lyricists. New York, Oxford: Oxford University Press 1990; the 1992 edition used here. On William Carlos Williams, p. 102; see also the particular example of Porter's 'Anything Goes', p.168; on e.e. cummings, pp.128, 166. As my colleague Dr Peter Kuch pointed out, this converging of interests on the return of the poetic/musical voice to common speech was apparent in other areas, including Irish theatre and poetry from early in the century.

46 · When János Maróthy analyses the rise of the bourgeois ego as reflected in music, he uses as his point of departure the lyrics of Cole Porters 'Night and Day'; János Maróthy *Music and the Bourgeois, Music and the Proletarian,* trans Eva Rona. Budapest: Akadémiai Kiadó 1974, p.43.

47 · See Peter Kirkpatrick, *The Sea Coast of Bohemia: Literary Life in Sydney's Roaring Twenties.* Queensland: Queensland University Press 1992, pp.271–273, 269. The *Australian Musical News* item is quoted in Whiteoak 1999, p.111.

48 · Richard Haese, *Rebels and Precursors: The Revolutionary Years in Australian Art* Penguin, Ringwood Vic 1981, p.3.

49 · The Melbourne *Argus,* 6 September 1924, 22 November 1924.

50 · Norman Lindsay cited in John E Williams, *Quarantined Culture: Australian Reactions to Modernism 1913–1939.* Melbourne: Cambridge University Press 1995, p. 175; Lionel Lindsay cited in Waterhouse 1995, p 140; J.S. MacDonald cited in Haese 1981, p.4. See similarly David Walker in P. Spearritt & D. Walker (eds) *Australian Popular Culture.* Sydney: George Allen & Unwin 1979, p.5.

51 · See for example Johnson 1987, pp.99–103.

52 · See further, chapters 3 and 4, pp.38–98. The connections are confirmed from the side of the visual arts, for example in Haese 1981, pp.72–5. For debate regarding the Communist connection see the following articles in *Jazz: The Australasian Contemporary Music Magazine:* Bruce Johnson 'Graeme Bell At Seventy', Winter/Spring 1984, pp.8–11; Jack Mitchell 'Jazz, Art and the Communist Party' Winter/Spring 1985, pp.16–18; Harry Stein 'If

Those Walls Could Only Speak' pp.22–26, and 'Bruce Johnson Comments', Summer/Autumn 1986, pp.26–27.

53 · See for example Haese 1981, p.238

54 · See 'Introduction' (pp 20, 35, 44) to Janine Burke (ed), *Dear Sun: The Letters of Joy Hester and Sunday Reed.* Port Melbourne: William Heinemann Australia 1995.

55 · Bell 1988, pp.56, 255–6; Christopher Heathcote, *A Quiet Revolution. The Rise of Australian Art 1946–1968.* Melbourne: The Text Publishing Company 1995, pp.158–9.

56 · See [Mike Sutcliffe], Australian Jazz Compositions' Part 3, *Australian Record and Music Review,* 32, January 1997, p.22; Johnson 1984, p.9.

57 · See Bruce Clunies-Ross, An Australian Sound: Jazz in Melbourne and Adelaide, 1941–51', in P. Spearritt & D. Walker (eds) *Australian Popular Culture.* Sydney: George Allen & Unwin, 1979, pp.62–80, and Dean Bruton, *The Contemporary Art Society of South Australia 1942–86: Recollections.* Bedford Park SA: Flinders University 1986.

58 · See for example his article 'Lunching at Smacka's Place' in Max Harris, *The Angry Eye.* Potts Point NSW: Pergamon Press 1973, pp. 13–15.

59 · E.G. Whitlam's 'Introduction' to Scott Murray, *Australian Cinema,* speaks of the 'moribund condition' of the industry between the wars and lasting until the 60s. St Leonards: Allen & Unwin/Australian Film Commission 1994, pp.1–3.

Chapter 2

60 · Marshall Berman, *All That Is Solid Melts Into Air: The Experience of Modernity.* London and New York: Verso, 4th Impression 1989, p. 16; J.F. Williams 1995, pp.16, 18–19.

61 · See for example, Patrick Brantlinger, *Bread and Circuses: Theories of Mass Culture as Social Decay.* Ithaca: Cornell University Press, 1983.

62 · TJ Clark, 'Clement Greenberg's Theory of Art', in Francis

Frascina, *Pollock and After: The Critical Debate.* London: Harper & Row 1985, p.47. Quotes from Greenberg are from the essays published in this collection.

63 · See for example Frascina 1985-

64 · This is abundantly exemplified in Kirk Varnedoe and Adam Gopnik, *High and Low, Modem Art and Popular Culture.* New York: the Museum of Modern Art 1991.

65 · Jay Winter, *Sites of Memory, Sites of Mourning: The Great War in European Cultural History.* Cambridge: Cambridge University Press 1995, p.120.

66 · On the growing market for such products in Australia, see Gaye Poole, *The Big Day: Scoring the Wedding.* Unpub paper presented at the 6th Annual Conference of the International Association for the Study of Popular Music, Adelaide, June 1998.

67 · The position of intellectuals within the cultural field is one of the pervasive themes of Bourdieu's *oeuvre.* Apart from work referred to below, I draw particular attention to: Pierre Bourdieu, *The Field of Cultural Production: Essays on Art and Literature,* ed Randal Johnson. Cambridge. Polity Press 1993; *Language and Symbolic Power,* trans Gino Raymond and Matthew Adamson, ed John B. Thompson. Cambridge: Polity Press 1992. These elaborate some of the positions which, not so much underpin, as constitute points *of* departure for this book.

68 · Walter Benjamin, 'The work of art an the age of mechanical reproduction', in *Illuminations,* ed Hannah Arendt, trans Harry Zohn. London. Jonathan Cape, 1970, pp 219–254.

69 · Thomas Crow, 'Modernism and mass culture in the visual arts' in Francis Frascina, *Pollock and After: The Critical Debate.* London: Harper & Row 1985, p.259.

70 · Richard Ohmann, *Selling Culture: Magazines, Markets, and Class at the Turn of the Century.* London: Verso 1996, p. 14.

71 · See Max Horkheimer and Theodore Adorno, *The Dialectic of Enlightenment.* trans John Cumming. NY: Continuum Press 1972; in particular their essay The Culture Industry: Enlightenment

as Mass Deception'. As early as 1952, David Riesman recognised that popular culture cannot be understood without reference to the active process of consumption (see Peter Goodall, *High Culture, Popular Culture: The Long Debate.* St Leonards NSW: Allen & Unwin 1995, p.68). Subsequent developments and variations are to be found in the work of Pierre Bourdieu, notably *Distinction: a social critique of the judgement of Taste.* trans Richard Nice. Cambridge Mass: Harvard University Press 1984; first published in French, 1979), Michel de Certeau, *The Practice of Everyday Life.* trans Steven Rendall. Berkeley: University of California Press 1984), John Fiske, *Reading the Popular.* Boston: Unwin Hyman 1989 and *Understanding Popular Culture.* Boston: Unwin Hyman 1989. Paul Willis sets out case studies in a counter-aesthetic of consumption (see for example Paul Willis, with Simon Jones, Joyce Canaan, Geoff Hurd, *Common Culture: Symbolic work at play in the everyday cultures of the young.* Milton Keynes; Open University Press reprint of 1996); a problematisation of the case is put by, inter alia, James Walter, 'Controlling the Technology of Popular Culture: The Introduction of Television in Australia' in Ian Craven (ed) *Australian Popular Culture.* Cambridge, New York, Melbourne: Cambridge University Press 1994, pp.66–78. Useful overviews of the history of these debates may be found in, for example, Dominic Strinati, *An Introduction to Theories of Popular Culture.* London & New York: Routledge 1995; an invaluable collection of primary twentieth century texts is published in Charles Harrison and Paul Wood (eds), *Art in Theory 1900–1990: An Anthology of Changing Ideas.* Oxford UK and Cambridge USA: Blackwell 1992. There is considerable literature on the connections between Australian mass culture, technology, the United States, modernisation, and the framework of cultural values; see for example Philip and Roger Bell, *Implicated: The United States in Australia.* Melbourne: Oxford University Press 1993; Goodall 1995; J.F. Williams 1995. My purpose is not to go over ground that has already been excellently covered, but to situate music within that field.

72 · Antony Easthope, *Literary into Cultural Studies.* London and New York Routledge 1991, p.79

73 · For a spirited 'no-prisoners' elaboration of this point, specifically in relation to popular music, see Neil Nehring, *Popular Music, Gender, and Postmodernism: Anger is an Energy.* Thousand Oaks California, London, New Delhi: Sage Publications 1997, in particular, chapter 2, 'The vicious history of aesthetics' pp.21–53.

74 · See in particular such pioneering studies as Ruth Finnegan, *The Hidden Musicians: music-making in an English town.* Cambridge, 1989; and Sara Cohen, *Rock Culture in Liverpool: popular music in the making.* Oxford 1991. More recently, reflections on the meaning of music from a cross section of 'consumers' have been assembled in Susan D. Crafts, Daniel Cavicchi, Charles Keil, *My Music.* Hanover New Hampshire: Wesleyan University Press 1993.

75 · Frascina 1985 p. 17 (authors italics).

76 · Anne-Marie Willis, *Illusions of Identity: The Art of Nation.* Sydney: Hale & Iremonger 1993, p.129.

77 · Heathcote 1995, pp.206, 209. My word 'largely' acknowledges, among other things, that this act of exclusion is itself also part of the dialectic of Australian modernity.

78 · See for example Anne-Marie Willis 1993, pp.131–3.

79 · See J.F. Williams 1995, pp.79, 120–125; Goodall 1995 pp.79–113.

80 · See Bell & Bell 1993, esp Part II.

81 · Willis 1993, pp. 133–147; see also Graeme Turner, *Making it National: Nationalism and Australian Popular Culture.* St Leonards NSW: Allen & Unwin 1994, p.97.

82 · Mary Eagle, 'Modernism in Sydney in the 1920s', in Ann Galbally and Margaret Plant (eds) *Studies in Australian Art.* Melbourne 1978.

83 · Kirkpatrick 1992, see for example pp.271, 273.

84 · Mary Mackay, 'Almost Dancing: Thea Proctor and the modern woman', in Maryanne Dever (ed), *Wallflowers and Witches: Women and Culture in Australia 1910–1945.* Queensland:

University of Queensland Press 1994, p.29.

85 · See in particular Andreas Huyssen's analyses of the attempt to gender modern mass culture as female, in *After the Great Divide: Modernism, Mass Culture, Postmodernism.* Indianapolis: Indiana University Press 1986.

86 · Billie Melman, *Women and the Popular Imagination in the Twenties: Flappers and Nymphs.* New York, St Martin's Press 1988, pp. 15–37.

87 · See for example G. Stedman-Jones, 'Working-Class Culture and Working-Class Politics in London, 1870–1900: Notes on the Remaking of a Working Class', *Journal of Social History,* VII, Summer 1974, pp.460–508.

88 · Bolton 1992, p.17; Hilary M. Carey, *Believing in Australia: a cultural history of religions.* St Leonards NSW: Allen & Unwin 1996, pp.4, 16. See further Waterhouse 1995, pp.10–12; Goodall 1995 pp.84–5. See also Bell and Bell 1993, p.23: '... an entrenched order was reluctant to share power, other than with the "respectable classes"'.

89 · J.F. Williams 1995, p.217

90 · Sections of the following are to a great extent a summary of J.F. Williams 1995, chapters 1, 8, 10.

91 · The central role *of* women in early Australian modernist painting has been increasingly documented, notably in a special issue of *Journal of Australian Studies,* 32, March 1992; Maryanne Dever (ed), *Wallflowers and Witches: Women and Culture in Australia 1910–1945.* St Lucia Qld, University of Queensland Press 1994; Jeanette Hoorn (ed), *Strange Women: Essays in Art and Gender.* Carlton Vic: Melbourne University Press, 1994; Helen Topliss, *Modernism and Feminism: Australian Women Artists 1900–1940.* Roseville East NSW: Craftsman House 1996. See further, chapter 3 below.

92 · Heathcote 1995, pp.64–5, 155, 161, 166.

93 · Heathcote 1995, all quotes p.211.

94 · See further Nehring 1997, pp.21–53, which concludes 'Much of

postmodernism is not really "post" at all in its warmed-over rehash of romantic and modernist prejudices',

95 · Letter from Kandinsky to Marc, cited by Winter 1995, p.149. See further Varnedoe and Gopnik 1991.

96 · See further Bruce Johnson, Art, Jazz and Uncle Tom's Cabin', *Jazzchord,* 13, May/June 1993, p.8. I have documented this adaptive process in both musical and discursive practice in Johnson, 'Jazz and the cultural politics of Australian music', *Context,* 10, Summer 1995, pp. 11–26 (Johnson 1995A).

97 · See John Whiteoak, 'Robert Rooney and the McKimm/Rooney/Clayton Music Collaboration: Melbourne, 1960s' in Jenepher Duncan and Merryn Gates (eds) *From the Homefront: Robert Rooney Works 1953–1988.* Monash University, Clayton Vic: Monash University Gallery 1990, pp. 15–21.

98 · Steven Paul Scher, *Music and Text: Critical Enquiries.* Cambridge: Cambridge University Press 1992, p.xiv. See also Joseph Kerman *Musicology* London; Collins 1985, p.17. Extended affirmations to this effect may be found in, inter alios, C. Dahlhaus, *Foundations of Music History,* trans. J.B. Robinson. Cambridge: Cambridge University Press 1983; Middleton 1990; Charles Seeger *Studies in Musicology 1937–75.* Berkeley and Los Angeles: University of California Press, 1977; Philip Tagg, 'Music for Moving Pictures: Academia, Education and Independent Thought'. Unpub. Paper, Colloquium *Musica e Cinema*, Siena August 1990.

99 · Richard Middleton 1990 p.103. See similarly, John Shepherd, *Music as Social Text.* Cambridge: Polity Press 1991, p.5. Van Der Merwe 1989 is a useful starting point for a discussion of the relationship between 'popular' and 'classical' musics.

100 · Kerman 1985, p. 14. Schwartz and Godfrey also identify Schoenberg's *Pierrot Lunaire* and Stravinsky's *Rite of Spring* as pivotal works in the transition to modern music, noting also the 'romantic legacy' in both: Elliott Schwartz and Daniel Godfrey, *Music Since 1945: Issues, Materials and Literature.* New York: Schirmer/Macmillan 1993, pp.4–5.

101 · Marshall Brown, 'Origins of modernism: musical structures

and narrative forms', in Steven Paul Scher, *Music and Text: Critical Enquiries.* Cambridge: Cambridge University Press 1992, pp.79–80.

102 · Schwartz and Godfrey 1993, pp.9–25.

103 · Although Romain described this in an interview with me, Whiteoak 1999, p.183, must take the credit for seeing the larger significance of the practice as summarised here.

104 · Waterhouse 1995, p.186.

105 · Covell 1967, p.152.

106 · Carl Vine, 'Art for Whose Sake?', *ABC Radio 24 Hours,* August 1993, pp.44, 45.

107 · The interest shown by Stravinsky, Ravel, et al., in the possibilities of jazz are sufficiently well known Ernest Ansermet's prediction in 1919 that Afro-American music, specifically jazz, was the 'highway' to the future of the world's music has been oft-quoted; see for example John Chilton, *Sidney Bechet: The Wizard of jazz.* London, Basingstoke: Macmillan 1987, p.40. Among more general music historians, see Charles Nanry 'Jazz and Modernism: Twin-born Children of the Age of Invention', *Annual Review of Jazz Studies,* I, 1982, pp. 146–154, and Henry Pleasants, *The Agony of Modern Music.* New York: Simon & Schuster, 1955.

108 · Lawrence Levine 1988, p. 145, observes a parallel process in the United States itself: 'American nature became worthy of consideration only after it was filtered through European sensibilities'. Lawrence W Levine, *Highbrow/Lowbrow: The, Emergence of Cultural Hierarchy in America.* Cambridge Massachusetts: Harvard University Press 1988, p. 145.

109 · I have developed and exemplified this further in 'Towards a new cartography: rethinking Australia's music history' in Nicholas Brown et al (ed) *One Hand on the Manuscript: Music in Australian Cultural history 1930–60.* Canberra: The Humanities Research Centre 1995, pp 243–257. Sections of that article provide part of the basis for the following.

110 · See for example, Covell 1967, pp. 178–80; Ann Carr-Boyd 'Australia', in H. Ryker (ed), *New Music in the Orient: Essays on Composition in Asia since World War II*. Buren, The Netherlands: Frits Knuf Publishers 1991, p.53; James Murdoch, *Australia's Contemporary Composers*. South Melbourne and North Sydney: Macmillan 1972, p.16; Andrew McCredie, *Musical Compositions in Australia, including select bibliography and discography*. Canberra: Australian Government Printing Office 1969, p. 14.

111 · Don Banks, *De Berg Tapes*, National Library 1972, Transcription 626:1/7. See also Whiteoak 1999, pp.255–6, which includes an invaluable revision of this conventional construction of Banks' career.

112 · John Whiteoak, *Early Modern Jazz in Australia The Introduction of Bop*. Unpub. Honours Diss., Dept of Music, La Trobe University, Vic 1986, p.83.

113 · Mitchell 1988, refer index.

114 · This session is among those listed in the journals of Ray Marginson.

115 · For example, Whiteoak 1999, pp.257–263.

116 · Don Banks, 'Expanding the World of Sound: Electronic Composer Don Banks talks to Di Gaston', *Soundblast*, May 1973, pp.17, 21; Murdoch, 1972, p.18.

117 · My source for this information is a conversation with Bell. In his biography *Sidney Nolan: Such is Life*. Milson's Point NSW: Vintage, Random House Australia, edition of 1992, pp.53–65, Brian Adams reports the event in a way that leaves unresolved the question of whether or not the classical music event took place. Haese 1981, p.72, writes, 'The response of local classical composers and performers was disappointing, but Don Banks and the Graeme Bell jazz band helped make the night of 28 October a heady experience'. When I raised this question with Graeme Bell in conversation in July 1997, he was unable to recall that the classical music concert had taken place.

118 · Quoted from the Melbourne *Truth* by Haese 1981, pp.72–3.

Chapter 3

119 · See in particular Diane Collins, 'The Movie Octopus', in P. Spearritt & D. Walker (eds) *Australian Popular Culture*. Sydney: George Allen & Unwin 1979, pp.102–120.

120 · The earliest event that might be categorised as a festival of jazz recorded in *The New Grove Dictionary of Jazz* was in 1926 (Kernfeld 1988 p.361).

121 · See Johnson 1987, p.4; Andrew Pike & Ross Cooper, *Australian Film 1900–1977: A Guide to Feature Film Production.*, Melbourne: Oxford University Press 1980, p. 118.

122 · Collins 1979, p.116.

123 · Katharine Brisbane (ed), *Entertaining Australia: an illustrated history*. Sydney: Currency Press 1991, pp.202, 166.

124 · See Leslie Heath, *Sydney Literary Societies of the Nineteen Twenties: Cultural Nationalism and the Promotion of Australian Literature*. Unpub Doctoral Diss, Schools of English and History, University of NSW 1996, p 81.

125 · Eagle 1978, p.89. These arguments have since been developed by Eagle and others, notably in Jeanette Hoorn, 'Misogyny and Modernist Painting in Australia: How Male Critics Made Modernism Their Own', *Journal of Australian Studies*, 32, March 1992, pp.7–17; J. Pigot '"Decadent, Savage and Primitive": Hilda Rix Nichols and Modernism', *Journal of Australian Studies*, 32, March 1992, pp.26–33; Dever 1994; Hoorn 1994; Topliss 1996.

126 · Angela Philp, 'From Wallflowers to Tall Poppies? The Sydney Society of Women Painters, 1910–1934', in Dever 1994, pp. 1–2. See also Katie Holmes, '"Diamonds of the Dustheap"? women's diary writing between the wars', in Dever 1994, p.46.

127 · Quoted by Mackay 1994, p.29.

128 · See Waterhouse 1995, p. 11.

129 · See for example, Susan McClary, *Feminine Endings: Music, Gender and Sexuality*. Minneapolis: University of Minnesota Press 1991.

130 · Diller-Anderson has studied this process by focussing on the Sydney Tivoli from 1895–1917; Gae M. Diller-Anderson, *The First Twenty-five Years of Vaudeville at the Sydney Tivoli, 1893–1917: Sexual Difference and the Female Vaudevillian.* Unpub. Diss., MA (Hons), University of New South Wales 1991, see particularly pp.39–40.

131 · See further Bruce Johnson, 'Resituating Improvisation', *Journal of Improvisational Practice,* 2/1, 1996, pp.6–1 1; Bruce Johnson, 'In the Jumble, the Genre Jumble: the prison house of popular music discourse'. Unpub Paper delivered at *Rock as a Research Field* Symposium, University of Aarhus, Denmark, 4–10 April 1997. A version on-line as 'Watching the Watchers' under Archive link: A version on-line as 'Watching the Watchers' under Archive link: www.arts.unsw.edu.au/jazz/

132 · Phyllis McCorquodale gives a sample listing of public dance halls which opened in Australia from 1913 into the twenties, in *The Lure of the Dance: some aspects of ballroom dancing in Australia in the inter-war years.* Unpub Hons Diss, School of History, University of New South Wales 1985, pp. 9–13. See further, Jill Julius Matthews, 'Dancing modernity', in Barbara Came & Rosemary Pringle (eds), *Transitions: New Australian Feminisms,* St. Leonards NSW: Allen & Unwin 1995, pp. 74–87.

133 · See for example Waterhouse 1995, pp.22, 40, 83. See also McCorquodale 1985 on the moral anxiety aroused by public dancing; pp.44–50.

134 · Waterhouse 1995. p.177.

135 · The other, and for the same reasons, is singing, which I discuss below.

136 · See Drew Cottle, 'Dancing Out The Depression: The Sydney Trocadero's earliest years, 1936–39', *New Music Articles (NMA),* 3, 1984, p.38.

137 · See further, Chapter Six. Since I wrote this chapter, John Whiteoak's similar discussion *of* the social meaning and function of colonial, and later ragtime, dance in Australia has appeared; Whiteoak 1999, pp.54–5, 150–3.

138 · The earliest Australian jazz bands billed as such performed in venues such as Fuller's Bijou Theatre with other vaudeville acts; see Johnson 1987 pp 3, 64–5.

139 · See McCorquodale, 1985, pp.29–32, 38.

140 · See Frank Kermode, 'Poet and Dancer before Diaghilev' in *Modern Essays.* Great Britain: Fontana 1971, p.20.

141 · Kay Ferres, 'How to be a singer though married', in Ian Craven (ed), *Australian Popular Culture.* Melbourne: Oxford University Press 1994, p. 156.

142 · See Johnson 1987, p.6.

143 · In her account of Australian flappers, Barbara Cameron specifically lists smoking, drinking and applying makeup in public as transgressive gestures associated with female emancipation; Barbara Cameron, 'The Flappers and the Feminists', in Margaret Bevege, Margaret James, Carmel Shute (eds), *Worth Her Salt: Women at Work in Australia.* Sydney: Hale & Iremonger 1982, in particular pp.257–9.

144 · Johnson 1987, pp.3, 64–5.

145 · John Hasse (ed), *Ragtime: its History, Composers and Music.* London: Macmillan 1985, p.20.

146 · See for example Whiteoak 1999, pp 14, 66; quote from p.61. Further light is cast on the role of women in Australian dance bands by Kay Dreyfus' *Sweethearts of Rhythm: the story of Australia's all-girls bands and orchestras to the end of the second world war,* Sydney, Currency Press, 1999.

147 · James Sabine, *A Century of Australian Cinema.* Port Melbourne: William Heinemann Australia 1995, p.86; Waterhouse 1995, p.87.

148 · Brisbane 1991, p.212.

149 · Few of these films survive intact, and I therefore also rely on the summaries provided for each in Pike & Cooper, 1980.

150 · My thanks to Gaye Poole whose detailed knowledge of Australian film pointed me towards thematic patterns and other aspects of early Australian cinema that inform this discussion.

151 · In the following discussion, passages quoted from the films' captions are signified in the running text within single inverted commas.

152 · The butterfly girl image seems to have been standard currency in the twenties, and reappears implicitly in the title of, and explicitly in the publicity for, the 1928 film *Caught in the Net* (Pike and Cooper, 1980, p. 1 89). Cameron 1982, p.260, reports what was evidently a fashion among Australian flappers of painting butterflies on their knees.

153 · The same name, incidentally, as the city 'butterfly girl' in *Moonbi*. It is spelled thus in the film's titles, but sometimes spelled 'Marjorie' in publicity and commentary. Likewise 'Gavin', alternatively 'Garvin'.

154 · Waterhouse 1995, p.82 . Waterhouse also records that in Melbourne it was illegal for women to bet with bookmakers, leading to an increase in women's gambling with the introduction of sophisticated totalisators in the thirties (p.169).

155 · In some matters of detail the shooting script does not correspond to the surviving footage, as for example in the absence of any reference to the dancing scene. Nor, apart from the musicians, are there any men visible at the lawn party, though the shooting script refers to their presence (Shot 68). See also in reference to being 'sheiked', below.

156 · The synopsis is reproduced in Susanne Chauvel Carlsson, *Charles and Elsa Chauvel: Movie Pioneers*. St Lucia, Queensland: University of Queensland Press 1989, p.54.

157 · Stuart Cunningham, *Featuring Australia: The Cinema of Charles Chauvel*. North Sydney: Allen & Unwin 1991, p.49.

158 · It is an aside that is relevant to the 'reading' of old movies, that the sense of dated grotesquerie can be largely dissipated by shuttling frame by frame, which also foregrounds the ecstatically abandoned dimensions *of* the dance.

159 · The figure/ground dualism emerges in Maróthy's study of the nexus between the rise of capitalism, the bourgeois ego, and the development of monocentricity in literature, painting and

music. Within this framework he analyzes the ideological underpinnings of musical properties which are commonly reified as autonomously aesthetic in new approaches to tonality, closure, polyphony, in the form for example of the appetite for the liberated soloistic melody'; János Maróthy 1974, p.104. He provides a succinct summary on the historical stages of this process, pp.116–126. Philip Tagg uses this figure/ground model as the basis of a stimulating approach to contemporary rave music in 'From Refrain to Rave: The Decline of Figure and the Rise of Ground', published in *Popular Music,* 1994, also online at www.liv.ac.uk/ipm/tagg/taggwbtx.htm. In the case of Margery's 'soloing' as a departure from the heterosexual model, it must be borne in mind of course that with an all-female guest-list, there was no male partner available in any case. The point still holds, however: the script did not have to call for her to dance at all. Chauvel chose to use this action as a way *of* establishing Margery as the independent modern woman.

160 · Belinda Quirey, *May I Have the Pleasure? The story of popular dancing.* London: Dance Books 1987, p.68. Although originally a dance in which power was shared equally by each member of the couple, in crowded ballrooms it became necessary for one to lead, and this became the male partner; see Gerald Jonas, *Dancing: The Power of Dance Around the World.* London: BBC Books 1992, p. 124. I wish to thank former student Melissa Skinner for drawing my attention to these sources.

161 · See Murray 1994, p. 10; Pike & Cooper 1980, pp.130, 135–6.

162 · Brisbane 1991, p.192.

163 · Waterhouse 1995, p. 181; Melman 1988, pp.89–104. *Moonbi* and *Greenhide* are two of four films bracketed for examination by M. Ruth Megaw in '"Happy Ever After"; the image of women in four Australian feature films of the Nineteen Twenties', *Journal of Australian Studies,* 7, November 1980. Megaw justly notes the masculinist imprint of Chauvel's hand, though on the basis of the particular reading I have given and the gendered market for film at that time, I can't share her confidence that for this film

'there can be no doubt that the ideal spectator is conceived of as male' (p.63).

164 · Copies of the publicity are included in Carlsson 1989, pp.55–7. The complete absence of maternal figures in both *Moonbi* and *Greenhide* is notable in this connection. Cunningham's 1991 study overwhelmingly makes the case for Chauvel's position on contemporary gender politics.

165 · According to the shooting script, this is glimpsed in a closeup shot of her legs as she arrives in a jalopy at Walloon (Shot 131). Megaw 1980 includes this shot as evidence that Chauvel is playing to a voyeuristic male audience (see fn 110). Certainly the shooting script specifies several leg shots, but its stipulation of a specifically *jazz* garter introduces an image that goes beyond that reading.

Chapter 4

166 · See Paul Théberge, *Any Sound You Can Imagine: Making Music/ Consuming Technology*. Hanover, New Hampshire: Wesleyan University Press 1997, pp. 122–5.

167 · Among the abundant literature on music and affect, Tagg 1979 remains a benchmark.

168 · On Caccini, see below. See further John Potter, *Vocal Authority: Singing Style and Ideology*. Cambridge: Cambridge University Press 1998, for example pp.93, 96, 154. I thank colleague Richard Madelaine for suggesting the term 'naturalism' in this context.

169 · Roland Gelatt, *The Fabulous Phonograph 1877–1977*, Second Revised Edition. New York & London: Collier Macmillan 1977, p.115. The development of recording technology is chronicled in a number of studies. The main sources used here are Gelatt 1977 and Peter Copeland, *Sound Recordings*. London: British Library 1991.

170 · Simon Frith, 'Art versus technology: the strange case of popular music', *Media, Culture and Society*, 8/3, July 1986, pp.263–79.

171 · Cited by Cyril Ehrlich, *The Piano: A History*. London: JM Dent & Sons Ltd 1976, p.85.

172 · Cited by Ronald Pearsall, *Popular Music of the Twenties.* Totowa NJ: Roman & Littlefield 1976, p.102.

173 · Waterhouse 1995, pp. 182–5.

174 · See for example Frith 1986.

175 · Regarding this Summit, see further, [Peter Rix?], *Contemporary Music Summit: Report on the Contemporary Music Summit for the Minister for Communications and the Arts, Michael Lee.* Canberra: Dept of Communications and the Arts 1995; Bruce Johnson, 'The Music Industry: Selling Empty Boxes', *Realtime*, 9, October-November 1995, p.l5.

176 · See for example Gelatt 1977 on recording and T. Lewis, *Empire of the Air: The men who made radio.* New York: Edward Burlingame 1991.

177 · See Copeland 1991, pp. 19–21, 24.

178 · Evan Eisenberg, *The Recording Angel: Explorations in Phonography.* New York: McGraw Hill 1987, p.115.

179 · Schwartz and Godfrey 1993, pp.110 ff.

180 · Cited by Steve Jones, *Rock Formation: Music, Technology, and Mass Communication,* Foundations of Popular Culture 3. Newbury Park, London, New Delhi: Sage Publications 1992, p.131.

181 · Copeland 1991, pp.10–15.

182 · Steve Jones 1992, p.173. Frith points out that 'while *classical* divisions of record companies have led the way in studio technology, their pursuit of authenticity has limited their studio imagination'; Simon Frith, 'The Industrialisation of Popular Music' in James Lull (ed), *Popular Music and Communication.* Newbury Park, Beverly Hills, London: Sage Publications 1987, p.65. Italics in the original.

183 · For succinct summaries and critiques of Adornos positions on popular music, see Richard Middleton 1990, pp.37 ff.; Alistair Williams, *New Music and the Claims of Modernity.* Aldershot England: Ashgate Publishing 1997. pp.3–21.

184 · Eisenberg 1987, pp.145–8.

185 · Brad Kay, sleeve note to *Reflections in Ellington: The 1932 band in true stereo, and on the road with the great 1940 band*, Everybodys EV—3005, 1985. When, in 1981, record collector Steve Lasker had noticed a discrepancy in matrix and take numbers on two copies of the same Ellington session, he brought this to the attention of Kay, who first realised that these were the two components of a stereo recording, setting off further research which unearthed examples by other groups.

186 · These two hypotheses regarding the origins of the early stereo recordings are summarised in Kernfeld 1988, pp.358–9.

187 · Stanley Dance, *Duke Ellington.* Alexandria, Virginia: Time-Life Records 1978, p.5.

188 · See the example of avant-gardist Milton Babbit, who preferred his work to be purged of any corporeal component that could contaminate the cognitive realm; see Schwartz and Godfrey 1993, pp.86–7.

189 · Jones 1992, p.124; also Stephen Struthers, 'Technology in the art of recording' in Avron White (ed) *Lost in Music: Culture, Style and the Musical Event,* Sociological Review Monograph 34. London & NY: Routledge & Kegan Paul 1987, see especially pp.242–3.

190 · See Kernfeld 1988, pp.218, 224, 233; Jim Haskins, *The Cotton Club.* New York, Random House 1977, pp.29–33. A photograph taken of Pete Lala's shortly before it was demolished in 1954, is published in Orrin Keepnews and Bill Grauer's *A Pictorial History of Jazz.* UK: Spring Books, New Revised Edition 1966, p.15.

191 · Kernfeld 1988, p.233.

192 · See Potter 1998, p.51.

193 · Henry Pleasants, *The Great American Popular Singers,* New York: Simon and Schuster 1974, pp. 134, 136.

194 · Quoted in Bob Rogers and Denis O'Brien, *Rock'n Roll Australia: The Australian Pop Scene 1954–1964.* Stanmore NSW & North

Melbourne Vic: Cassell Australia, 1975, p 31. Photographs of O'Keefe confirm the phallic prominence of the microphone in his live performance.

195 · John Rickard, 'Music and Cultural Hierarchy', in Nicholas Brown, Peter Campbell, Robyn Holmes, Peter Read, Larry Sitsky (eds), *One Hand on the Manuscript: Music in Australian Cultural History 1930–1960*. Canberra: The Humanities Research Centre 1995, p.183.

196 · Quoted in Johnson 1987, p.71.

197 · Brisbane 1991, p.216. This venue is sometimes spelled 'Palais Royale', but I have adopted the alternative form throughout.

198 · See further, K.S. Inglis, *This is the ABC: The Australian Broadcasting Commission 1932–1983*. Carlton Victoria: Melbourne University Press 1983, pp.5–24.

199 · The two class system of broadcasting licenses very broadly corresponds to government and commercially funded stations (A and B respectively). See K.S. Inglis 1983, pp.6–18.

200 · Hammet in *Australian Music-Maker and Dance Band News (AMM&DBN)*, 1 November 1933, p.23; on 3LO see for example *AMM&DBN* 1 February 1933, p.12; 1 March 1933, p. 12; 1 August 1933, p. 16; 1 September 1933, p.5; 1 October 1933, p.7; 1 January 1934, p.24; 1 February 1934, p.5. On 2GB, *AMM&DBN*, 1 December 1933, p.52. On Cecil Fraser, *AMM&DBN*, 1 December 1933, pp.27, 50. In dating the various events reported in *AMM&DBN* and *Australian Dance Band News*, cited below, it is important to understand the sometimes confusing process of publication. The journals always dated themselves strictly in monthly sequences, although they did not always appear at those precise intervals. It appears that editorial copy would accumulate until factors such as advertising enabled the production of an issue, which would then appear using enough accumulated copy to produce the issue. Other material would be held over until the next issue could be produced. This often resulted in an event being foreshadowed and reviewed in the same issue. Unless actual dates are given

in the copy, the most that can be deduced from the date of the issue is that events reported to have taken place had certainly done so by then, but possibly longer ago than the month of the previous issue.

201 · Reg Oxford, 'Sound amplification an integral part of modern band presentation in *AMM&DBN,* 1 January 1935, p.47.

202 · 'Twentieth Century Blues', in *AMM&DBN,* 1 August 1933, p.25; Davidsons recordings, see above Chapter 1; 'Big Bad Wolf', in *AMM&DBN,* 1 January 1934, p.28; Carioca, in *AMM&DBN,* 1 April 1934, p. 19.

203 · On the appointment of 'Coughlin', in *Australian Dance Band News (ADBN*), 1 August 1932, p.8; on 'girl' singers, in *AMM&DBN,* 1 August 1933, p. 14.

204 · *ADBN,* 1 July 1932, p.24; *AMM&DBN,* 1 September 1933, p.9.

205 · The size of a band of course always varies according to circumstances ranging from architecture to economics, and small venues would still present a solo pianist or a duo. But the maximum size of bands continues to increase throughout the thirties, as evidenced in personnel listings and recordings. It was reported in *AMM&DBN,* 1 March 1934 that in Melbourne 'Bands everywhere are being enlarged' (p.22).

206 · *AMM&DBN,* 1 June 1933, p.18, and 1 May 1934, p.15.

207 · Earls Court, in *AMM&DBN,* 1 December 1933, pp.10, 44; the Rex, in *AMM&DBN,* 1 June 1934, p.7; Palais de Danse and Palais Royal, in *AMM&DBN,* 1 May 1934, pp.5, 7, June 1934 p.104, September 1934, p.33; Albert Palais, in *AMM&DBN,* 1 May 1934, p.9, 1 June 1934, p. 11; the Orchestrola, in *AMM&DBN,* 1 September 1934, p.42; the Amplivox, in *AMM&DBN,* 1 November 1934, p.4.

208 · On the arrival of the electric guitar see for example Charles [Charlie] Lees 'The Electric Guitar', in *AMM&DBN*, August 1936, and on Lees, Johnson 1987 p. 195.

209 · Brisbane 1991, p.251.

210 · 'Exceptions' include Stockhausen's opera *Donnerstag*, and Berio's *Sinfonia* and *Laborintus*, written for amplified voices (Potter 1998, p. 171).

211 · See in this connection Potter's comments on duets between Freddie Mercury of Queen and Monserrat Caballé (Potter 1998, pp. 187–9).

212 · See for example *ADBN*, 1 June 1932, p.21, *AMM&DBN*, 1 June 1933, p.16, and 1 January 1934, p.14.

213 · Al Bowlly 'Modern Style Singing (Crooning)', in *AMM&DBN*, 1 March 1934, p.31. Other Bowlly articles referred to in my discussion are 'Crooning—and the microphone', in *AMM&DBN*, 1 May 1934, p.38, and 'Modern style singing', in *AMM&DBN*, 1 April 1935, p.27. There was a fourth one by Bowlly published in *AMM&DBN*, 1 July 1934, p.29, but this is a beginner's guide to reading music and has no particular relevance to crooning. There were in addition other articles published at this time on the subject, but more frequently they were comedy pieces which throw little light just here, as for example those by Jack Davey including 'The Greeks had a word for it', in *AMM&DBN*, June 1936, p. 11.

214 · Pleasants 1974, p.61.

215 · Pleasants 1974, p.61

216 · Eisenberg 1987, p. 156.

217 · Bowlly 1 March 1934.

218 · Al Bowlly 'Crooning—and the microphone', in *AMM&DBN*, 1 May 1934, p.38.

219 · Quoted in Rickard 1995, pp.182–3.

220 · On Foster, in *AMM&DBN*, 1 September 1933, p.11; Crosby, in *AMM&DBN*, 1 February 1934, p.12; Hennessy, in *ADBN*, 1 October 1932, p.5.

221 · These were custom pressed, but were much later issued as a set on *The Troc* MBS Jazz 8, Linehan Series (1991).

222 · Laurie Lewis, *Arthur and the Nights at the Turntable: The Life and*

Tinies of a Jazz Broadcaster. London: First pub, Excalibur Press, 1996; this edition, Wingen NSW: K'Vrie Press 1997, pp 53–67.

223 · Potter 1998, pp.47*, 56–58, 53*, 53, 63–65, 151–2* (*quotations).

224 · Pleasants 1974, pp. 17, 45.

225 · Pearce responded, incidentally, by illustrating the banality of opera libretti when read separately from the music; and commented, 'Yet thousands of educated people who profess complete admiration for these grotesque fairy stories as the greatest musical contribution to the world, sneer and scoff at all popular music—good or bad, although it expresses the natural inclinations and instincts in the everyday life of the great public' Lewis 1997, p.62.

226 · Frith 1986, p.270.

227 · See also Frith 1986, pp.269–70; Potter 1998, p.88.

228 · Andrew Chester, 'Second Thoughts on a Rock Aesthetic: The Band', *New Left Review*, 62, 1970, pp.78–79: italics in the original.

229 · I would like to thank Dr Jill Stubington, School of Music and Music Education at the University of NSW, for the benefit of her own interpretation of Chester's distinction. While it differs in some details from my own, I believe the general terms in which I have paraphrased it here accommodate both views.

230 · See Furia 1992, p.246.

231 · Whiteoak 1999, chapter 11, pp.111–167.

232 · In *AMM&DBN,* 1 October 1933, p. 10. it was reported that Romains singing voice had led at least one of his female fans to rank him above Rudy Vallee.

233 · Brisbane 1991, p. Brisbane 1991, p. 181.

Chapter 5

234 · The interviews with Barbara James are as follows: with Lyn Markham (broadcast on 20/4/85 on ABC's *The Coming Out Show*); with Mike Sutcliffe (recorded) 22/5/92; and the following with Bruce Johnson: recorded 25/6/93; notes of telephone

conversation, 5/12/97; recorded 9/12/97; notes of telephone conversation 10/12/97.

235 · See Louise Douglas, *Truckin' at the Troc.* Unpub. Diss., Macquarie University, NSW 1983, and Bruce Johnson, Sleeve Notes for *The Troc*, CD Recording, Linehan Series, MBS Jazz 8, 1991. Frank Coughlan's daughter has published a personal memoir of the venue: Joan Ford, *Meet me at the Trocadero.* Cowra NSW: Joan Ford, 1995. See further, Patricia Hale, 'The Dancing Years: Popular Dancing and the Trocaderos', *Public History Review,* 1997, pp. 99–115

236 · Reg Lewis died in 1977, and at the time *of* writing, Barbara James lives in Kings Cross. A more comprehensive overview of their careers, with a discography and filmography, is published in Bruce Johnson and Mike Sutcliffe, 'Barbara James: a career in Australian popular music', in *Australasian Drama Studies,* 21, October 1992, pp.123–137.

237 · See for example J.F Williams 1995, pp.200–210; Bell & Bell 1993, pp.65–87; John Potts, *Radio in Australia.* Kensington NSW: University of New South Wales Press 1989, pp.50–51.

238 · Monique Geitenbeck, 'The Role of Women in the Australian Music Examinations Board from 1930 to 1950', in Nicholas Brown et al, *One Hand on the Manuscript: Music in Australian Cultural History 1930–1960* (Humanities Research Centre Monograph Series No. 9. Canberra: Australian National University 1995, pp 189–200.

239 · Geitenbeck 1995, pp.189–91, pp.192–3.

240 · Peter Dunbar-Hall, *Strella Wilson: The Career of an Australian Singer.* Chatswood NSW: Redback Press 1997.

241 · Recounted in an interview with the author, Sydney, 20/3/98

242 · The most comprehensive discography of her work is published in Johnson & Sutcliffe 1992, pp.136–7.

243 · The accompanist is pianist Beryl Newell, who shows no awkwardness. From western NSW, she moved to Adelaide where she worked on stage. Moving to Sydney in the late

twenties, she became musical director for Parlophone; see *ADBN*, February 1 1933, pp.9, 25; [Mike Sutcliffe], 'Des Tooley', *Australian Record and Music Review*, 8, January 1991, pp.8–13. Her facility in the modern style is striking, and the obscurity into which she has fallen is one of the lamentable silences in the history of Australian music, inviting further parallels with the gender politics of modernist Australian painting.

244 · Roland Barthes, 'The Grain of the Voice', *Image-Music-Text*, trans Stephen Heath. Great Britain: Fontana/Collins 1977, p.188.

245 · I wish to thank John Colborne-Veel for checking my analysis. As an orchestral composer, former President of the Fellowship of Australian Composers, and a jazz musician, his 'amphibious' perspective was invaluable. The definitions of soprano and contralto are based on Nikolay Rimsky-Korsakov's summary of the ranges for solo voices in his *Principles of Orchestration, with musical examples drawn from his own works*, trans Edward Agate. New York: Dover Publications Inc. 1964, pp. 134–6.

246 · It is impossible to know whether this decision was based on the model she might have used, or the strength of her voice at that pitch. Whatever might have been indicated by a written orchestration is irrelevant, as Barbara learned her repertoire from recordings (see below). Among the available models was a version of the song recorded in New York, issued in Australia, by vocalist Mark Fisher on February 2 1933, just over four months prior to Barbara's version Fisher also finishes on a sixth, with a brief downward slur. Thanks to Bill Haesler for assisting in tracing this, and in fact playing his copy of this version (and other recordings) for me over the telephone.

247 · I owe this identification of the vocalist to discussion with Mike Sutcliffe, who in turns bases the opinion on a combination of aural evidence and the information available in professional journals of the time. The Llewellyn track has been issued on *King of the Trocadero*; *Frank Coughlan,* Larrikin LRH 428.

248 · Unless otherwise indicated, all the interview material in the following section is from Johnson 9/12/97.

249 · Tooley's recordings are virtually unavailable, An excellent anthology was produced in 1975 by Sydney jazz pianist Graham Grant, but according to his report in a gig conversation with me, following poor sales, the remaining pressings were pulped. Like many other jazz-accented musicians of the late twenties, Tooley's career was partly killed by the Depression, to which the spirit of her major recorded output was inappropriate, and she had fallen into complete obscurity by the time of her death in 1957. For further detail on her life and career see [Sutcliffe] 1991, pp.8–13.

250 · See for example *ADBN* 1 October 1932, p.3, and 1 December 1932, p.4. Armstrong's version of this song was reviewed in *ADBN*, 1 October 1932, p.21. Nigel Buesst's video documentary on Featherstone throws no further light on Featherstone's vocal style.

251 · On scat singing see for example *AMM&DBN*, 1 June 1934, p.26.

252 · For a brief overview of these debates, see Goodall 1995, pp.97–102. Waterhouse 1995, pp.182–5, notes the contribution made to the high/low model by radio programming policy.

253 · Kernfeld 1988, p.52. See similarly Leonard Feather, *The New Edition of The Encyclopedia of Jazz.* NY: Horizon Press 1960, p. 108, and Pleasants 1974 p.144.

254 · Kernfeld 1988, p.256. See also, Pleasants 1974, pp. 136–42.

255 · The great majority of singers identified as 'crooners' in Australia during the early thirties were men, including: Billy Foster in *ADBN*, 1 November 1932, p.4; Bert Mar (aka Mars) in *ADBN*, 1 February 1933, p. 10; Abe Romain in *AMM&DBN*, 1 October 1933, p.10; Walter Smith in *AMM&DBN*, 1 January 1934, p.34; and most notably Jack Davey, who is discussed below. Occasionally women were however, declared by reviewers to be crooners: Marjorie Nicholson in *AMM&DBN*, September 1 1934, p.33; Belle Sylvia in retrospect in *AMM&DBN*, 1 December 1933, p.15; and Barbara James in *AMM&DBN*, 1 March 1934, p.5. An article called 'The gentle art of crooning' in 1936 listed a number of current Australian dance-band vocalists, of whom

ten were explicitly identified as crooners, and of whom only two were women (*AMM&DBN*, June 1936, p.7).

256 · Bisset 1987, p.47; *AMM&DBN*, 1 March 1934, p.8.

257 · There is a more extended discussion of James' professional and personal relationships, carried forward into her later life, in Johnson and Sutcliffe 1992, from which sections of this discussion have been adapted.

258 · Bisset 1987, p.67.

259 · Marjorie Stafford ('she was to Melbourne what I was to Sydney' 10/12/97), Joan Clark (Melbourne), and Sydney singers Doris Turner, Joan Wilton, Norma Francis, Alice Smith, Gloria Ashcroft, Margaret Kerr, Jean Cerchi, Des Tooley, Grace Quine, and the Lester sisters.

260 · 'Barbara Does Her Crooning', in *Victorian Dance News*, 23 June 1934. My thanks to Mike Sutcliffe who drew this article to my attention.

261 · The following, to the end of the paragraph, is mainly from Johnson 25/6/93 and 10/12/97.

262 · Stanley Sadie (ed), *The Norton/Grove Concise Encyclopedia of Music*. New York and London: W.W. Norton & Co 1994, p. 182.

263 · In this connection, the relationship scripted by Barbara James for herself and Reg Lewis for their broadcasts in Australia and for the BBC presents points of interest. See Johnson & Sutcliffe 1992, pp. 129–130.

Chapter 6

264 · See for example [Eric Myers] 'Reviews of Bernie McGann Trio in Canada, *Jazzchord*, Sep/Oct 1993, p.6; 'Bernie McGann Again Praised Overseas', *Jazzchord*, Mar/Apr 1994, p.7. Encomiums in overseas reviews include: Larry Hollis in *Cadence*, December 1987; Victor Schonfield in *Jazz Journal*, January 1988; *Coda*, April/May 1988; Brian Davis and Keith Cox in *Jazz Forum*, February 1989. McGann's CD 'Playground' was included in *Coda*'s 1997 Writers' Choice Top Ten Recordings (Jane March, SIMA

[Sydney Improvised Music Association] Program, March 1998, Email version).

265 · The activities of this band are hilariously chronicled by George Melly in *Owning Up*. Harmondsworth Middlesex: Penguin 1970.

266 · See [Mike Sutcliffe], 'Tony Newstead in the USA' *Australian Record and Music Review*, 25, April 1995, pp.20–21.

267 · Some accounts of the AJQ's work in the United States may be found in the following articles by Eric Myers in *Jazz: The Australasian Contemporary Music Magazine*: 'Errol Buddle: A New Era', August 1982, pp.4–8; 'Errol Buddle: Some earlier eras', October 1982, pp.20–23; 'Errol Buddle and the AJQ', January/February 1983, pp.22–26. See also Clare 1995, pp.34–38.

268 · The summary given here is abstracted from Terry McCardell's contemporary accounts, reprinted as a 200 print-run monograph, *Jazz Speaks All Languages*. Sydney: Australian Jazz Convention Trust Fund 1985.

269 · See [Mike Sutcliffe] 'Australians Overseas: The Three Australian Boys', *Australian Record and Music Review* 1, April 1989, p.2.

270 · Anonymous, 'Played With Whiteman In The "King Of Jazz": Clarrie Collins Returns', *AMM&DBN*, 3 Dec 1933, pp.29, 47.

271 · Sources for Collins' early career include: *Australasian Band and Orchestra News*, January 1929; 26/3/30, p.19; 26/4/30 pp.25–6; 26/5/31, p.5; December 1931; *AMM&DBN*, 1/12/33 pp.29,47; *Music Maker*. 21/10/46, p.20. For a summary (unsourced) of his whole career see [Mike Sutcliffe], 'The Career of Clarrie Collins', *Australian Record and Music Review*, 7, October 1990, pp.3–10.

272 · See further [Mike Sutcliffe], 'The Career of Abe Romain', *Australian Record and Music Review*, 19, October 1993, pp.3–13.

273 · See further [Mike Sutcliffe], 'The Career of Abe Walters', *Australian Record and Music Review*, 9, April 1991, pp.3–12.

274 · *AMM&DBN*, 1 September 1933, p. 10.

275 · See further Johnson Sutcliffe, 1992, p.126.

276 · Apart from specific references provided, for further details regarding most of the musicians mentioned in the foregoing, see their entries in Johnson 1987 and Warren Bebbington (ed), *The Oxford Companion to Australian Music*. Melbourne: Oxford University Press 1997.

277 · The following narrative is amplified in a number of sources, including Bell 1988, pp.63–118; Bell, Graeme, 'Czechoslovak Journey II', in *Quarterly Rag, 70*, January 1994, pp.21–22; the Bell scrapbooks and journals; Bisset 1987, pp. 131–132; Jim Godbolt, *A History of Jazz in Britain 1919–50*. London: Quartet 1984, pp.212–215; Jim Godbolt, *All This and 10%*. London: Robert Hale 1976; Bruce Johnson, 'Is There an Australian Jazz?', *Jazz: The Australasian Contemporary Music Magazine*, Part I, December 1981, pp.6–8; Part II, February 1982, pp.20–23; Johnson 1984; Johnson 1986; Humphrey Lyttelton, *I Play As I Please: The Memoirs of an Old Etonian Trumpeter*. London, MacGibbon & Kee 1954, pp. 147–161; Stein 1986; Harry Stein, 1994; Bruce Johnson, 'Australian Jazz in Post-war Europe: a case study in musical displacement', *Perfect Beat—The Pacific Journal of Research into Contemporary Music and Popular Culture*, 2/3, July 1995, pp.49–64. I am aware of other non-English sources and for this reason am particularly grateful to Czech researcher Aleš Opekar for his comments.

278 · The journal of the Sydney Jazz Club, *Quarterly Rag*, 70, Jan. 1994, has published some of the letters written by band manager Mel Langdon during this period. In one of them he describes a stadium concert at which 9,500 people passed through the gates (H.M. Harris 1994, p.4). This is confirmed by Graeme Bell (11 April 1994) who locates the concert at Riegrovy Sady (Park) in Prague. I have viewed the footage of film shot in Prague; there is a belief in some circles that the film crew was actually Russian.

279 · The recordings are listed under Bell's name in Mitchell 1988.

280 · *Melody Maker and Rhythm*, 22 May 1948. In a reprint of this passage in the Australian journal *Radio Call*, July 8 1948 the article was attributed to George Avakian, but published in the

U.S. journal *Down Beat,* 19 May 1948, it carried the byline of Monte Ballou.

281 · See Jack Mitchell, 'Graeme Bell in Europe 1947–1948: Recordings Known, and Radio Broadcasts Which May Have Been Recorded', *Australian Record and Music Review* 16, January 1993, pp.14–17.

282 · There is extensive literature on this subject, much of it reviewed and placed in some context in Julian Croft, 'Responses to Modernism, 1915–1965' in Laurie Hergenhan (ed), *The Penguin New Literary History of Australia.* Ringwood Vic: Penguin 1988, pp.409–429.

283 · The most substantial publications on jazz in Czechoslovakia remain untranslated into English. The following is constructed to some extent from Joseph Škvorecký, *The Bass Saxophone.* Toronto: Lester & Orpen Denny 1980, and *Talkin Moscow Blues,* ed Sam Solecki. London: Faber & Faber edition 1989, the impressions of members of the Bell band, and a considerable number of Czech musicians, writers, historians, including most prominently L. Dorůžka, A. Opekar, P. Sedlak, J. Škvorecký, L. Sváb, including conference papers delivered by Dorůžka in Darmsdadt and Lugano in 1993. Tony Mitchell also makes reference to the tour in the context of his discussion of popular music and politics in Czechoslovakia, in *Popular Music and Local Identity: Rock, Pop and Rap in Europe and Oceania.* London and New York: Leicester University Press 1996, pp. 105–6.

284 · There had been a 'good selection' of American records available in Prague until the United States entered the war, when supplies virtually ceased. During the two years between the end of the war and Bell's arrival, records covering a wide range of jazz-based styles were beginning to become available again (Dorůžka Aug. 14 1994).

285 · Ludwíg Sváb, letter to author, 14 March 1994. See further Škvorecký 1980, pp.7–21.

286 · Uggé 1947a*. The full details for these Czechoslovakian sources are given at the conclusion of these endnotes. All

material marked with an asterisk gives the text as it was kindly translated into English for Graeme Bell by Mr and Mrs Jan Jirasek in 1985; see Bibliography for detail.

287 · Uggé, 1947a*.

288 · Dorůžka 1947*.

289 · Uggé 1947b*.

290 · The newspaper *Ohlas* in Melnik, Bohemia, 16 October 1947*.

291 · The newspaper *Osvobozeny* [sic] in Olomouc, Moravia, 11 November 1947*.

292 · Škvorecký 1980, p.16.

293 · Dorůžka 1994.

294 · Letter to author, received February 1994.

295 · Dorůžka 1994. I gratefully acknowledge Dorůžka's account in this connection. It was confirmed in broad outline by Aleš Opekar during our discussions in Liverpool (1994) and Prague (1997).

296 · Bell reports being told, 'The records of your old band were our Bible' (Bell 1994), and his account of his reception (Bell/Anna Tousikova 1993) is confirmed by all other informants.

297 · The main source for this information is Godbolt 1976 and 1984 In conversation in March 1994, the Director of Liverpool's Institute of Popular Music David Horn reported that research into service bands based in England during the war indicates the need for a more nuanced account.

298 · The main published sources for this background include Bell 1988, Godbolt 1976 and 1984, Johnson 1984, Lyttelton 1954, Bruce Turner, *Hot Air, Cool Music*. London, Quartet 1984.

299 · Rex Harris, *Jazz*. Harmondsworth Middlesex: Penguin 1952, p.220.

300 · Peter Lewis, *The Fifties: Portrait of a Period*. London: Cupid Press 1989, p. 131; D Bradley, *Understanding Rock'n'Roll: Popular Music in*

Britain 1955–1964. Buckingham, Open University Press 1992, p.56.

301 · Lyttelton 1954 and Turner 1984, provide colourful accounts of the perils of playing saxophone in the context of post-war British jazz.

302 · In every one of the extended visits I have made to Britain since the late 1960s, I have heard local traditional jazz bands pull out songs introduced by the Bell band, including as recently as 1996 when Liverpool's Merseysippi Jazz Band performed an Ade Monsbourgh composition during their Monday night gig at Hartleys in the Albert Dock.

303 · Lyttelton 1954, pp. 150–2. For further accounts of the ecstatic improvised dancing introduced to the jazz scene by the Bell band policy, see Godbolt 1976, pp.44–5, 122; Godbolt 1984, p.213; Harris 1952, p.22.

304 · Lyttelton 1954, p. 149.

305 · Godbolt 1984, p.215; Harris 1952, pp.226, 245.

306 · Max Harris, *The Angry Eye.* Potts Point, NSW: Pergamon Press. 1973, p. 14.

307 · Haese 1981, p.282.

308 · Godbolt 1984, p.213.

309 · See for example Kernfeld 1988, pp.601–602.

310 · See for example Geoff Bull, in an interview with Eric Myers published in *Jazz: The Australasian Contemporary Music Magazine*, December 1981, p. 19.

311 · See Bisset, 1987 pp.114–117; Johnson 1987, pp.99–100. There is a detailed comparison of the two bands in Bruce Johnson December 1981 and February 1982.

312 · See for example Clunies-Ross 1979, and Johnson 1987, pp.87–90, 205–207.

313 · See further Johnson 1998.

314 · Clunies-Ross 1979, pp.75–77, summarises the jazz coverage in *Angry Penguins.*

315 · This has been a continuing project in the work of Dave Dallwitz in particular; sec further Clunies-Ross 1979 and the following articles in *Jazz: The Australasian Contemporary Music Magazine*: Bruce Johnson, 'Dave Dallwitz and the Southern Jazz Group' Part 1, March/April 1982, pp. 10–13; Part 2, May/June 1982, pp.10–13; Part 3, August 1982, pp.10–13; Norman Linehan 'Dave Dallwitz: The Creation of a Myth', January/February 1983, pp.20–2 L Bruce Clunies-Ross, 'Dave Dallwitz & Australian Jazz: A Reply To Mr Linehan', May/June 1983, pp.6–8.

316 · Clunies-Ross 1979, p.63. On the evolution of the music, sec p.73.

317 · 'Dave Dallwitz' in the Australian Composers series produced by the Australia Music Centre, January 1981. Although unsigned, the narrative was written by Eric Myers, as disclosed in an editorial appendix to Linehan 1983, p.21.

318 · Harris 1973, pp. 13, 14, 15. The question is also taken up in Johnson 1981 and 1982.

319 · Sec for example Bull in Myers 1981.

320 · Ian Carr, Digby Fairweather, Brian Priestley, *Jazz: The Essential Companion*. London: Paladin, Grafton Books 1990, p.17.

321 · Godbolt 1976, p.49.

322 · H.M. Harris 1994, p.5; Godbolt 1984, p.212.

323 · The role of amateurism in traditional jazz is taken up also in Bruce Johnson, 'Traditional Jazz in Australia', *Jazz: The Australasian Contemporary Music Magazine,* December 1982, p.5.

324 · See Clunies-Ross 1979, pp.67–70; Johnson 1982, p.22.

325 · During nationwide research on the history of Australian jazz I gathered evidence of this, some of which appears incidentally in the biographical entries in Johnson 1987. In Adelaide, the example of the Southern Jazz Group is representative, with members ranging at various times from trades, professions, and, in the case of Kym Bonython, one of South Australia's wealthiest dynasties.

326 · Among the extensive literature on the problematics of national

identity, see for example the benchmark study by Benedict Anderson, *Imagined communities: reflections on the origin and spread of nationalism.* London: Verso 1983; in the case of music, see for example Martin Stokes (ed), *Ethnicity Identity and Music: The Musical Construction of Place,* Oxford/Providence USA: Berg 1994.

327 · Godbolt 1976, p.49.

328 · **Czechoslovakian journals**

Anonymous (trans. Jirasek) 1947. 'The Australian Orchestra in Prague', in *Mladá Fronta* (17 August)

Anonymous (trans. Jirasek) 1947. 'Australian Jazz played farewell for them', in *Svobodné Slovo* (11 December). This is probably by Uggé.

Anonymous (trans. Jirasek) 1947. 'Jack Varney Married in Prague', in *Mladá Fronta* (undated beyond year)

Anonymous (trans. Jirasek) 1947. 'I played together with Don Roberts', in *Jazz* (Prague, 31 October). This is probably by 'Johnny' Kraus

Anonymous (trans. Jirasek) 1947. 'History of jazz in one concert', in *Mladá Fronta* (28 September). This is probably by Uggé

Anonymous (trans. Jirasek) 1947. Review in *Ohlas* (Melnik, Bohemia, undated beyond year)

Anonymous (trans. Jirasek) 1947. Review in *Osvobozeny* [sic] (Olomouc, Moravia, undated beyond year)

Uggé, E. (trans. Jirasek) 1947a 'New Orleans in Prague', in *Mladá Fronta* (17 August)

Uggé, E. (trans. Jirasek) 1947b *MY 47,* Prague (16 June?)

Chapter 7

329 · Mileham Hayes, Ray Scribner, Peter Magee, *The Encyclopedia of Australian Jazz* (no publisher, place or date, but ca 1976); Bisset 1979/1987; Johnson 1987; Clare 1995; Mitchell 1988 and 1998; Australia Music Centre, *Catalogues of Australian Compositions VIII: Jazz.* Sydney: Australia Music Centre 1978.

330 · Geoff Page, *Winter Vision*. Queensland: University of Queensland Press 1989; Mandy Sayer, *Mood Indigo*. Sydney: Allen & Unwin 1990; Kerry Greenwood, *The Green Mill Murder*. Ringwood Victoria: McPhee Gribble 1993.

331 · See bibliography.

332 · Australian Bureau of Statistics, *Cultural Trends in Australia: A Statistical Overview 1997*. ABS Cat. 4172.0, Canberra, p.8.

333 · Covell, 1967; Philip J. Drummond, *Australian Directory of Music Research*. Sydney: Australia Music Centre 1978; Deborah Crisp, *Bibliography of Australian Music: an index to monographs, journal articles and theses*, Australian music Studies 1. Armidale 1982.

334 · Murray 1994, pp.337–8; Brian Reis, *Australian Film: A Bibliography*. London & Washington: Mansell 1997.

335 · See Bruce Johnson 1995A, p.12.

336 · These figures are taken from the list of grants in Australia Council, *Annual Report*. Sydney: Australia Council 1995–6, pp.98–105. As the jazz recipients are not differentiated as such I have relied on my own knowledge to identify them in the listings, erring on the optimistic side, as in the example of broad-based improvisational groups. In my study of 1993–4 the figures, which were also cross-checked by Australian and National Jazz Co-ordinator, were of about the same order: jazz received 9.4% of the money disbursed to music for 13.7% of the successful applications.

337 · A detailed analysis of the relative levels of audience and musician participation in jazz and classical music, based on figures published by such bodies as the ABS and the AC, is provided in Bruce Johnson, 'The Production and Consumption of Jazz in Live Performance in Australia', *Jazzchord*, 25, Jun/Jul 1995, 6–7.

338 · *The Australian Opera Annual Report 1995*. For detail, see p. 15.

339 · Commonwealth Government of Australia, *Creative Nation: Commonwealth Cultural Policy October 1994*. Canberra: National Capital Printing 1994.

340 · 'Eric Myers writes', *Jazzchord* 19, May/June 1994, p.5.

341 · Stokes 1994, p.3.

342 · Kater 1992; S. Frederick Starr, *Red and Hot: The Fate of Jazz in the Soviet Union 1917–1980*. New York/Oxford: Oxford University Press 1983.

343 · These and related issues are developed in Bruce Johnson, 'In the Jumble, the Genre Jumble: the prison house of popular music discourse'. Unpub Paper delivered at *Rock as a Research Field* Symposium, University of Aarhus, Denmark, 4–10 April 1997. On such distinctions as 'folk', 'art music' see for example Middleton 1990, pp. 127–146.

344 · Bruce Johnson 1992A, 'Orality and jazz education', *New Music Articles,* 10, 1992, pp.39–43, 46.

345 · Paul F. Berliner, *Thinking in Jazz: The Infinite Art of Improvisation.* Chicago and London: The University of Chicago Press 1994. Berliner's work provides documentation for virtually every aspect of jazz practices referred to in my inquiry.

346 · Among the growing historiography and critique of the autonomy of art see for example the work of Janet Wolff, including *Aesthetics and the Sociology of Art,* Second Edition. London: Macmillan 1993, and in a musical context, her 'Foreword—the ideology of autonomous art' in Richard Leppert and Susan McClary (eds), *Music and Society: the politics of composition, performance and perception.* Cambridge UK: Cambridge University Press 1987, pp.1–12. In music in particular, see the essays in that collection. Lawrence Kramer briefly outlines the rise of the doctrine in *Music as Cultural Practice.* Berkeley, Los Angeles, London: University of California Press 1990, esp. pp, 1–5. Alistair Williams 1997 returns to the topic at several points, for example pp.15–16, as a corollary to commodification

347 · Tim Rowse, *Arguing the Arts: the funding of the arts in Australia.* Ringwood Vic: Penguin 1985; Gay Hawkins, *From Nimbin to Mardi Gras: constructing community arts.* St Leonards NSW: Allen & Unwin 1993.

348 · See for example Potter 1998, p.49.

349 · Berliner 1994, is for example an Associate Professor of Ethnomusicology at Northwestern University.

350 · See above, chapter 4.

351 · Grainger quoted in Charles Keil and Steven Feld, *Music Grooves.* Chicago: University of Chicago Press 1994, p. 121 fn 5; on 'engendered meaning', p.55.

352 · Keil and Feld 1994, pp.96–108; Charles Keil, 'The Theory of Participatory Discrepancies: a Progress Report', *Ethnomusicology: Journal of the Society for Ethnomusicology,* 39/1, Winter 1995, pp. 1–19. This issue of the journal is largely devoted to debate on the theory.

353 · J.A .Prögler, 'Searching for Swing: Participatory Discrepancies in the Jazz Rhythm Section', *Ethnomusicology: Journal of the Society for Ethnomusicology,* 39/1, Winter 1995, pp.21–54. For the information regarding Yamaha, see Prögler in Charles Keil and J.A. Prögler, 'Rejoinders', *Ethnomusicology: Journal of the Society for Ethnomusicology*, 39/1, Winter 1995, p. 101.

354 · Brian Brown, interview with author, Melbourne 24 July 1991.

355 · See further Johnson 1996.

356 · Pressing, 'The Micro- and Macrostructural Design of Improvised Music', *Music Perception,* 5/2, 1987, pp. 132–72. My thanks to John Whiteoak for drawing this particular article to my attention. My own library does not hold this issue, and the text is quoted from a MS.

357 · On the non-musical determinants of improvisation, see further Bruce Johnson, 'Klactoveesedstene—Music, Soundscape and Me', in Helmi Järviluoma (ed) *Soundscapes: Essays on Vroom and Moo.* Finland: Dept of Folk Tradition, University of Tampere 1994, pp.39–47.

358 · See further Johnson 1992A; Bruce Johnson, 'The Great Divide—Australian Traditional Jazz and the Academies', *Journal of Australian Studies*, 34, September 1992, pp.32–42 (1992B); Bruce Johnson, 'Jazz: A Test Case for Popular Music in the Australian

Academies', *Institute of Popular Music Occasional Paper 3*. Liverpool: University of Liverpool 1992 (1992C).

359 · As listed in Eric Myers (ed) *Australian Jazz Directory 1998*. Millers Point NSW: Jazz Co-ordination Association of New South Wales 1998, pp.97–101.

360 · Exceptions as disclosed, for example, in interviews with educators: Brian Brown (Melbourne July 29 1991); Judy Bailey (Sydney on numerous occasions, but for formal attribution February 20 1998); Maurie Le Doeuff (Adelaide August 7 1991); Pat Crichton (Perth August 13 1991).

361 · See further Johnson 1992B, 1992C.

362 · See for example Clunies-Ross 1979.

363 · Ade Monsbourgh, interview with Bruce Johnson, Melbourne 30/7/91. In Johnson 1992A and 1992B I provide further evidence of the neglect of these traditions in Australian jazz, to the point of active resistance on the part of program directors.

364 · See for example Valerie Wilmer, *As Serious as Your Life: The Story of the New Jazz*. Melbourne, New York, London: Quartet 1977, p.41.

365 · H.O. Munn, *The Story of the Original Dixieland Jazz Band*. Louisiana: Louisiana State University Press 1960, p. 101.

366 · Quoted in Jacques Chailley, *40,000 Years of Music: Man in Search of Music*, trans Rollo Myers. London: Macdonald 1964, p.104. See also the epigraph to this chapter, Boulez on the centrality of the score: 'If it works, it's wonderful' interview with Warren Burt, *Meanjin*, 2, Winter 1988, p.256; on institutional exclusiveness: Boulez and Michel Foucault, 'Contemporary music and its public', *Melbourne Journal of Politics*, 17, 1985/86, p.43.

367 · This is developed further in Johnson 1993A.

368 · The reference is to Edgar Allan Poe's short story, one of the most succinct early realisations of the dislocated urban psyche.

COPYRIGHT

First published in 2000 by Currency Press

This edition published in 2021 by Ligature Pty Limited
34 Campbell St · Balmain NSW 2041 · Australia
www.ligatu.re · mail@ligatu.re

e-book ISBN: 9781922749246

ligature *un*tapped

This print edition published in collaboration with Brio Books, an imprint of Booktopia Group Ltd

Level 6, 1A Homebush Bay Drive · Rhodes NSW 2138 · Australia

Print ISBN: 9781761280771

briobooks.com.au

The paper in this book is FSC® certified.
FSC® promotes environmentally responsible, socially beneficial and economically viable management of the world's forests.